Contemporary Japanese Workbook

AN INTRODUCTORY WORKBOOK
FOR STUDENTS OF JAPANESE

Volume 2

by Eriko Sato, Ph.D.

TUTTLE PUBLISHING
Tokyo · Rutland, Vermont · Singapore

Published by Tuttle Publishing, an imprint of Periplus Editions (HK) Ltd., with editorial offices
at 364 Innovation Drive, North Clarendon, Vermont 05759 U.S.A. and 130 Joo Seng Road #06-01, Singapore 368357.

ISBN-10: 0-8048-3812-7
ISBN-13: 978-0-8048-3812-2

Distributed by:

North America, Latin America & Europe
Tuttle Publishing
364 Innovation Drive
North Clarendon, VT 05759-9436 U.S.A.
Tel: 1 (802) 773-8930
Fax: 1 (802) 773-6993
info@tuttlepublishing.com
www.tuttlepublishing.com

Japan
Tuttle Publishing
Yaekari Building, 3rd Floor
5-4-12 Osaki
Shinagawa-ku
Tokyo 141 0032
Tel: (81) 03 5437-0171
Fax: (81) 03 5437-0755
tuttle-sales@gol.com

Asia Pacific
Berkeley Books Pte. Ltd.
130 Joo Seng Road #06-01
Singapore 368357
Tel: (65) 6280-1330
Fax: (65) 6280-6290
inquiries@periplus.com.sg
www.periplus.com

Indonesia
PT Java Books Indonesia
Kawasan Industri Pulogadung
Jl. Rawa Gelam IV No. 9
Jakarta 13930
Tel: (62) 21 4682-1088
Fax: (62) 21 461-0206
cs@javabooks.co.id

10 09 08 07 6 5 4 3 2 1

Printed in Singapore

Preface

Contemporary Japanese Workbook was created as a supplementary material for *Contemporary Japanese*: *An Introductory Textbook for College Students*. While it is best used for reviewing and reinforcing the concepts and learning materials introduced in the textbook, this workbook is also designed to function as a stand alone comprehensive workbook. Some of the features included for this purpose are (a) presentation of a brief note on the concept tested before every question, (b) providing of vocabulary and kanji glossaries on unfamiliar words, and (c) an audio input by native speakers ⊙. This workbook also offers materials in the business, traveling and daily life contexts, in addition to the college life context featured greatly in the textbook.

Structure

Contemporary Japanese Workbook series comes in two volumes, consisting of 26 chapters (Chapter One to Fourteen in Volume One and Chapter Fifteen to Twenty-Six in Volume Two) in all. It integrates all the information provided in the textbook. Each chapter in the workbook has specific objectives and includes the following six sections.

• **Kanji and Vocabulary**
• **Grammar**
• **Conversation and Usage**
• **Listening Comprehension**
• **Reading Comprehension**
• **Writing**
• **New Vocabulary Reference List**

Orthography

In **Contemporary Japanese Workbook**, hiragana characters are introduced in Chapter One in the form of questions along with audio recordings, and are used in subsequent chapters without ruby, in this case in romaji. Katakana characters are introduced in Chapter Four, also in the form of questions, and are used in subsequent chapters without ruby. Kanji characters are introduced in the form of questions, accompanied by detailed information such as meanings, component equations, remembering guides 📖, stroke order, and usage examples. The required kanji characters in every chapter are introduced without ruby. When they appear again in the following chapters, ruby is sparingly provided, wherever it is thought to be helpful, and the use of this pronunciation guide is gradually reduced. Nonrequired kanji characters occasionally appear with ruby to help learners get accustomed to kanji and thus, able to see the phrase boundaries in a sentence easily.

Reference

Henshall, Kenneth G. (1988) A Guide To Remembering Japanese Characters, Charles E. Tuttle Publishing Co., In

Acknowledgment

Special appreciation goes to Doreen Ng and many other staff of Tuttle Publishing for their enthusiasm, expertise, creativity and professionalism in making this workbook a reality.

Contents

CHAPTER FIFTEEN
Exchanging Opinions

Objectives:

- to form the plain forms of verbs and adjectives
- to form embedded sentences with verbs such as 思う (*to think*)
- to express ideas using modals かもしれません and でしょう
- to ask or state reasons
- to describe weather and physical conditions
- to name the people and items in a college

Kanji and Vocabulary

1. Reading and Writing Kanji Characters

A) Let's read each of the following kanji words or phrases aloud several times.

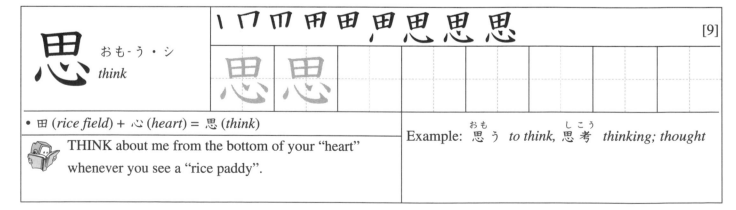

おも
思う *to think*

てんき
天気 *weather*

あめ
雨 *rain*

ゆき
雪 *snow*

でんわ
電話 *telephone*

でんき
電気 *electricity*

でんしゃ
電車 *train*

で
出る *to come out, to attend, to leave*

びょうき
病気 *sickness*

げんき
元気だ *healthy, fine*

びょういん
病院 *hospital*

いた
痛い *painful*

もんだい
問題 *question, issue, problem*

しつもん
質問 *question, inquiry*

しゅくだい
宿題 *homework*

ぶんか
文化 *culture*

ほんとう
本当だ *true*

B) In the boxes provided, write each kanji character following the correct stroke order.

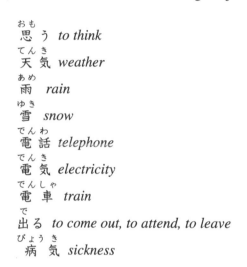

思 おも-う・シ *think*	丨 冂 冊 冊 田 田 思 思 思							[9]
	思	思						

- 田 (*rice field*) + 心 (*heart*) = 思 (*think*)

THINK about me from the bottom of your "heart" whenever you see a "rice paddy".

Example: おも 思う *to think*, しこう 思考 *thinking; thought*

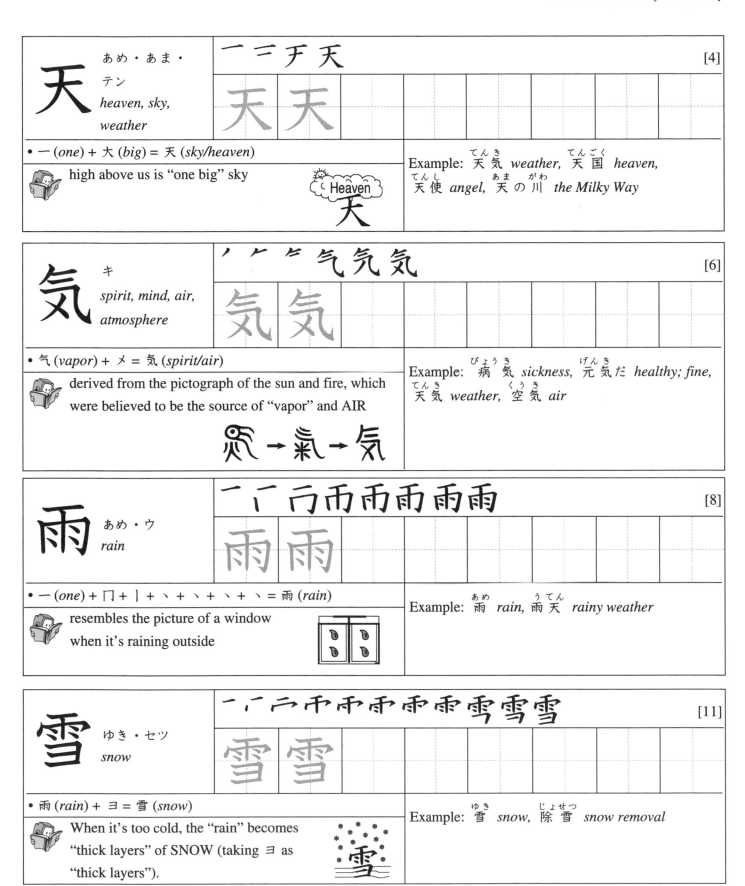

天 あめ・あま・テン
heaven, sky, weather

一 二 チ 天 [4]

天 天

• 一 (one) + 大 (big) = 天 (sky/heaven)

high above us is "one big" sky

Heaven 天

Example: 天気 weather, 天国 heaven, 天使 angel, 天の川 the Milky Way

気 キ
spirit, mind, air, atmosphere

丿 气 气 气 気 気 [6]

気 気

• 气 (vapor) + メ = 気 (spirit/air)

derived from the pictograph of the sun and fire, which were believed to be the source of "vapor" and AIR

Example: 病気 sickness, 元気だ healthy; fine, 天気 weather, 空気 air

雨 あめ・ウ
rain

一 丆 丏 币 雨 雨 雨 雨 [8]

雨 雨

• 一 (one) + 冂 + | + 丶 + 丶 + 丶 + 丶 = 雨 (rain)

resembles the picture of a window when it's raining outside

Example: 雨 rain, 雨天 rainy weather

雪 ゆき・セツ
snow

一 丆 冖 币 币 雨 雨 雪 雪 雪 [11]

雪 雪

• 雨 (rain) + ヨ = 雪 (snow)

When it's too cold, the "rain" becomes "thick layers" of SNOW (taking ヨ as "thick layers").

雪

Example: 雪 snow, 除雪 snow removal

電 デン
electricity

一 ニ � 币 币 雨 雨 雷 雷 雷 雷 電 電 [13]

電 電

- 雨 (*rain*) + 电 (*lightning*) = 電 (*electricity*)

  The "lightning" that occurs during a heavy "rain" is a form of ELECTRICITY.

- The kanji sharing a component with 電 (*electricity*) is 雪 (*snow*).

Example: 電車 でんしゃ *electric train*, 電気 でんき *electricity*, 電話 でんわ *telephone*

病 ビョウ
sick

' 亠 广 广 疒 疒 疒 病 病 病 [10]

病 病

- 疒 (*sickness*) + 丙 (*third*) = 病 (*sick*)

  resembles a sickly person being cared of under one roof

Example: 病気 びょうき *sickness*, 病院 びょういん *hospital*

元 もと・ゲン・ガン
origin, source, base

一 ニ テ 元 [4]

元 元

- 二 (*two*) + 儿 (*human legs*) = 元 (*origin*)

  We are "two-legged" creature from the same ORIGIN.

Example: 元気です げんき *fine (mentally and physically)*, 元日 がんじつ *New Year's Day*, 元通り もとどお *as before*

院 イン
hall, house, institute

ㄱ ㄋ � 阝 阝' 阝' 阧 陊 陊 院 [10]

院 院

- 阝 (*hill*) + 完 (*completion*) = 院 (*institute*)

  The "completed" building on the "hill" is an INSTITUTION.

Example: 大学院 だいがくいん *graduate school*, 病院 びょういん *hospital*, 議院 ぎいん *the House*

痛

いた-い・いた-む・ツウ
pain

[12]

- 疒 (*sickness*) + マ + 用 (*use*) = 痛 (*pain*)

 Patients" suffering from serious "sickness" often "use" drugs to reduce PAIN (taking マ as "patients").

- The kanji sharing a component with 痛 (*pain*) is 病 (*sick*).

Example: 痛い *painful*, 苦痛 *pain*, 頭痛 *headache*

質

シツ・シチ
quality, question

゛゛゛゛゛゛゛゛゛゛゛゛゛質質 [15]

- 斤 (*ax*) + 斤 (*ax*) + 貝 (*shell*) = 質 (*quality*)

 Try to crack the "shell" with two "axes" to check its QUALITY—if it doesn't break, it is hard enough.

- The kanji sharing a component with 質 (*quality*) is 買 (*buy*).

Example: 質問 *question*, 品質 *quality*, 質屋 *pawnshop*

問

と-う・モン
inquire, question

丨冂冂冃冃門門門門問問問 [11]

- 門 (*gate*) + 口 (*mouth*) = 問 (*inquire*)

 Someone is INQUIRING at the "gate", and I can only see his "mouth".

- The kanji sharing a component with 問 (*inquire*) is 間 (*between*).

Example: 問題 *question; problem; issue*, 質問 *question*

題

ダイ
title, theme

丨冂冃日旦早早是是是匙匙題題題題題題題 [18]

- 是 (*approve*) + 頁 (*page/head/big shell*) = 題 (*title*)

 The "approved" TITLE is also printed on the first "page" of a book.

Example: 問題 *question; problem; issue*, 宿題 *homework*, 話題 *topic*, 題名 *title*

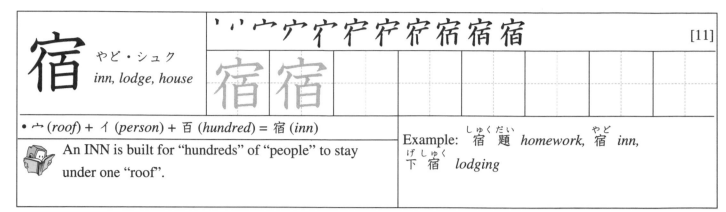

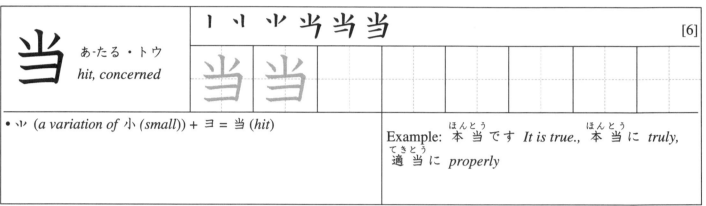

C) Let's read aloud to check how well you've mastered the kanji you've learned.

1. 明日の天気はあまりよくないと思います。雨がふるかもしれません。それか、雪がふるかもしれません。山田さんと、田中さんに電話をして、ピクニックはキャンセルします。

2. 昨日はせきが出て、あたまが痛くて、薬をのみました。それから、病院に行きました。ごごは楽になりました。今日はとても元気になりました。

3. 言語学のクラスは宿題が多くて、テストの問題が難しくて、たいへんです。でも、とてもおもしろくて、大好きです。クラスではいつも先生に質問します。

4. いつも電車や、車や、バスを使います。

5. 日本の文化とアメリカの文化は本当にちがいます。

D) Fill in the correct kanji characters in the boxes provided.

1. でん しゃ ☐☐ で びょういん ☐☐ に行きます。　3. ゆき ☐ がふります。

2. しゅくだい ☐☐ をします。　4. 日本の ぶん か ☐☐ が好きです。

2. Naming and Describing

A) From the list below, select an appropriate heading for each category of words.

{けいようし・どうし・めいし・じょし}

1. _____	2. _____	3. _____	4. _____
高い	本	〜は	食べる
安い	いす	〜が	思う
さむい	雨	〜も	ある
あつい	学生	〜を	いる
まじめ (な)	読書	〜に	読む

B) Look at the pictures below and describe how each person feels.

Example: ___さむい___ です   1. _____ です   2. _____ です   3. _____ です

C) The following is what Takako said about her college. Complete the paragraph by selecting appropriate words from the list below.

じむいん・きょうじゅ・じゅぎょう・じゅぎょうりょう・たんい・宿題

私の大学は_____が高いです。でも、とてもゆうめいな_____が
たくさんいます。今とっている文学の_____はとてもおもしろいです。
_____はあまりありませんが、テストは難しいです。

D) Below is what Takeshi said to the doctor. Fill in the blanks with appropriate words.

あたまが_____です。のども少し_____です。くしゃみと、せき
が_____ます。ねつも_____ます。

Grammar

1. The Plain Forms and 〜と思います

The plain form is not just for informal conversation. In some cases, it is needed before a particle or an auxiliary even in the polite context. For example, verbs and adjectives must be in the plain form when followed by the phrase 〜と思います (*I think* ...). The following table summarizes both the polite and plain forms of verbs and adjectives.

<table>
<tr><th colspan="6">Verbs and Adjectives in the Plain and Polite Forms</th></tr>
<tr><th colspan="2"></th><th colspan="2">Affirmative</th><th colspan="2">Negative</th></tr>
<tr><th colspan="2"></th><th>Polite</th><th>Plain</th><th>Polite</th><th>Plain</th></tr>
<tr><td rowspan="2">Verb</td><td>present</td><td>食べます</td><td>食べる</td><td>食べません</td><td>食べない</td></tr>
<tr><td>past</td><td>食べました</td><td>食べた</td><td>食べませんでした</td><td>食べなかった</td></tr>
<tr><td rowspan="2">Noun + copula</td><td>present</td><td>学生です</td><td>学生だ</td><td>学生じゃありません</td><td>学生じゃない</td></tr>
<tr><td>past</td><td>学生でした</td><td>学生だった</td><td>学生じゃありませんでした</td><td>学生じゃなかった</td></tr>
<tr><td rowspan="2">Na-type adjective</td><td>present</td><td>便利です</td><td>便利だ</td><td>便利じゃありません</td><td>便利じゃない</td></tr>
<tr><td>past</td><td>便利でした</td><td>便利だった</td><td>便利じゃありませんでした</td><td>便利じゃなかった</td></tr>
<tr><td rowspan="2">I-type adjective</td><td>present</td><td>高いです</td><td>高い</td><td>高くありません</td><td>高くない</td></tr>
<tr><td>past</td><td>高かったです</td><td>高かった</td><td>高くありませんでした</td><td>高くなかった</td></tr>
</table>

Note: ありません and ありませんでした in the negative forms in the above table can be ないです and なかったです, respectively, for some speakers. じゃ in the negative forms in the above table can be では in some cases.

Fill in the blanks with correctly conjugated forms of the items in the parentheses.

1. あの人は ＿＿＿＿＿＿＿＿＿＿ と思います。（てんいんです）

2. 父は 7 時に ＿＿＿＿＿＿＿＿＿＿ と思います。（帰ります）

3. チェンさんは中国に ＿＿＿＿＿＿＿＿＿＿ と思います。（帰りました）

4. 昨日のパーティーは ＿＿＿＿＿＿＿＿＿＿＿＿＿ と思います。（おもしろかったです）

2. 〜かもしれません and 〜でしょう

To express possibility or probability, make a statement using the plain form and add the phrase 〜かもしれません (*It may be the case that ...*), or 〜でしょう (*It is probably the case that ...*) after it. In either case, just make sure to remove the だ that appears at the end of a copula and a na-type adjective in the plain present affirmative form.

Fill in the blanks using the correct form of the phrases in the parentheses.

1. 今晩は雨が ＿＿＿＿＿＿＿＿＿ かもしれません。でも、明日は ＿＿＿＿＿＿＿＿＿ でしょう。
   （ふります）　　　　　　　　　　　　　　　　　　　（はれます）

2. ＿＿＿＿＿＿＿＿＿ でしょう。でも、＿＿＿＿＿＿＿＿＿ かもしれません。
   （かぜです）　　　　　　　　（はいえん(pneumonia)です）

3. あの人はたぶん ＿＿＿＿＿＿＿＿＿ でしょう。
   （けっこんしています）

4. たけしくんは ＿＿＿＿＿＿＿＿＿ かもしれません。
   （べんごしになります）

3. ～と思います, ～かもしれません and ～でしょう

Following the example, convert each phrase to three different forms.

Example: 日本人です ⟶ 日本人だと思います
　　　　　　　　　　　日本人かもしれません
　　　　　　　　　　　日本人でしょう

1. さむくありません ⟶ ＿＿＿＿＿＿＿＿＿＿＿＿＿＿
   ＿＿＿＿＿＿＿＿＿＿＿＿＿＿
   ＿＿＿＿＿＿＿＿＿＿＿＿＿＿

2. 帰りました ⟶ ＿＿＿＿＿＿＿＿＿＿＿＿＿＿
   ＿＿＿＿＿＿＿＿＿＿＿＿＿＿
   ＿＿＿＿＿＿＿＿＿＿＿＿＿＿

3. 難しかったです ⟶ ＿＿＿＿＿＿＿＿＿＿＿＿＿＿
   ＿＿＿＿＿＿＿＿＿＿＿＿＿＿
   ＿＿＿＿＿＿＿＿＿＿＿＿＿＿

4. かぜです ⟶ ＿＿＿＿＿＿＿＿＿＿＿＿＿＿
   ＿＿＿＿＿＿＿＿＿＿＿＿＿＿
   ＿＿＿＿＿＿＿＿＿＿＿＿＿＿

5. うそでした ⟶ ＿＿＿＿＿＿＿＿＿＿＿＿＿＿
   ＿＿＿＿＿＿＿＿＿＿＿＿＿＿
   ＿＿＿＿＿＿＿＿＿＿＿＿＿＿

4. どうして～んですか and ～からです

For asking reasons, use the question word どうして (*why*) and end your question with the phrase ～んですか. Remember to replace the だ at the end of a copula or na-type adjective with a な when it comes before ～んですか, as in 学生なんですか and 便利なんですか. For giving reasons, add the phrase ～からです at the end of your statement. The verbs and adjectives right before ～からです must be in the plain form.

Following the examples, convert the sentences in the parentheses into a question and its answer.

Example: A: どうして<u>日本語をとっている</u>んですか。（日本語をとっています）

B: <u>日本の文化にきょうみがある</u>からです。（日本の文化にきょうみがあります）

1. A: どうして_____。（薬をのみました）

   B: _____ からです。（あたまが痛かったです）

2. A: どうして_____。（会社をやめました）

   B: _____ からです。（きゅうりょうが安かったです）

3. A: どうして_____。（そうじをしています）

   B: _____ からです。（おきゃくさんが来ます）

4. A: どうして_____。（たけしさんが好きです）

   B: _____ からです。（やさしい人です）

Conversation and Usage

1. 成田空港からホテルまで

Every airport in Japan has more than one ground transportation that can take you to the places you want to go. You can check with the information booth to find out about the transportation most convenient for you.

Justin has just arrived at the Narita Airport in Japan and he is talking with a lady at the ground transportation information booth. Listen to their conversation carefully and answer the questions that follow.

ジャスティン　：　すみません。

女の人（おんな ひと）　：　はい。

ジャスティン　：　東京（とうきょう）まで行（い）きたいんですが、いくらぐらいかかりますか？

女の人　：　成田（なりた）エクスプレスでは 2,940 円、リムジンバスでは 3,000 円です。

ジャスティン　：　ああ、そうですか。時間（じかん）はどれぐらいかかりますか。

女の人　：　成田（なりた）エクスプレスでは約（やく）1 時間（じかん）、リムジンバスでは約（やく）1 時間（じかん）半（はん）です。

ジャスティン　：　じつは高輪（たかなわ）プリンスホテルに行きたいんですが。

女の人　　　　　：では、リムジンバスが便利だと思います。高輪プリンスホテルにとまりますから。

ジャスティン　　：ああ、そうですか。じゃあ、リムジンバスにします。切符はどこで買えますか。

女の人　　　　　：ここで買えますよ。

ジャスティン　　：ああ、そうですか。じゃあ、大人1枚お願いします。

[*Unfamiliar words:* 成田エクスプレス *Narita Express (train)*, リムジンバス *limousine bus*, 約 *approximately*, じつは *actually; as a matter of fact*, 〜にとまる *to stop at ...*, 高輪プリンスホテル *Takanawa Prince Hotel*, では（＝じゃあ）*then*, 〜にする *to decide on ...*, 切符 *ticket*, 大人 *adult*]

1. Which is a more expensive transportation to Tokyo from the Narita Airport, by Narita Express (train) or limousine bus? _____

2. Which is a faster transportation to Tokyo from the Narita Airport, by Narita Express (train) or limousine bus? _____

3. Why did Justin decide to take the limousine bus? _____

2. 宅配便

When the Japanese travel, they often use the delivery service called 宅配便 to deliver their baggage from their home to the airport and vice versa. One can arrange for this service at the 宅配便 counters right after arriving at the airport, and the baggage will be delivered to most places in Japan within a day.

Susan has just arrived at the Narita Airport. She is arranging for her baggage to be delivered to her friend's house where she will be staying while she is in Japan. Listen carefully to her conversation with a man at the 宅配便 counter, then answer the questions that follow.

スーザン　：すみません。これをお願いします。

(Susan gives the suitcase to the man at the counter.)

男　の　人：はい。ありがとうございます。じゃあ、ここに受取人の方のお名前と、御住所と、お電話番号を書いて下さい。

スーザン　：すみませんが、これを見て、書いて下さいませんか。

(Susan shows her address book to the clerk.)

男の人　　：はい。わかりました。

(The man writes the name, address and telephone number of the recipient.)

スーザン　：明日までに届きますか。

男の人　　：はい。たぶん、明日の午前中に届くでしょう。

スーザン　：ああ、よかった。いくらですか。

男の人　　：1,920 円です。

[**Unfamiliar words:** 受取人 *recipient*, 御住所 *address (polite)*, お電話番号 *telephone number (polite)*, お客様 *customer*, 届く *be delivered, arrive*]

1. Who wrote the recipient's address? _____
2. When will the suitcase be delivered? _____
3. How much does it cost? _____

Listening Comprehension

天気

 Listen carefully to the weather forecast on the CD and answer the following questions in English.

1. How is the weather in Tokyo in the afternoon? _____
2. How is the weather in Nagoya in the morning? _____
3. How is the weather in Osaka in the afternoon? _____

Reading Comprehension

薬のふくろ

Below is the medicine bag (薬 の 袋) received by Takashi from the doctor he has seen. Read the label on the bag and answer the questions. There are some unfamiliar words in the label, but you should be able to answer the questions.

1.　１日に何回薬をのみますか。(*How many times a day does he have to take the medicine?*)

　　_____

2.　1回にカプセルをいくつのみますか。(*How many capsules does he have to take at a time?*)

　　_____

3.　薬は何日分ありますか。(*How many days does the prescribed medicine last?*)

　　_____

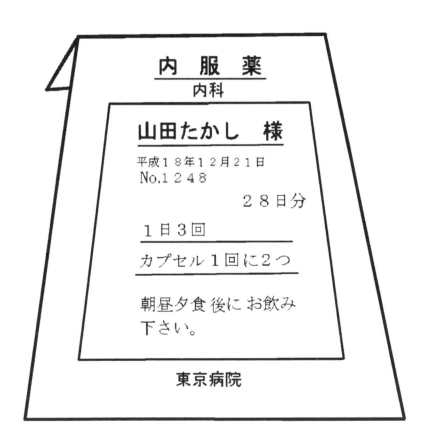

内　服　薬
内科

山田たかし　様

平成１８年１２月２１日
No.１２４８

　　　　　２８日分

１日３回

カプセル１回に２つ

朝昼夕食後にお飲み
下さい。

東京病院

Writing

入国・出国記録カード

When visiting Japan, a foreigner must fill out the 入国・出国記録カード (*Disembarkation/Embarkation Card*) before going through the immigration. Shown below is a sample of the card. The Disembarkation Card (part 1) will be retained by the immigration officer, and the Embarkation Card (part 2) will be stapled to the passport.

Pretend that you have just arrived at the Tokyo International Airport from your home country by your favorite airline. Fill out the Disembarkation/Embarkation Card below as much as you can.

New Vocabulary Reference List

NOUN

あめ（雨）*rain*

いけばな（生け花）*flower arranging*

おなか（お腹）*abdomen, stomach*

かつよう（活用）*conjugation*

かんじゃ（患者）*patient*

きょうじゅ（教授）*professor*

きょうみ（興味）*interest*（～に興味がある *to be interested in …*）

くしゃみ *sneeze*（くしゃみが出る／くしゃみをする *to sneeze*）

くも（雲）*cloud*

けいようし（形容詞）*adjective*

じむいん（事務員）*office worker, clerk*

じゅぎょう（授業）*class, lesson*

じゅぎょうりょう（授業料）*tuition*

じょし（助詞）*particle*

せき（咳）*cough*（咳が出る／咳をする *to cough*）

たんい（単位）*(academic) credit*

てんき（天気）*weather*

どうし（動詞）*verb*

ねつ（熱）*fever, temperature, heat*（熱がある *to have a fever*）

のど（喉）*throat*

びょうき（病気）*sickness, illness*

ぶんか（文化）*culture*

ほか（他）*another item/other items*（他の車 *other cars*）

めいし（名詞）*noun*

もんだい（問題）*question, issue, problem*

ゆき（雪）*snow*

QUESTION WORD

どうして *why*

ADJECTIVE

さむい（寒い）*cold (weather)*

あつい（暑い）*hot (weather)*

あたたかい（暖かい）*warm (weather)*

すずしい（涼しい）*cool (weather)*

ADVERB

たぶん（多分）*probably, maybe, perhaps*

うまく *well, right*

ほんとうに（本当に）*truly*

VERB (Ru-verb)

でる（出る）*to come out, to attend, to leave*（くしゃみが出る *to sneeze*, セミナーに出る *to attend the seminar*, レストランを出る *to leave the restaurant*）

はれる（晴れる）*to become clear (sky)*

VERB (U-verb)

おもう（思う）*to think*（～と思う *to think that …*）

ふる（降る）*to fall (rain/snow)*

くもる（曇る）*to become cloudy*

いる（要る）*to be required, to be needed*（単位がいる *(I) need credits.*）

IRREGULAR VERB

きんちょうする（緊張する）*to become tense or nervous*

PARTICLE

～と embedded sentence particle, quotation particle

OTHERS

～でしょう *It is probably the case that …* (plain form: ～だろう)

～かもしれない *It may be the case that …* (polite/neutral form: ～かもしれません)

つぎの～（次の～）*next …*

だいじょうぶです（大丈夫です）*It is all right.*

ほんとうです（本当です）*(It) is true.*

～からです *It is because …*

CHAPTER SIXTEEN
Permission and Obligation

Objectives:
- to ask permission and to ask about requirements
- to name different parts of a house
- to describe job conditions
- to read and write a resume

Kanji and Vocabulary

1. Reading and Writing Kanji Characters

A) Let's read each of the following kanji words or phrases aloud several times.

きょうしつ
教室 *classroom*

き
気をつける *to be careful*

こま
困る *to be in trouble*

へや
部屋 *room*

や
～屋 *store that sell ...*

おぼ
覚える *to memorize*

しごと
仕事 *job*

べんり
便利だ *convenient*

ふべん
不便だ *inconvenient*

まいにち
毎日 *every day*

まいしゅう
毎週 *every week*

まいつき
毎月 *every month*

まいとし
毎年 *every year*

さが
探す *to search*

B) In the boxes provided, write each kanji character following the correct stroke order.

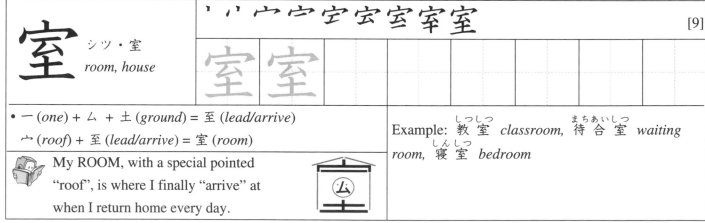

室 シツ・室
room, house

`` ` `` `宀` `宀` `宀` `空` `空` `空` `室` `室` [9]

- 一 (*one*) + ム + 土 (*ground*) = 至 (*lead/arrive*)
  宀 (*roof*) + 至 (*lead/arrive*) = 室 (*room*)

My ROOM, with a special pointed "roof", is where I finally "arrive" at when I return home every day.

Example: しっしつ 教室 *classroom*, まちあいしつ 待合室 *waiting room*, しんしつ 寝室 *bedroom*

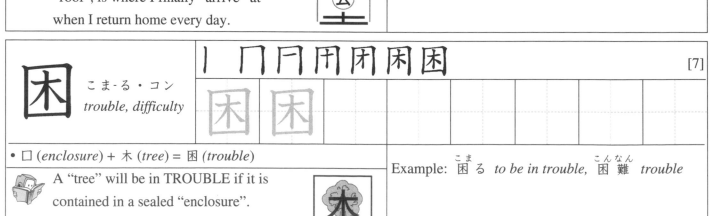

困 こま-る・コン
trouble, difficulty

`|` `冂` `冂` `用` `用` `困` `困` [7]

- 囗 (*enclosure*) + 木 (*tree*) = 困 (*trouble*)

A "tree" will be in TROUBLE if it is contained in a sealed "enclosure".

Example: こま 困る *to be in trouble*, こんなん 困難 *trouble*

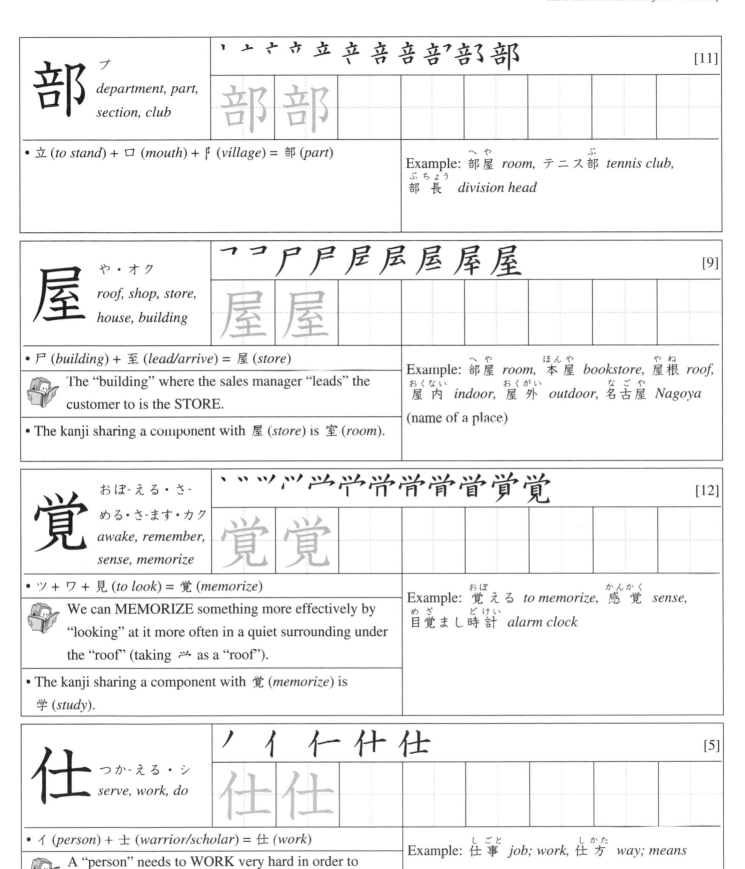

部 ブ
department, part, section, club

丶 ㇒ 亠 ナ ㇆ 立 ㇒ 音 音 音 音³ 部³ 部 [11]

部 部

• 立 (to stand) + 口 (mouth) + ㇌ (village) = 部 (part)

Example: 部屋 (へや) room, テニス部 (ぶ) tennis club, 部長 (ぶちょう) division head

屋 や・オク
roof, shop, store, house, building

㇆ ㇆ 尸 尸 尸 屏 屏 屋 屋 [9]

屋 屋

• 尸 (building) + 至 (lead/arrive) = 屋 (store)

The "building" where the sales manager "leads" the customer to is the STORE.

• The kanji sharing a component with 屋 (store) is 室 (room).

Example: 部屋 (へや) room, 本屋 (ほんや) bookstore, 屋根 (やね) roof, 屋内 (おくない) indoor, 屋外 (おくがい) outdoor, 名古屋 (なごや) Nagoya (name of a place)

覚 おぼ-える・さ-める・さ-ます・カク
awake, remember, sense, memorize

丶 ㇜ ㇜ ㇜ 宀 宀 宀 営 営 覚 覚 [12]

覚 覚

• ツ + ワ + 見 (to look) = 覚 (memorize)

We can MEMORIZE something more effectively by "looking" at it more often in a quiet surrounding under the "roof" (taking 宀 as a "roof").

• The kanji sharing a component with 覚 (memorize) is 学 (study).

Example: 覚 (おぼ) える to memorize, 感覚 (かんかく) sense, 目覚 (めざ) まし時計 (どけい) alarm clock

仕 つか-える・シ
serve, work, do

ノ イ 仁 什 仕 [5]

仕 仕

• イ (person) + 士 (warrior/scholar) = 仕 (work)

A "person" needs to WORK very hard in order to become a "scholar" (or "warrior" in the old days).

Example: 仕事 (しごと) job; work, 仕方 (しかた) way; means

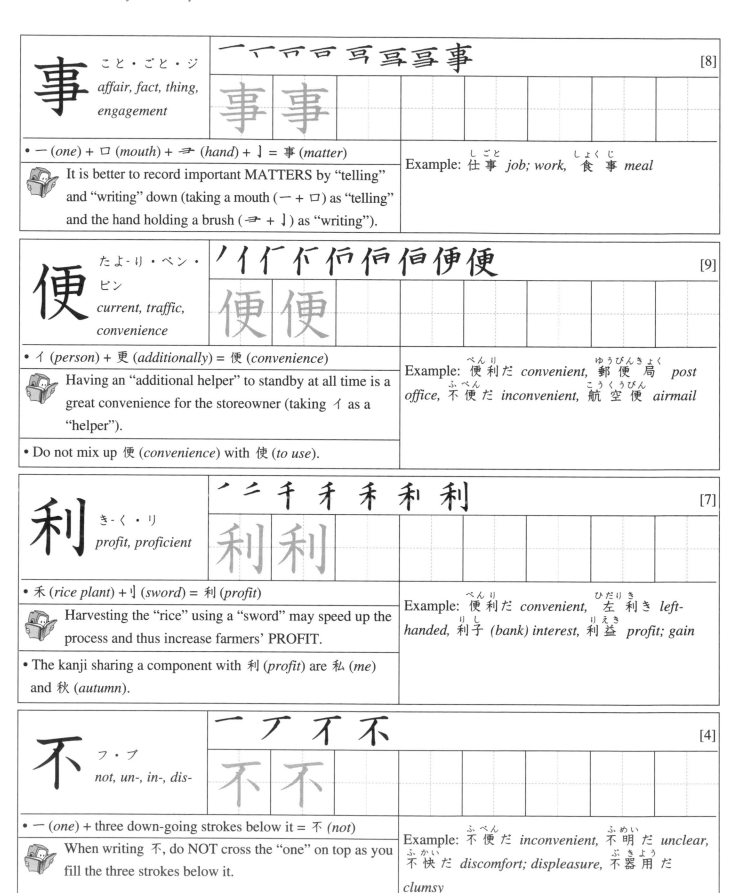

事 こと・ごと・ジ
affair, fact, thing, engagement

一 ナ 一 写 写 写 事 事 [8]

- 一 (one) + 口 (mouth) + ⺕ (hand) + ⎟ = 事 (matter)

It is better to record important MATTERS by "telling" and "writing" down (taking a mouth (一 + 口) as "telling" and the hand holding a brush (⺕ + ⎟) as "writing").

Example: 仕事 しごと *job; work*, 食事 しょくじ *meal*

便 たよ-り・ベン・ピン
current, traffic, convenience

ノ イ イ イ 佰 佰 佰 便 便 [9]

- イ (person) + 更 (additionally) = 便 (convenience)

Having an "additional helper" to standby at all time is a great convenience for the storeowner (taking イ as a "helper").

- Do not mix up 便 (convenience) with 使 (to use).

Example: 便利 べんり だ *convenient*, 郵便局 ゆうびんきょく *post office*, 不便 ふべん だ *inconvenient*, 航空便 こうくうびん *airmail*

利 き-く・リ
profit, proficient

ノ 二 千 千 禾 利 利 [7]

- 禾 (rice plant) + 刂 (sword) = 利 (profit)

Harvesting the "rice" using a "sword" may speed up the process and thus increase farmers' PROFIT.

- The kanji sharing a component with 利 (profit) are 私 (me) and 秋 (autumn).

Example: 便利 べんり だ *convenient*, 左利き ひだりきき *left-handed*, 利子 りし *(bank) interest*, 利益 りえき *profit; gain*

不 フ・ブ
not, un-, in-, dis-

一 ア 不 不 [4]

- 一 (one) + three down-going strokes below it = 不 (not)

When writing 不, do NOT cross the "one" on top as you fill the three strokes below it.

Example: 不便 ふべん だ *inconvenient*, 不明 ふめい だ *unclear*, 不快 ふかい だ *discomfort; displeasure*, 不器用 ぶきよう だ *clumsy*

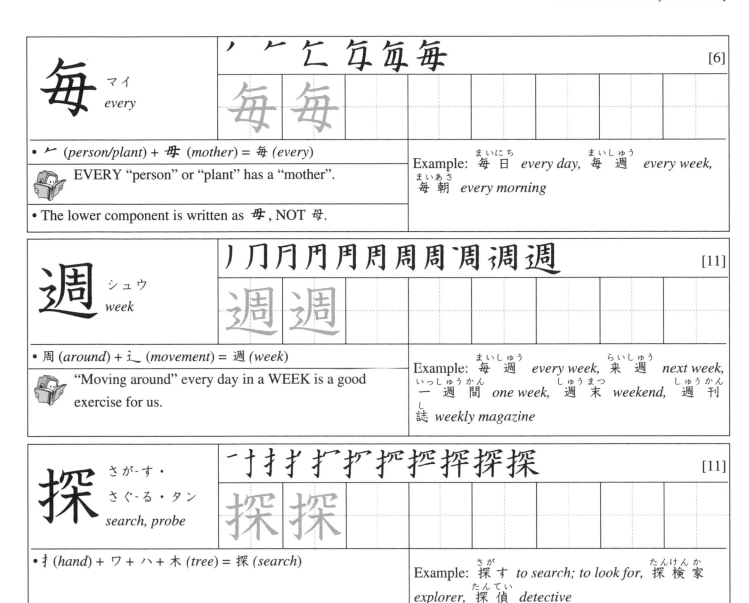

毎 マイ every

ノ 亠 仁 勾 毎 毎 [6]

毎 毎

• 亠 (person/plant) + 母 (mother) = 毎 (every)

EVERY "person" or "plant" has a "mother".

• The lower component is written as 毋, NOT 母.

Example: 毎日 every day, 毎週 every week, 毎朝 every morning

週 シュウ week

丿 刀 月 円 円 円 周 周 `周 调 週 [11]

週 週

• 周 (around) + 辶 (movement) = 週 (week)

"Moving around" every day in a WEEK is a good exercise for us.

Example: 毎週 every week, 来週 next week, 一週間 one week, 週末 weekend, 週刊誌 weekly magazine

探 さが-す・さぐ-る・タン search, probe

一 寸 扌 扩 扩 护 挧 挧 探 探 [11]

探 探

• 扌 (hand) + ワ + ハ + 木 (tree) = 探 (search)

Example: 探す to search; to look for, 探検家 explorer, 探偵 detective

C) Let's read aloud to check how well you've mastered the kanji you've learned.

1. 毎日たんごを七つ覚えます。クラスで毎日たんごクイズがあります。

2. このじしょは小さくて便利です。毎日使っています。教室にももって行きます。でも、あのじしょは大きくて不便です。いつも部屋で使っていますが、教室にはもって行きません。毎週、漢字テストがあります。とても難しくて、困っています。今、いい漢字のテキストを探しています。

3. 毎月、仕事で外国に行きます。かん国や、中国や、シンガポールに行きます。いつも便利で、安いホテルを探します。食べものには気をつけています。

4. 毎年、子供の夏休みにはかぞくでハワイに行きます。シュノーケリングをします。おみやげにネックレスやマカデミアンナッツを買います。

D) Fill in the correct kanji characters in the boxes provided.

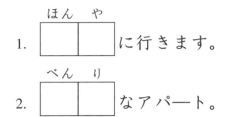

1. ほん や　□□ に行きます。

2. べん り　□□ なアパート。

3. かぎを □ しています。　さが

4. まい にち　□□ 、 し ごと □□ をします。

2. Naming Various Occupations

The following passage is about a family members' occupation. Fill in the blanks by selecting appropriate words from the list below.

> じきゅう・きゅうりょう・ざんぎょう・つうきん・さらあらい

　弟は毎週日曜日にレストランで働いています。_____ をしています。_____ は900円です。5時間働いて、一日に4,500円もらいます。兄は貿易会社で働いています。毎日_____ は便利です。地下鉄で15分です。_____ があるので、うちには10時ごろに帰ります。

3. Naming Different Parts of a House

The following passage is about Akiko's house. Fill in the blanks appropriately.

　私のうちの_____ (kitchen) はとても広いです。_____ (toilet) は2つあります。_____ (straw mat) の部屋が2つと、_____ (carpet) の部屋が1つあります。

Grammar

1. 〜てもいい and 〜てはいけない 1

To express a permission, combine a conditional phrase in the form of 〜ても (*even if ...*) with an approval phrase such as いいです (*it is fine.*) For example, テレビを見てもいいです (literally *even if you watch TV, it is fine*) means *you may watch TV*. On the other hand, to express a prohibition, combine a conditional phrase in the form of 〜ては (*if ...*) and a denial phrase such as いけません (*it is bad.*) For example, テレビを見てはいけません (literally *if you watch TV, it is bad*) means *you may not watch TV*.

For each phrase, construct a statement expressing a permission and a statement expressing a prohibition.

Example: お酒を飲む   →   Permission: お酒を飲んでもいいですよ。

                                   Prohibition: お酒を飲んではいけませんよ。

1. タバコをすう   →   Permission: _____

                                     Prohibition: _____

2. じしょを見る   →   Permission: _____

                                     Prohibition: _____

3. 友達に言う   →   Permission: _____

                                     Prohibition: _____

4. 会社の車を使う   →   Permission: _____

                                     Prohibition: _____

2. 〜てもいい and 〜てはいけない 2

The constructions 〜てもいい and 〜てはいけない can be used not only with a verb, but also with a copula and an adjective for expressing permissible and impermissible, or acceptable and unacceptable. For example, じゅうたんは古くてもいいです means *an old carpet is acceptable*, and じゅうたんは古くてはいけません means *an old carpet is not acceptable*.

Takeshi is looking for an apartment. Below is a passage describing the conditions of a prospective apartment. Complete the passage by filling in the blanks with appropriate words.

今、アパートを探しています。友達といっしょに住むつもりです。ですから、寝室 (bedroom)が2つなくては_____。料理はしませんから、台所はなくても_____。あまりお金がありませんから、家賃は_____いけません。ちょっと不便でも_____。あまりきれいじゃなくても_____。

3. 〜なくてはいけない and 〜なくてもいい

To express an obligation, combine a negative conditional phrase in the form of 〜なくては (*if you do not ...*) and a denial phrase like いけません (*it is bad.*) For example, 宿題をしなくてはいけません (literally *if you do not do your homework, it is bad*) means *you must do your homework*. To express a discretion, combine a negative conditional phrase in the form of 〜なくても (*even if you do not ...*) and an approval phrase like いいです (*it is fine.*) For example, 宿題をしなくてもいいです (literally *even if you do not do your homework, it is fine*) means *you do not have to do your homework*. Both can be applied to an adjective and a copula.

For each phrase, construct a statement expressing an obligation and a statement expressing a discretion.

Example: そうじをする ⟶ Obligation: そうじをしなくてはいけません。

Discretion: そうじをしなくてもいいです。

1. 漢字（かんじ）を覚える ⟶ Obligation: _____

Discretion: _____

2. ざんぎょうをする ⟶ Obligation: _____

Discretion: _____

3. だいどころは広い ⟶ Obligation: _____

Discretion: _____

4. ワインは赤だ ⟶ Obligation: _____

Discretion: _____

Conversation and Usage

アパート探し

 Lyn is moving to Nagoya for her new job as a proofreader in a translation company in Nagoya. She is talking to a realtor about finding an apartment near the company. Listen carefully to their conversation and then answer the questions.

リン　　　　：あのう、4月（しがつ）から桜町（さくらまち）にアパートを借（か）りたいんですが。

不動産屋（ふどうさんや）：お一人（ひとり）で住（す）むんですか。

リン　　　　：はい。

不動産屋　　：(The realtor starts checking the information.) ええと、桜町、桜町。

リン　　　　：インターナショナルー・センター・ビルの近（ちか）くがいいんですが。

不動産屋　　：ああ、あの高（たか）いビルですね。

リン　　　　：ええ。

不動産屋　　：家賃（やちん）はいくらぐらいで？

リン　　　　：5万円以下（まんえんいか）で。

不動産屋　　：うんんん。ちょっと5万円以下では難（むずか）しいと思（おも）いますよ。

リン　　　　：そうですか。

不動産屋　：ちょっとこれを見て下さい。(The realtor shows the layout of an apartment.) これは6畳の和室が1つと、台所が1つです。インターナショナル・センター・ビルから歩いて10分です。でも、家賃は9万円。

リン　　　：高いですね。

不動産屋　：(The realtor shows the layout of another apartment.) これは桜町から地下鉄で20分。洋室が1つと、ダイニングキッチンで、5万円ですが。

リン　　　：ああ。

不動産屋　：あっ、でも、これは7月までは空きません。

リン　　　：それは困ります。私は4月1日までに入らなくてはいけないんです。*1

不動産屋　：じゃあ、これは？(The realtor shows the layout of another apartment.) これは4万円ですよ。

リン　　　：ああ、安い！それに、洋室と、和室と、ダイニングキッチンがありますね。近くに地下鉄の駅はありますか。

不動産屋　：いいえ。

リン　　　：やっぱり。桜町まではどれぐらいかかりますか。

不動産屋　：バスで40分ぐらいです。

リン　　　：バスで40分ですか。じゃあ、オートバイでも買おうかな。

不動産屋　：オートバイですか？気をつけて下さいよ。

リン　　　：ええ、だいじょうぶ。じゃあ、このアパートをお願いします。

[*Unfamiliar words:* 不動産屋 is the informal way of saying 不動産業者 *(real estate agent),* 桜町 the name of a town, ええと is the interjection used when one needs time to figure out the right reply or response (like *"Well..."*), インターナショナルー・センター・ビル *International Center Building,* 〜以下 *... or less,* 6畳 *six-tatami-mat room,* 和室 *Japanese-style room,* 洋室 *Western-style room,* ダイニングキッチン *eat-in-kitchen,* 空く *to become vacant,* やっぱり *as one expected,* オートバイ *motorcycle,* 買おう the volitional form (the speaker's volition or will to do something) of, 買う *to buy,* かな a sentence-ending particle that indicates a question to oneself (like *"I wonder"*)]

Note: (*1) までに (the combination of particles まで and に) expresses a deadline when used with a time phrase.

1. When does Lyn want to move into the new apartment? _____

2. Was Lyn able to find an apartment near the International Center Building with a rent below 50,000 yen?

_____

3. What kind of apartment did Lyn decide to move to? Describe. _____

_____

Listening Comprehension

仕事のルール

Ken is working at a store part-time and there are some rules that the employees must follow. Listen to the narrative on the CD and answer the questions that follow.

1. What are forbidden? List them all. _____

    _____

2. What are required? List them all. _____

    _____

Reading Comprehension

りれきしょ (Resume)

The following is a relatively simple resume (履歴書 りれきしょ) written by Manabu Takabe (高部 学 たかべまなぶ) on September 5, 2006 (平成 へいせい 18年9月5日), for applying for a part-time job. Read it carefully and then answer the questions. You may encounter several unfamiliar words, but you should be able to answer the questions.

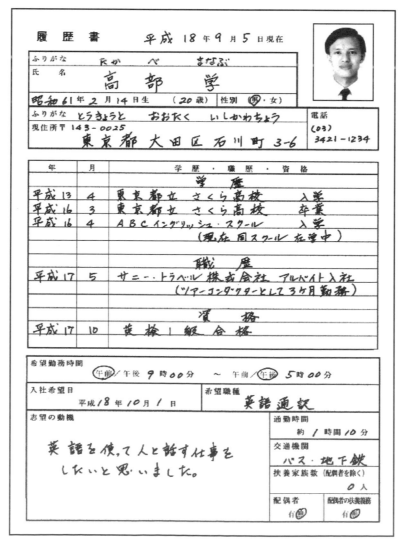

[*Unfamiliar words:* 平成 *Heisei* (Japanese era name), 学歴 *academic career*, 職歴 *professional career*, 資格 *qualification*, 入学 *to be admitted to a school*, 卒業 *to graduate from a school*]

1. When did Manabu graduate from high school? _____

2. What did he study after he graduated from high school? _____

3. What did he do at Sunny Travel, Inc? _____

Writing

りれきしょ (Resume)

Pretend that the table below is part of your resume. Complete it by filling out your academic career, professional career and qualifications in Japanese.

年	月	学 歴 ・ 職 歴 ・ 資 格

New Vocabulary Reference List

NOUN

きょうしつ (教室) *classroom*

さらあらい (皿洗い) *dish-washing*

ざんぎょう (残業) *overtime work*

じきゅう (時給) *hourly wage*

じゅうたん *carpet*

スリッパ *slippers*

せわ (世話) *care, aid* (犬 (いぬ) の世話をする *to take care of the dog*)

だいどころ (台所) *kitchen*

たたみ (畳) *tatami mat, straw mat*

つうきん (通勤) *commute to work*

トイレ *toilet*

ふろ・おふろ (風呂・お風呂) *bath*

まいしゅう (毎週) *every week*

まいつき (毎月) *every month*

まいとし (毎年) *every year*

まいにち (毎日) *every day*

ADVERB

ぜったい(に) (絶対(に)) *absolutely* (絶対にいけません。 *Absolutely not permitted.*)

VERB (Ru-verb)

おぼえる (覚える) *to memorize* (単語を覚える *to memorize vocabulary words*)

VERB (U-verb)

こまる (困る) *to be in trouble*

さがす (探す) *to search ..., to search for ..., to look for ...* (かぎを探す *to look for the key*, へやの中を探す *to search the room*)

IRREGULAR

しんぱいする (心配する) *to worry* (子供のことを心配する *to worry about one's child*)

OTHERS

きをつける (気をつける) *to be careful* (車に気をつける *to watch out for the car*)

～までに *by ... (deadline)* (9時までに帰ります。 *I will return by 9 o'clock.*)

CHAPTER SEVENTEEN
Comparison

Objectives:

- to name sets and classes
- to name the four Japanese islands
- to make comparison and express superlatives

Kanji and Vocabulary

1. Reading and Writing Kanji Characters

A) Let's read each kanji word or phrase aloud several times.

北海道 *Hokkaido* (Japanese island)　　　森田 *Morita* (family name)

本州 *Honshu* (Japanese island)　　　　川 *river*

九州 *Kyushu* (Japanese island)　　　　湖 *lake*

四国 *Shikoku* (Japanese island)　　　　海 *sea, ocean*

土地 *land*　　　　　　　　　　　　泳ぐ *to swim*

地下 *basement, underground*　　　　肉 *meat*

人口 *population*　　　　　　　　　魚 *fish*

同じ *same*　　　　　　　　　　　色 *color*

〜の方 *...'s side*　　　　　　　　一番 *the most, the best, the first*

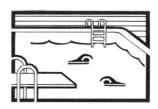

B) In the boxes provided, write each kanji character following the correct stroke order.

うみ・カイ
sea, ocean

丶　亠　氵　氵　汇　汇　海　海　海　　　[9]

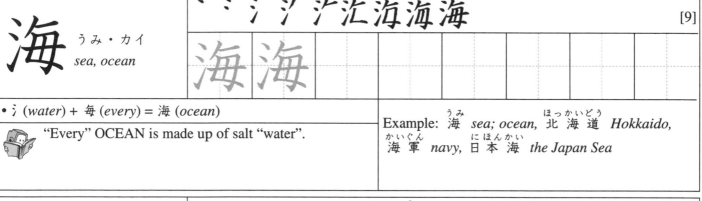

- 氵 (water) + 毎 (every) = 海 (ocean)

　"Every" OCEAN is made up of salt "water".

Example: 海 *sea; ocean*, 北海道 *Hokkaido*,
海軍 *navy*, 日本海 *the Japan Sea*

州
シュウ・す
state, province, sandbank

丶　丿　丿　州　州　州　　　[6]

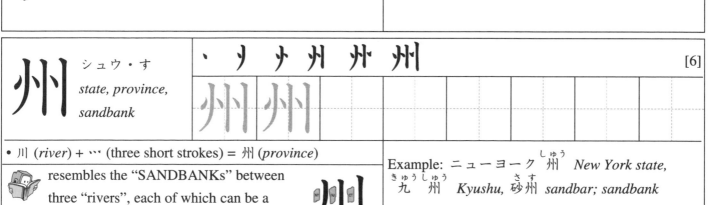

- 川 (river) + 丶丶丶 (three short strokes) = 州 (province)

　resembles the "SANDBANKs" between three "rivers", each of which can be a PROVINCE

Example: ニューヨーク州 *New York state*,
九州 *Kyushu*, 砂州 *sandbar; sandbank*

地 チ・ジ
ground, land

一 十 土 圡 地 地 [6]

地 地

• 土 (*soil*) + 也 (*to be*) = 地 (*ground*)

"Soil" is considered "to be" the main component that makes the GROUND.

Example: 土地 *land*, 地下 *basement*, 地下鉄 *subway*

同 おな-じ・ドウ
same

｜ 冂 冂 同 同 同 [6]

同 同

• 冂 + 一 (*one*) + 口 (*mouth*) = 同 (*same*)

This character is more or less symmetrical—the left side is almost the SAME as the right side.

同

Example: 同じ *the same*, 同時に *simultaneously*

方 かた／がた・ホウ
direction, way, side, means

丶 一 方 方 [4]

方 方

• 丶 + 万 (*ten thousand*) = 方 (*way/direction*)

Can you believe it? The boy who was lost in the jungle was saved by "ten thousand ants" that form a line which showed him the WAY out (taking 丶 as an ant).

Example: 〜の方 *...'s side*, この方 *this person* (polite), 夕方 *evening*, 方向 *direction*, 仕方 *method*

森 もり・シン
forest

一 十 才 木 朩 杧 柰 柰 森 森 森 森 [12]

森 森

• 木 (*tree*) + 木 (*tree*) + 木 (*tree*) = 森 (*forest*)

a "tree" is often above other "trees" in the FOREST

木
林

Example: 森 *forest*, 森田 *Morita* (family name)

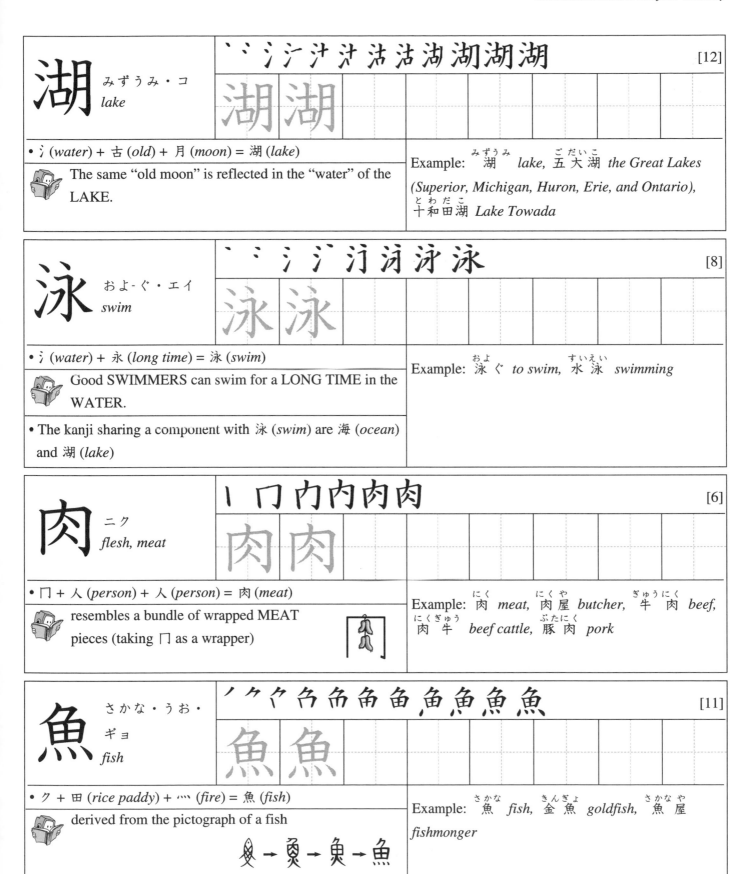

湖
みずうみ・コ
lake

ヽ ヽ シ シ 汁 汁 沽 沽 汮 湖 湖 湖 [12]

湖 湖

• シ (water) + 古 (old) + 月 (moon) = 湖 (lake)

The same "old moon" is reflected in the "water" of the LAKE.

Example: 湖 (みずうみ) lake, 五大湖 (ごだいこ) the Great Lakes (Superior, Michigan, Huron, Erie, and Ontario), 十和田湖 (とわだこ) Lake Towada

---

泳
およ-ぐ・エイ
swim

ヽ ヽ シ シ 汀 汀 汯 泳 [8]

泳 泳

• シ (water) + 永 (long time) = 泳 (swim)

Good SWIMMERS can swim for a LONG TIME in the WATER.

• The kanji sharing a component with 泳 (swim) are 海 (ocean) and 湖 (lake)

Example: 泳ぐ (およぐ) to swim, 水泳 (すいえい) swimming

肉
ニク
flesh, meat

ヽ 冂 内 内 肉 肉 [6]

肉 肉

• 冂 + 人 (person) + 人 (person) = 肉 (meat)

resembles a bundle of wrapped MEAT pieces (taking 冂 as a wrapper)

Example: 肉 (にく) meat, 肉屋 (にくや) butcher, 牛肉 (ぎゅうにく) beef, 肉牛 (にくぎゅう) beef cattle, 豚肉 (ぶたにく) pork

---

魚
さかな・うお・ギョ
fish

ノ ク ケ 夕 各 各 角 魚 魚 魚 魚 [11]

魚 魚

• ク + 田 (rice paddy) + 灬 (fire) = 魚 (fish)

derived from the pictograph of a fish

Example: 魚 (さかな) fish, 金魚 (きんぎょ) goldfish, 魚屋 (さかなや) fishmonger

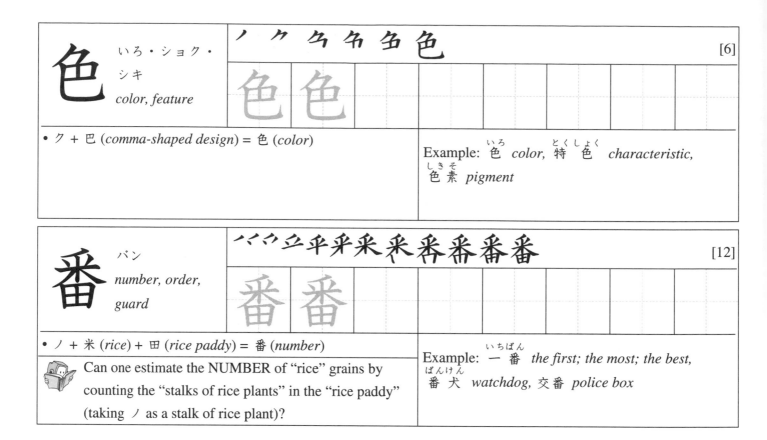

色 いろ・ショク・シキ color, feature	ノ ク ク 名 色 色							[6]
	色 色							

• ク + 巴 (comma-shaped design) = 色 (color)

Example: 色 (いろ) color, 特色 (とくしょく) characteristic, 色素 (しきそ) pigment

番 バン number, order, guard	ハ ヘ ヘ 平 平 来 来 来 番 番 番							[12]
	番 番							

• ノ + 米 (rice) + 田 (rice paddy) = 番 (number)

Can one estimate the NUMBER of "rice" grains by counting the "stalks of rice plants" in the "rice paddy" (taking ノ as a stalk of rice plant)?

Example: 一番 (いちばん) the first; the most; the best, 番犬 (ばんけん) watchdog, 交番 police box

C) Let's read aloud to check how well you've mastered the kanji you've learned.

1. 日本は土地がせまくて、人口が多いです。高いたてものがたくさんあります。地下にもショッピングモールがたくさんあります。やちんは高いです。食べものも高いです。日本の肉や魚は高いですが、とてもおいしいです。

2. 私は泳ぐのが大好きです。プールで泳ぐより、海や、川や、湖で泳ぐ方が好きです。湖で泳ぐのは一番楽しいです。毎年、カナダのともだちのうちに行きます。近くに湖があります。ともだちといっしょに泳ぎます。

D) Fill in the correct kanji characters in the boxes provided.

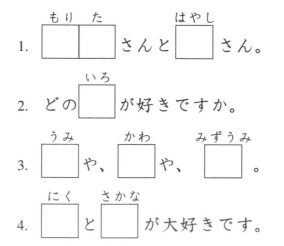

1. [もり][た]さんと[はやし]さん。

2. どの[いろ]が好きですか。

3. [うみ]や、[かわ]や、[みずうみ]。

4. [にく]と[さかな]が大好きです。

2. Grouping Items

Fill in the category to which each set of items belong.

Example: <u>のみもの</u>:　コーヒー・オレンジジュース・コーラ

1. _____:　キャベツ *cabbage*・ピーマン *pepper*

2. _____:　バナナ *banana*・りんご *apple*・いちご *strawberry*

3. _____:　牛肉 *beef*・豚肉 *pork*・鶏肉 *chicken*

4. _____:　鮭 *salmon*・鮪 *tuna*・鯛 *red snapper*

5. _____:　春・夏・秋・冬

6. _____:　日本・アメリカ・フランス・タイ

3. Naming Japanese Islands

Write the names of the four largest Islands of Japan in kanji and hiragana.

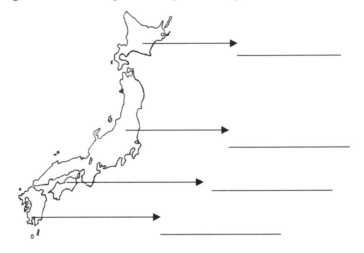

Grammar

1. 〜より

> In Japanese, it is not required to conjugate the adjectives or adverbs in a sentence that expresses a comparison. To compare two items, simply add the particle より (*than*) to the item being compared with the topic item. For instance, スミスさんはやさしいです means *Mr. Smith is kind*, and スミスさんはリーさんよりやさしいです means *Mr. Smith is kinder than Mr. Lee.*

 Following the example below, form a sentence that compares the item in the parentheses with the item in each sentence.

Example: 中国は広いです。（日本）　⟶　中国は日本より広いです。

1. 漢字は難しいです。（カタカナ）　⟶　_____。

2. 犬はかわいいです。（ねこ）　⟶　_____。

3. 魚はからだにいいです。（肉）　⟶　_____。

4. 母はやさしいです。（父）　⟶　_____。

2. どちら

When forming a question that compares two items X and Y, begin with the phrase Xと、Yとでは, followed by どちら or どちらの方 (which one) before completing the sentence. では is not used in some cases. The answer to a どちら-question begins with 〜の方が, as below:

A: 漢字と、カタカナとでは、どちらの方が難しいですか。

Which is more difficult, kanji or katakana?

B: 漢字の方が難しいです。

Kanji is more difficult (than katakana.)

Look at the following illustrations. Form a question that compares the two items in each set. Be creative.

1. 魚　　 肉　　4. 北海道　　九州

2. 犬　　 ねこ

3. ひこうき　　 車　　5. こんにちは！: 日本語　　*Ni hao* 你好: 中国語

1. _____

2. _____

3. _____

4. _____

5. _____

3. 〜と同じぐらい〜 and 〜ほど〜ない

Equivalence is expressed by the phrase 〜と同じぐらい, as in メアリーさんはけい子さんと同じぐらい背が高いです (*Mary is as tall as Keiko*). The degree of some property of an item that does not match or less than the item compared with can be indicated using the particle ほど, along with a negative adjective or verb. For example, メアリーさんはけい子さんほど背が高くありません means *Mary is not as tall as Keiko*.

1. けい子さんはメアリーさん_____背が高_____。

2. けい子さんはアン_____背が高_____。

3. けい子さんはよう子さん_____背が高_____。

よう子　けい子　メアリー　アン

4. ～の

When comparing activities using verbs, add the noun-maker の at the end of the verb and place it before other particles such as が, は and で. However, please note that の is not usually used when a verb occurs right before より, and is never used before ほど and 方（ほう） in this construction.

Examples: 漢字（かんじ）を書（か）くのは ひらがなを書（か）くより 難（むずか）しいです。

Writing kanji is more difficult than writing hiragana.

ピアノをひくのは うたをうたうのと 同（おな）じぐらい 楽（たの）しいです。

Playing the piano is as fun as singing a song.

話（はな）すのは書（か）くほど 難（むずか）しくありません。

Speaking is not as difficult as writing.

A: 勉強（べんきょう）するのと、遊（あそ）ぶのとでは、どちらの方（ほう）が好（す）きですか。

Which do you like better, studying or playing?

B: 遊ぶ方が勉強するより好きです。

I like playing better than studying.

Answer the following questions.

1. スポーツをするのと、スポーツを見るのとでは、どちらの方が好きですか。

   _____

2. りょうりをするのと、さらを洗うのと、どちらの方が好きですか。

   _____

3. 日本語を話すのと、日本語を聞くのとでは、どちらの方が難しいですか。

   _____

Note: When the particle も follows a question word such as どちら or どの～, it indicates "both" or "all". Example:

どちらも好（す）きです。 *I like both.*

どの学生（がくせい）も来（き）ました。 *All the students came.*

However, if the verb or the adjective of the sentence is negative, the particle も indicates "either", "neither" or "no/none," Example:

どちらも好きじゃありません。 *I like neither one of them./I don't like either one of them.*

どの学生も来ませんでした。 *No student came.*

5. いちばん

The superlative of an adjective is expressed simply by adding the adverb 一番（いちばん）. For instance, スミスさんは背（せ）が高（たか）いです means *Mr. Smith is tall*, and スミスさんは一番背が高いです means *Mr. Smith is the tallest*. The basis of superlative can be a list of items or a set, as in 兄（あに）と姉（あね）と私の中（なか）では、私が一番背が高いです or うちの中では私は一番背が高いです.

Question words used for comparison			
	People	Location	Others
Two items	どちら	どちら	どちら
Three or more items	だれ	どこ	どれ
Set	だれ	どこ	何

Following the example, underline the appropriate question word in the parentheses.

Example: クラスでは、（どれ・だれ・どちら）が一番背（せ）が高（たか）いですか。

1. としょかんと、りょうと、ラボの中では、（どれ・どこ・何）が一番しずかですか。
2. ねこと、犬（いぬ）と、さるの中では、（どれ・何・だれ）が一番好（す）きですか。
3. どうぶつでは、（どれ・何・だれ）が一番好きですか。
4. ピザと、ハンバーガーと、すしの中では、（どれ・どちら・何）が一番好きですか。
5. 食べものの中では、（どれ・どちら・何）が一番好きですか。
6. 今（いま）、（どれ・何・だれ）が一番したいですか。

Conversation and Usage

日本への留学

Kelly would like to go for a study abroad（留学（りゅうがく））program in Japan. She is getting some advice from her Japanese friend, Toshihiko, on which city is best for her. Listen to the conversation carefully and answer the questions that follow.

ケリー　：日本に留学（りゅうがく）したいんだ。

としひこ：本当（ほんとう）？

ケリー　：うん。東京（とうきょう）か、大阪（おおさか）か、名古屋（なごや）か、京都（きょうと）。

としひこ：ああ。

ケリー　：でも、東京（とうきょう）はぶっかが高（たか）いよね。

としひこ：うん。一番（いちばん）高いよ。

ケリー　：じゃあ、無理ね。大阪と、名古屋と、京都では、どこが一番おもしろい？

としひこ：日本の古い文化は好き？

ケリー　：うん、大好き。お寺や、神社。きものや、いけばなも。

としひこ：それなら、京都が一番おもしろいと思うよ。お寺や、神社が多いから。

ケリー　：名古屋は？

としひこ：名古屋は日本で3番目に大きい都市。東京と大阪の次。

ケリー　：東京から遠いの？

としひこ：東京から新幹線で2時間ぐらい。

ケリー　：ああ、近いじゃない。

としひこ：うん。でも、片道一万円ぐらいかかるよ。

ケリー　：じゃあ、遠いね。

[**Unfamiliar words:** 留学 *study abroad,* 無理 *impossible,* お寺 *temple,* 神社 *(Shinto) shrine,* それなら *if so,* 都市 *city,* 新幹線 *Shinkansen (bullet train),* 片道 *one way*]

1. What is the disadvantage of living in Tokyo for Kelly?　_____
2. What is the advantage of living in Kyoto for Kelly?　_____
3. What are the three largest cities in Japan?　_____
4. How long does it take from Tokyo to Nagoya by Shinkansen?　_____

Listening Comprehension

家のサイズ

Listen carefully to a narrative about the houses of 山田さん, 田中さん, 川口さん and 石田さん. Then state which illustration below correctly shows the relative size of their houses.

A.

C.

B.

Reading Comprehension

長生きした人

The following passage is about the longest living persons in the world, as recorded in the Guinness Book of World Record. Let's read it carefully and then answer the questions.

　2005年のギネス・ワールド・レコードによると、世界で一番長生きした男性は日本人の泉重千代さんだ。彼は1865年に生まれ、1986年に120オで亡くなった。世界で一番長生きした女性はフランス人のジャンヌ・カルマンさんだ。彼女は1875年に生まれ、1997年に122オで亡くなった。世界で一番長生きした双子の姉妹は成田きんさんと、蟹江ぎんさんだ。2人は1892年に生まれ、きんさんは2000年に107オで亡くなり、ぎんさんは2001年に108オで亡くなった。2人とも19世紀、20世紀、21世紀を生きた。きんさんは子供を11人産み、孫が11人、曾孫が7人、玄孫が1人いた。ぎんさんは子供が5人、孫が4人、曾孫が9人いた。

[*Unfamiliar words:* 長生きする *to live long,* 男性 *man; male,* 生まれる *to be born,* 亡くなる *to die,* 女性 *woman,* 双子 *twin,* 姉妹 *sisters,* ～世紀 *the ...th century,* 生きる *to live,* 子供を産む *to give birth to a child,* 孫 *grandchild,* 曾孫 *great-grandchild,* 玄孫 *great-grand-grandchild*]

1. How old was Mr. Shigechiyo Izumi when he died? _____
2. Who is the longest living woman in the world as of 2005? _____
3. How old were Kin and Gin when they died? _____
4. Who gave birth to more children, Kin or Gin? _____

Writing

日本語の学生

The table below lists the top ten countries with the biggest number of people learning the Japanese language in 1998 and 2003. Study it carefully and write down your observations in Japanese.

Country	1998	2003	Change
1. Korea	948,104	894,131	-5.7%
2. China	245,863	387,924	+57.8%
3. Australia	307,760	381,954	+24.1%
4. USA	112,977	140,200	+24.1%
5. Taiwan	161,872	128,641	-20.5%
6. Indonesia	54,016	85,221	+57.8%
7. Thailand	39,822	54,884	+37.8%
8. New Zealand	41,507	28,317	-31.8%
9. Canada	21,784	20,457	-6.1%
10. Brazil	16,678	19,744	+18.4%

The number of students of Japanese
(Source: Japan Foundation)

CHAPTER SEVENTEEN | New Vocabulary Reference List

[*Useful words:* ふえる *to increase,* へる *to decrease*]

_____

_____

_____

_____

_____

_____

_____

_____

_____

New Vocabulary Reference List

NOUN

かわ (川) *river*

きせつ (季節) *season*

くだもの (果物) *fruit*

さかな (魚) *fish*

じんこう (人口) *population*

せかい (世界) *world*

とち (土地) *land, estate*

にく (肉) *meat*

ぶっか (物価) *commodity price*

みずうみ (湖) *lake*

やさい (野菜) *vegetable*

PROPER NOUN

きゅうしゅう (九州) *Kyushu*

しこく (四国) *Shikoku*

ほっかいどう (北海道) *Hokkaido*

ほんしゅう (本州) *Honshu*

ADJECTIVE

あぶない (危ない) *dangerous*

あんぜんな (安全な) *safe*

ADVERB

ずっと *by far*

VERB (U-verb)

はしる (走る) *to run*

PARTICLE

～ほど (～ない) *(not) as ... as ...*

～より *than ...*

OTHERS

おなじ (同じ) *same*

～ほう (～方) *... side, ... direction*

－ 41 －

CHAPTER EIGHTEEN
When to Do What?

Objectives:

- to learn and use time adverbial phrases with 〜時に, 〜前に, 〜間に and 〜後に
- to express two actions that take place simultaneously using 〜ながら
- to practice common daily-life set phrases and action verbs
- to use the words related to college admission and graduation, food preparations and recipes

Kanji and Vocabulary

1. Reading and Writing Kanji Characters

A) Let's read each of the following kanji words or phrases aloud several times.

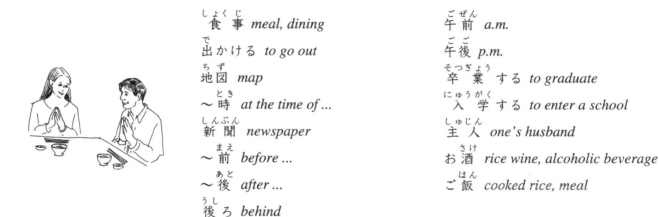

食事 *meal, dining*
出かける *to go out*
地図 *map*
〜時 *at the time of ...*
新聞 *newspaper*
〜前 *before ...*
〜後 *after ...*
後ろ *behind*

午前 *a.m.*
午後 *p.m.*
卒業する *to graduate*
入学する *to enter a school*
主人 *one's husband*
お酒 *rice wine, alcoholic beverage*
ご飯 *cooked rice, meal*

B) In the boxes provided, write each kanji character following the correct stroke order.

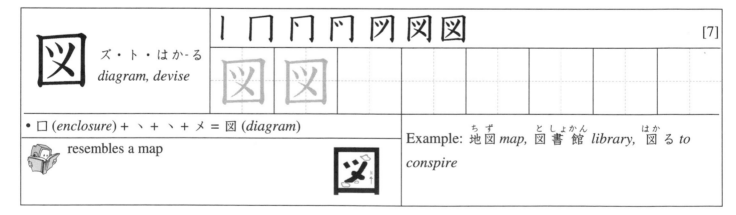

図 ズ・ト・はか-る
diagram, devise

一 冂 冂 冋 図 図 図 [7]

- 囗 (*enclosure*) + 丶 + 丶 + メ = 図 (*diagram*)
- resembles a map

Example: 地図 *map*, 図書館 *library*, 図る *to conspire*

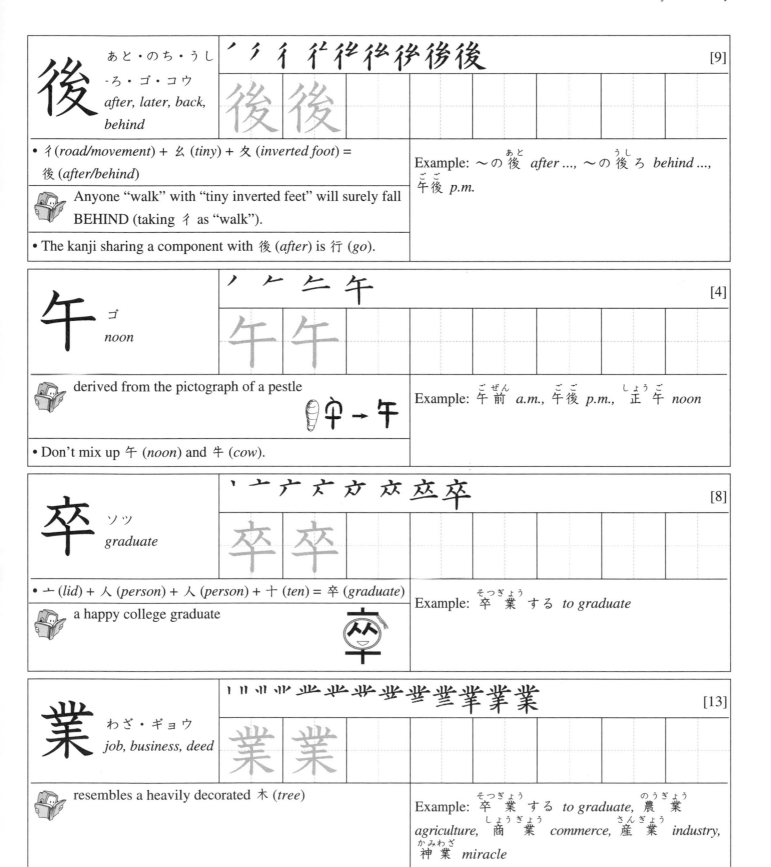

後	あと・のち・うし -ろ・ゴ・コウ after, later, back, behind	′ ク イ 彳 彴 徉 待 後 後						[9]

後 後

- 彳 (road/movement) + 幺 (tiny) + 夂 (inverted foot) = 後 (after/behind)
- Anyone "walk" with "tiny inverted feet" will surely fall BEHIND (taking 彳 as "walk").
- The kanji sharing a component with 後 (after) is 行 (go).

Example: 〜の後 after ..., 〜の後ろ behind ..., 午後 p.m.

午	ゴ noon	′ ╰ 二 午						[4]

午 午

- derived from the pictograph of a pestle
- Don't mix up 午 (noon) and 牛 (cow).

Example: 午前 a.m., 午後 p.m., 正午 noon

卒	ソツ graduate	′ 亠 广 亢 亢 众 众 卒						[8]

卒 卒

- 亠 (lid) + 人 (person) + 人 (person) + 十 (ten) = 卒 (graduate)
- a happy college graduate

Example: 卒業する to graduate

業	わざ・ギョウ job, business, deed	丨 丨丨 丨丨 业 业 业 业 业 丵 丵 業 業						[13]

業 業

- resembles a heavily decorated 木 (tree)

Example: 卒業する to graduate, 農業 agriculture, 商業 commerce, 産業 industry, 神業 miracle

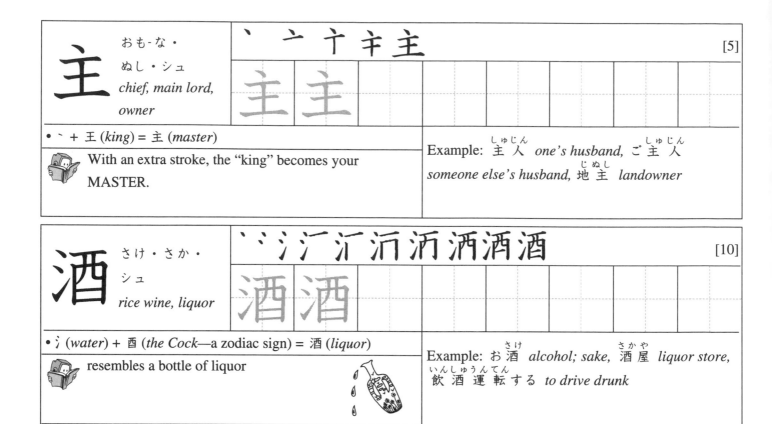

| 主 | おも-な・ぬし・シュ chief, main lord, owner | 丶 一 十 主 主 | | | | | | | | [5] |

• 丶 + 王 (*king*) = 主 (*master*)

With an extra stroke, the "king" becomes your MASTER.

Example: 主人 (しゅじん) *one's husband*, ご主人 (しゅじん) *someone else's husband*, 地主 (じぬし) *landowner*

| 酒 | さけ・さか・シュ rice wine, liquor | 丶 丶 氵 沂 沂 洒 洒 酒 酒 | | | | | | | | [10] |

• 氵 (*water*) + 酉 (*the Cock—a zodiac sign*) = 酒 (*liquor*)

resembles a bottle of liquor

Example: お酒 (さけ) *alcohol; sake*, 酒屋 (さかや) *liquor store*, 飲酒運転する (いんしゅうんてん) *to drive drunk*

• The kanji sharing a component with 酒 (*liquor*) are 海 (*ocean*), 湖 (*lake*) and 泳 (*swim*).

| 飯 | めし・ハン cooked rice, meal, food | ノ 𠆢 𠆢 今 今 仝 食 食 食 飮 飯 飯 | | | | | | | | [12] |

• 飠 (*eat*) + 反 (*opposite*) = 飯 (*meal*)

I like to sit "opposite" my little brother during a MEAL, watching his reaction when I "eat" his favorite food.

• The kanji sharing a component with 飯 (*meal*) is 飲 (*drink*).

Example: ご飯 (はん) *cooked rice; meal*, 釜飯 (かまめし) *rice, meat, and vegetables cooked together in a small pot*

C) Let's read aloud to check how well you've mastered the kanji you've learned.

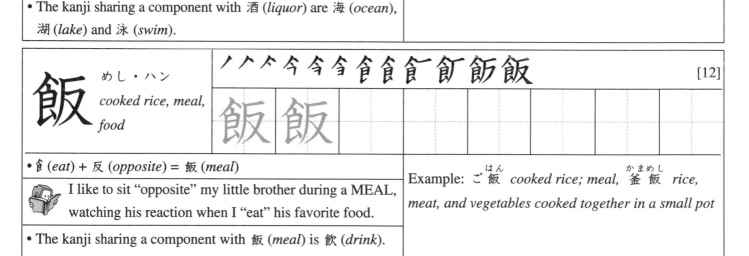

1. ひこうきはニューヨークを午後11時に出て、かん国のソウルにつぎの日の午前4時に着き(つ)ました。ひこうきに乗る前にお酒を買いました。ひこうきの中では新聞を読んで、かん国のえいがを見ました。食事はかん国のビビンバと、ご飯でした。とてもおいしかったです。食事の後に6時間ねました。私の後ろの人もよくねていました。ひこうきはあまりこんでいなかったので、よかったです。ソウルに着いた時に、ソウルの地図を買いました。ホテルに着いて、シャワーをあびた後に、一人で出かけました。(着く *to arrive*)

2. 私の主人は大学に入学しましたが、卒業しませんでした。卒業する前に、とてもいい会社にしゅうしょくしたからです。しゅうしょくした後は、いそがしくて、ぜんぜん勉強できませんでした。

D) Fill in the correct kanji characters in the boxes provided.

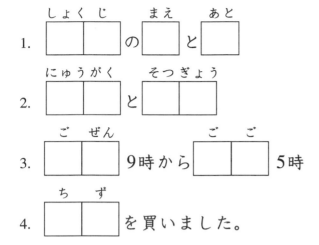

1. しょく じ ☐☐ の まえ ☐ と あと ☐

2. にゅうがく ☐☐ と そつぎょう ☐☐

3. ご ぜん ☐☐ 9時から ご ご ☐☐ 5時

4. ち ず ☐☐ を買いました。

2. Using Common Set Phrases and Action Verbs

A) In the following situations, what would you say in Japanese?

1. When you knock on the door of someone's house: _____

2. Right before eating: _____

3. Right after eating: _____

4. When leaving your home for work: _____

5. When you get home: _____

B) Fill in the blanks by selecting appropriate verbs from the following list. Conjugate the verbs if necessary.

> 入学する・卒業する・おわる・勉強する・のんびりする・とる・うける

　今年、高校を＿＿＿＿＿＿して、大学に＿＿＿＿＿＿しました。今学期はよく＿＿＿＿＿＿しました。クラスを5つ＿＿＿＿＿＿ました。先週文学のしけんを＿＿＿＿＿＿ました。難しくて、たいへんでした。来週ほかのクラスのしけんが＿＿＿＿＿＿ます。冬休みは＿＿＿＿＿＿したいです。

Grammar

1. ～時に 1

The present tense of a Japanese verb (such as 食べる) refers to the time right before the event, and the past tense of a Japanese verb (such as 食べた) refers to the time right after the event when used before 時. For example, 食べる時 means *right before eating* and 食べた時 means *right after eating*.

Translate each sentence into English, paying attention to the time of event.

1. バスに乗る時に、お金をはらいました。

_____

2. バスに乗った時に、お金をはらいました。

_____

3. 食べている時に、テレビを見ないで下さい。

_____

4. 食事の時に、話します。

_____

5. しずかな時に、本を読みます。

_____

6. 気分がいい時に、こうえんに行きます。

_____

2. 〜時に 2

Following the example, form a statement that shows when we use each set phrase below. Note that 「 and 」 are a pair of quotation marks in Japanese.

Example: 「いただきます」　⟶　食べる時に、「いただきます」と言います。

1. 「いってきます」　⟶　_____

2. 「ただいま」　⟶　_____

3. 「おやすみなさい」　⟶　_____

4. 「こんにちは」　⟶　_____

5. 「ごめんください」　⟶　_____

6. 「ありがとう」　⟶　_____

3. 〜前に・〜間に・〜後に

We can form a time adverbial phrase using the nouns 前 (beforehand), 後 (afterward) and 間 (during). These nouns usually follow another noun plus の or a verb in the plain form. The verb that precedes 前 must be in the present form as in 勉強する前に, the verb that precedes 後 must be in the past form as in 勉強した後に, and the verb that precedes 間 must be in the progressive form as in 勉強している間に, regardless of when the event takes place.

Following the example, join the two sentences in each set using 前 or 後.

Example: 朝ご飯を食べます。それから、新聞を読みます。

    ──→   朝ご飯を食べた後に、新聞を読みます。

    ──→   新聞を読む前に、朝ご飯を食べます。

1. 地図を見ます。それから、運転します。

   → _____

   → _____

2. 手を洗います。それから、ご飯を食べます。

   → _____

   → _____

3. シャワーをあびます。それから、出かけます。

   → _____

   → _____

4. 〜ながら

Two activities that take place at the same time are expressed using the suffix ながら. For example, 食べながらテレビを見ます means *I watch TV while eating*.

Complete the following sentences creatively.

1. 私は_____ながら勉強します。

2. 弟は_____ながら宿題をします

3. 兄は_____ながら運転します。

4. 父は_____ながらテレビを見ます。

5. 母は_____ながらりょうりをします。

Conversation and Usage

なまけものの奥さん

In colloquial conversations, the い in 〜ている is often dropped. For example, しっている becomes しってる.

Listen carefully to the conversation between a husband and a wife, and try to locate the sentence or phrase where い is dropped from ている.

夫 ： ただいま。

妻 ： おかえりなさい。あのう、晩ご飯、まだ、できてないの。*1 ごめんね。

夫　　：え？もう、7時だよ。

妻　　：ちょっと秋子と電話でしゃべってて。

夫　　：また長電話？

妻　　：30分しゃべっただけよ。*2

夫　　：毎日秋子さんと何をしゃべってるの？ぼくは、おなかがすいてるんだよ。

妻　　：ごめん、ごめん。すぐ作るから、ご飯の前にお風呂に入ってよ。

夫　　：ああ、いいよ。(He starts to undress in the bathroom.)

妻　　：あっ、ごめんなさい。お風呂をわかすの忘れた。

夫　　：え？本当に忘れっぽいね。

妻　　：ごめんなさい。私も忙しいから。

夫　　：何が忙しいの？働いてないでしょう。

妻　　：でも、主婦はいろいろ忙しいのよ。

夫　　：ああ、そう。それで、今日の晩ご飯は何を作るの？

妻　　：何がいい？

夫　　：まだ、考えてないの？

妻　　：うん。お魚がいい？それとも、お肉がいい？*3

夫　　：どっちが、あるの？

妻　　：ええと。(The wife checks the inside of the refrigerator.)魚だけ。

夫　　：じゃあ、魚。

[*Unfamiliar words:* 怠け者 *lazy person,* おかえりなさい *a reply to* ただいま, 長電話 *long telephone conversation,* ごめん (＝ごめんなさい) *I'm sorry,* お風呂をわかす *to heat the water of the hot bath,* 忘れる *to forget,* 忘れっぽい *forgetful,* 主婦 *housewife,* いろいろ *for all sorts of things,* 考える *to think,* どっち *the informal form of,* どちら *which one*]

Note:

(*1) The verb できる means *to be able to do, to be completed,* or *to be made.*

(*2) ～だけ means *just.*

(*3) The conjunction それとも is used when there are two yes-no questions, and it means *alternatively* or *or.*

Listening Comprehension

朝の日課

You will hear a narrative about Ken's 朝の日課 (morning routines) on the CD. Listen carefully and then specify what he does in the correct order.

_____ 朝ごはんを食べる   _____ シャワーをあびる

_____ 新聞を読む   _____ はをみがく

Reading Comprehension

おにぎりの作り方

The following is a step-by-step recipe which shows you how to make おにぎり (rice ball). Let's study it, then guess what the Japanese words in Box A mean and match them with the meanings in Box B.

1.  炊きたてのご飯と、梅干と、塩と、おわんを2つ用意する。

2.  2つのおわんをぬらす。

3.  1つのおわんにご飯を入れる。

4.  もう1つのおわんをかぶせる。

5.  2つのおわんをいっしょにまわして、中のご飯をボールのようにする。

6.  上のおわんをとって、ご飯の真ん中にあなをあける。

7.  あなに梅干を入れる。梅干を入れる前に、種はとる。

8.  手をぬらす。

9.  ぬらした手に塩をふる。

10. 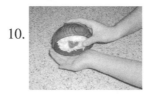 おわんの中の梅干の入ったご飯を手にのせる。

11.  ご飯を軽くにぎる。

12.  のりをまく。

13. できあがり！

[**Unfamiliar words:** 用意する *to prepare*, ぬらす *to make (something) wet*, 入れる *to put*, 〜をかぶせる *to let ... cover (something)*, まわす *to turn/rotate*, ボールのようにする *to shape it into a ball*, とる *to remove*, 真ん中 *middle*, あなをあける *to make a hole*, ふる(=ふりかける) *to sprinkle*, 〜をのせる *to put ... on something*, 軽く *lightly*, にぎる *to put pressure to shape*, 〜をまく *to wrap... around (something)*, できあがり! *Done!*]

Box A			Box B
おわん	•	•	freshly-cooked rice
炊きたてのご飯	•	•	seaweed
梅干	•	•	pickled ume (plum)
塩	•	•	salt
種	•	•	bowl
手	•	•	pit
のり	•	•	hand

Writing

レシピ

In the space provided below, write the recipe of a simple dish (such as a sandwich or salad) that you know.

New Vocabulary Reference List

NOUN

えんりょ (遠慮) hesitation, reservation (遠慮をする to hesitate)

きっぷ (切符) ticket

きぶん (気分) feeling (気分がいい to be in a good mood, 気分がわるい to be in a bad mood)

ぎょうぎ (行儀) manners, behavior

しゅじん・ごしゅじん (主人・御主人) husband

しょくじ (食事) meal (食事をする to dine)

ちず (地図) map

ADJECTIVE

ねむい (眠い) sleepy

めんどうな (面倒な) troublesome

ADVERB

とつぜん (突然) suddenly, abruptly

VERB (Ru-verb)

でかける (出かける) to go out

できる to be made, to be completed, to be able to do ...

VERB (U-verb)

もらう to receive

おわる (終わる) to be over, to end (クラスが終わった The class ended.)

かえす (返す) to return (本を返す to return the book)

なくなる to disappear, to run out (お金がなくなる to run out of money)

IRREGULAR VERB

そつぎょうする (卒業する) to graduate (大学を卒業する to graduate from a college)

にゅうがくする (入学する) to enter a school, to be admitted to a school (大学に入学する to enter a college)

のんびりする to relax

CONJUNCTION

それとも alternatively (買いますか。それとも、かりますか。 Will you buy it? Or, will you borrow it?) (cf. それか)

INTERJECTION

まあ Oh dear! (used by female)

PARTICLE

～ながら while doing ...

～から after ...

OTHERS

～あいだ(に) (～間(に)) during ...

～あと(に) (～後(に)) after ...

～たち (～達) plural suffix for nouns that denote people and animals (私達 we, 学生達 students, ねこ達 cats)

～だけです It's just that ... . (ちょっと会いたかっただけです I just wanted to see you.)

～とき(に) (～時(に)) at the time of ...

～ところです It is at the moment when ... . (今、食べているところです I am in the middle of eating now.)

～まえ(に) (～前(に)) before ...

いただきます (頂きます) a set phrase used right before eating

いってきます (行ってきます) a set phrase used before leaving one's home for work or school

おやすみなさい Good night!

ぎょうぎよく (行儀よく) with good manners (行儀よく食べる to eat with good manners)

ごちそうさま (ご馳走様) a set phrase used right after eating

ごめんください Hello! (used when one knocks on the door)

ただいま a set phrase used when one gets home

CHAPTER NINETEEN

Adding Implications

Objectives:

- to learn a variety of auxiliaries that add implications and nuances
- to review the te-form and stem form of verbs
- to name and describe the things in a room
- to make polite requests

Kanji and Vocabulary

1. Reading and Writing Kanji Characters

A) Let's read each of the following kanji words or phrases aloud several times.

重^{おも}い *heavy*

入^いれる *to put*

動^{うご}く *to move*

持^もつ *to hold or carry by hand*

物^{もの} *thing, object*

動物^{どうぶつ} *animal*

食^たべ物^{もの} *food*

苦^{くる}しい *distressful, uncomfortable*

始^{はじ}める *to start*

終^おわる *to finish*

〜個^こ ... *pieces*

竹下^{たけした} *Takeshita (family name)*

待^まつ *to wait*

忘^{わす}れる *to forget*

映画^{えいが} *movie*

絵^え *picture, painting, drawing, illustration*

開^あける *to open*

閉^しめる *to close*

B) In the boxes provided, write each kanji character following the correct stroke order.

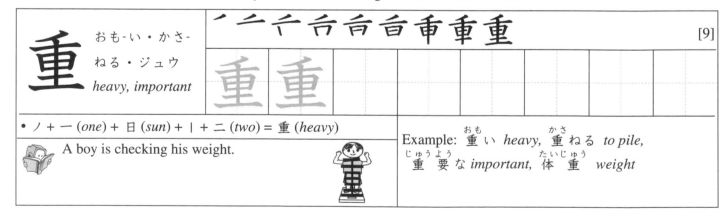

重 おも-い・かさ-ねる・ジュウ *heavy, important*	ノ 一 亻 亼 亩 盲 盲 重 重 [9] 重 重							

- ノ + 一 (*one*) + 日 (*sun*) + | + 二 (*two*) = 重 (*heavy*)

A boy is checking his weight.

Example: 重^{おも}い *heavy*, 重^{かさ}ねる *to pile*, 重要^{じゅうよう}な *important*, 体重^{たいじゅう} *weight*

動　うご-く・うご-かす・ドウ　move

ノ　ニ　イ　亡　盲　盲　重　重　重　動　動　[11]

動　動

- 重 (heavy) + 力 (strength) = 動 (move)

You can MOVE something "heavy" if you use more "strength"!

- The kanji sharing a component with 動 (move) is 働 (work).
- The last stroke in the left component should be short and slanting upward.

Example: 動く *to move*, ピアノを動かす *to move the piano*, 動物 *animal*, 自動車 *vehicle*, 行動する *to act*, 運動する *to exercise*

持　も-つ・ジ　hold

一　十　十　扌　打　护　拃　持　持　[9]

持　持

- 土 (soil) + 寸 (measure) = 寺 (temple)
- 扌 (hand) + 寺 (temple) = 持 (hold)

With a little trick, one can take a photo of someone appearing to HOLD a "temple" in one "hand".

- The kanji sharing a component with 持 (hold) is 探 (search).

Example: 持つ *to hold*, 持っている *to have*, 持って来る *to bring*, 気持ち *feeling*, 持続する *to sustain*

物　もの・ブツ・モツ　thing

ノ　ヒ　牛　牛　牛　物　物　物　[8]

物　物

- 牛 (cow) + 勿 (not) = 物 (thing)

A "cow" is "not" a THING, but an animal.

Example: 物 *thing*, 動物 *animal*, 食べ物 *food*, 飲み物 *beverage*, 貨物 *freight*

苦　くる-しい・にが-い・ク　bitter, painful

一　十　艹　艹　芊　芊　苦　苦　[8]

苦　苦

- 艹 (plant) + 古 (old) = 苦 (bitter)

Is it true that the tea leaves harvested from "old plants" are more BITTER?

Example: 苦しい *distressful; uncomfortable*, 苦い *bitter*, 苦手だ *not good at*, 苦痛 *pain; agony*

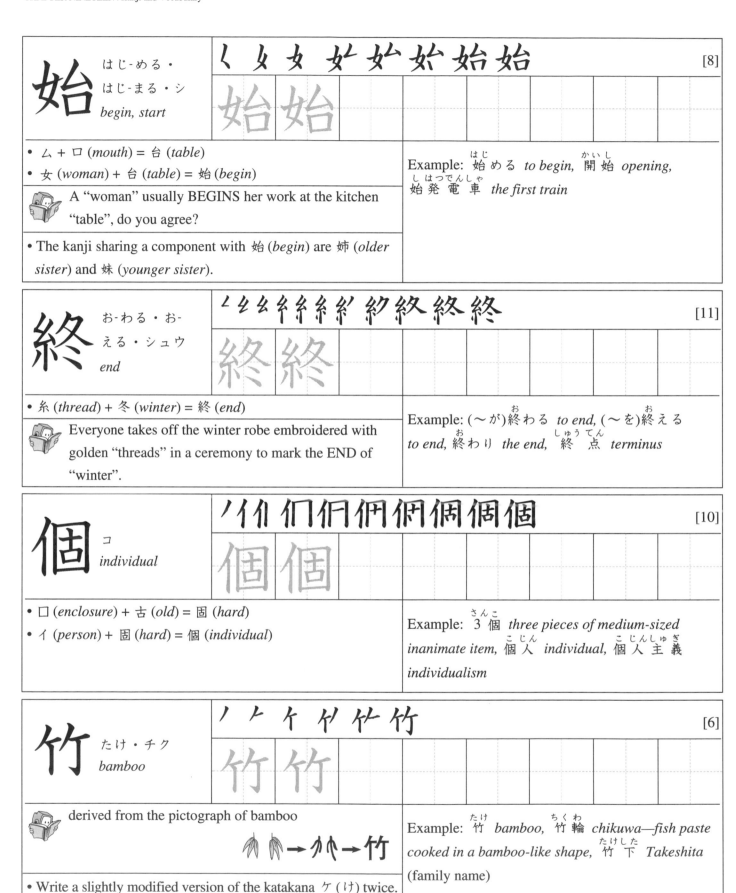

始 はじ-める・はじ-まる・シ
begin, start

く ﾑ 女 女 女 妒 始 始 [8]

- ﾑ + 口 (*mouth*) = 台 (*table*)
- 女 (*woman*) + 台 (*table*) = 始 (*begin*)

A "woman" usually BEGINS her work at the kitchen "table", do you agree?

- The kanji sharing a component with 始 (*begin*) are 姉 (*older sister*) and 妹 (*younger sister*).

Example: 始める *to begin*, 開始 *opening*, 始発電車 *the first train*

終 お-わる・お-える・シュウ
end

ﾉ ﾑ ﾑ 夂 糸 糸 糸' 糽 終 終 [11]

- 糸 (*thread*) + 冬 (*winter*) = 終 (*end*)

Everyone takes off the winter robe embroidered with golden "threads" in a ceremony to mark the END of "winter".

Example: (～が)終わる *to end*, (～を)終える *to end*, 終わり *the end*, 終点 *terminus*

個 コ
individual

ﾉ ｲ ｲ 们 们 佢 佣 個 個 個 [10]

- 囗 (*enclosure*) + 古 (*old*) = 固 (*hard*)
- ｲ (*person*) + 固 (*hard*) = 個 (*individual*)

Example: 3個 *three pieces of medium-sized inanimate item*, 個人 *individual*, 個人主義 *individualism*

竹 たけ・チク
bamboo

ﾉ ﾄ ﾑ 竹 竹 竹 [6]

derived from the pictograph of bamboo

- Write a slightly modified version of the katakana ケ (け) twice.

Example: 竹 *bamboo*, 竹輪 *chikuwa—fish paste cooked in a bamboo-like shape*, 竹下 *Takeshita* (family name)

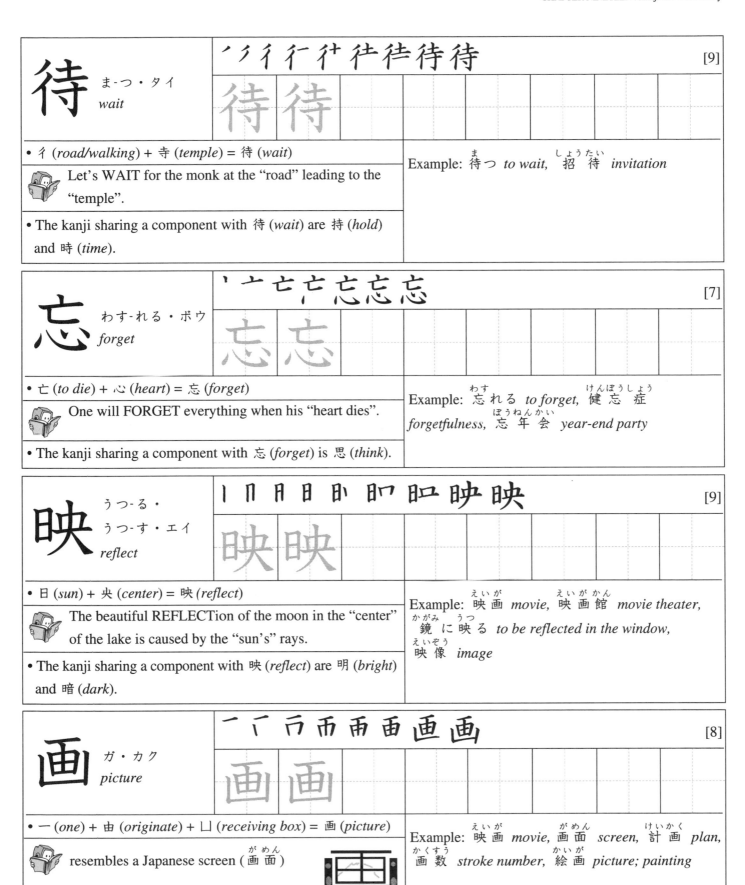

待 ま-つ・タイ wait

ノ ク イ 彳 彳 彳 待 待 待 [9]

• 彳 (road/walking) + 寺 (temple) = 待 (wait)

Let's WAIT for the monk at the "road" leading to the "temple".

• The kanji sharing a component with 待 (wait) are 持 (hold) and 時 (time).

Example: 待つ to wait, 招待 invitation

忘 わす-れる・ボウ forget

ヽ 亠 亡 亡 忘 忘 忘 [7]

• 亡 (to die) + 心 (heart) = 忘 (forget)

One will FORGET everything when his "heart dies".

• The kanji sharing a component with 忘 (forget) is 思 (think).

Example: 忘れる to forget, 健忘症 forgetfulness, 忘年会 year-end party

映 うつ-る・うつ-す・エイ reflect

丨 冂 月 日 日 旷 旷 映 映 [9]

• 日 (sun) + 央 (center) = 映 (reflect)

The beautiful REFLECTion of the moon in the "center" of the lake is caused by the "sun's" rays.

• The kanji sharing a component with 映 (reflect) are 明 (bright) and 暗 (dark).

Example: 映画 movie, 映画館 movie theater, 鏡に映る to be reflected in the window, 映像 image

画 ガ・カク picture

一 厂 冂 両 雨 面 画 画 [8]

• 一 (one) + 由 (originate) + 凵 (receiving box) = 画 (picture)

resembles a Japanese screen (画面)

Example: 映画 movie, 画面 screen, 計画 plan, 画数 stroke number, 絵画 picture; painting

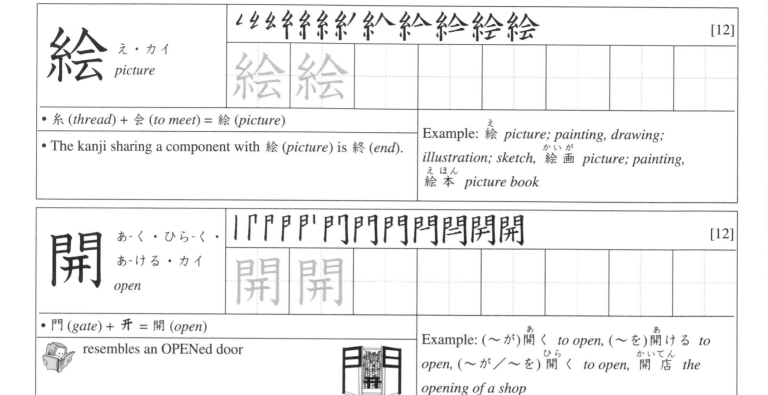

絵 え・カイ picture	‹ ‹ ‹ ‹ ‹ 糸 糸 糸 絆 絵 絵 絵								[12]
	絵 絵								

- 糸 (*thread*) + 会 (*to meet*) = 絵 (*picture*)
- The kanji sharing a component with 絵 (*picture*) is 終 (*end*).

Example: 絵 *picture; painting, drawing; illustration; sketch,* 絵画 *picture; painting,* 絵本 *picture book*

開 あ-く・ひら-く・ あ-ける・カイ open	l 冂 冂 冂 冂 門 門 門 門 閂 開 開								[12]
	開 開								

- 門 (*gate*) + 开 = 開 (*open*)

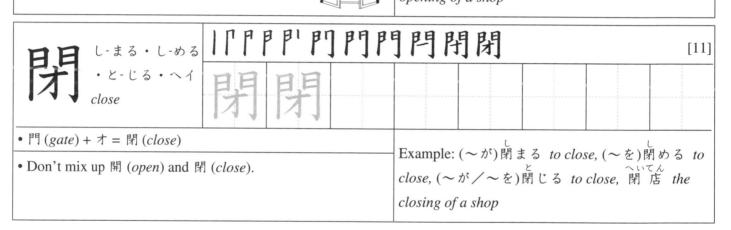 resembles an OPENed door

Example: (〜が)開く *to open,* (〜を)開ける *to open,* (〜が／〜を)開く *to open,* 開店 *the opening of a shop*

閉 し-まる・し-める ・と-じる・ヘイ close	l 冂 冂 冂 冂 門 門 門 門 閉 閉								[11]
	閉 閉								

- 門 (*gate*) + オ = 閉 (*close*)
- Don't mix up 開 (*open*) and 閉 (*close*).

Example: (〜が)閉まる *to close,* (〜を)閉める *to close,* (〜が／〜を)閉じる *to close,* 閉店 *the closing of a shop*

C) Let's read aloud to check how well you've mastered the kanji you've learned.

1. このかばんはとても重いです。大きいので、たくさんの物を入れられて便利ですが、とても持ちにくいです。

2. おいしい食べ物がたくさんあったので、ちょっと食べすぎました。ケーキも3個食べました。苦しくて、動けません。

3. 昨日は竹下さんと映画を見に行きました。ぼくはチケットを忘れたので、竹下さんは30分待たなくてはいけませんでした。

4. 今、絵をかいています。動物の絵です。ライオンです。しゃしんを見てかいています。1週間前に始めました。もうすぐ終わるところです。

5. まどは開けて下さい。でも、ドアは閉めて下さい。

D) Give as many as you can the kanji characters which contain each of the following as a component. You may add the okurigana or another kanji to form a word or compound.

1. サ  _____ _____ _____

2. イ _____ _____ _____

3. 寺 _____ _____ _____

4. 門 _____ _____ _____

5. カ _____ _____ _____

E) Fill in the correct kanji characters in the boxes provided.

1. どう ぶつ [ ][ ] が好きです。

3. 宿題を[わす]れました。

2. えい が [ ][ ] を見ます。

4. 勉強が[お]わりました。

2. Making Polite Requests

Fill in the blanks.

1. ちょっとかばんを_____下さい。 *Please hold this bag.*

2. ちょっと_____下さい。 *Please wait a little bit.*

3. テレビを_____下さい。 *Please turn off the TV.*

4. _____ないで下さい。 *Please don't move.*

5. カメラを_____ないで下さい。 *Please don't break the camera.*

3. Naming Common Objects in a Room

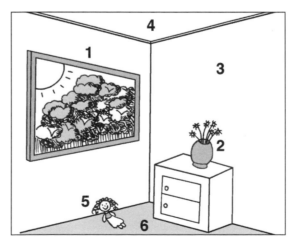

1. _____ 3. _____ 5. _____

2. _____ 4. _____ 6. _____

Grammar

1. ～にくい and ～やすい

The auxiliary adjectives ～にくい and ～やすい follow a verb in the stem form, and they express whether an action is easy or difficult to carry out. For example, 食べにくい means *to be difficult to eat* and 食べやすい means *to be easy to eat*.

Fill in the blanks creatively following the example.

Example: このかばんは大きくて、持ちにくいです。

1. このハンバーガーは大きくて、＿＿＿＿＿＿＿＿＿にくいです。

2. このペンは＿＿＿＿＿＿＿＿＿やすいです。

3. この本は難しい漢字が少なくて、とても＿＿＿＿＿＿＿＿＿やすいです。

4. 先生はやさしくて、とても＿＿＿＿＿＿＿＿＿やすいです。

5. このくつは＿＿＿＿＿＿＿＿＿にくいです。

2. ～すぎる

The auxiliary verb ～すぎる follows a verb or an adjective in the stem form, and it expresses the extent (too much or too little) of an action or a property is too great. For example, 食べすぎる means *to eat too much* and 古すぎる means *to be too old*.

Following the example below, rephrase each phrase by adding ～すぎる.

Example: ぎょうざを食べました。 ⟶ ぎょうざを食べすぎました。

1. ビールを飲みました。 ⟶ ＿＿＿＿＿＿＿＿＿＿＿＿＿＿＿

2. ようふくを買いました。 ⟶ ＿＿＿＿＿＿＿＿＿＿＿＿＿＿＿

3. 父はきびしいです。 ⟶ ＿＿＿＿＿＿＿＿＿＿＿＿＿＿＿

4. 兄はまじめです。 ⟶ ＿＿＿＿＿＿＿＿＿＿＿＿＿＿＿

5. このアパートはだいどころがせまいです。 ⟶ ＿＿＿＿＿＿＿＿＿＿＿＿＿＿＿

3. ～しまう

The auxiliary verb しまう follows a verb in the te-form. Depending on the context, it expresses the speaker's feelings (happy or regrettable), or it just emphasizes the completion of some action.

For each of the following sentences, state the speaker's feeling.

1. もう宿題をしてしまいました。 _____

2. さいふをおとしてしまいました。 _____

3. 姉とけんかをしてしまいました。 _____

4. 先生のかびんをこわしてしまいました。 _____

5. 朝ご飯を食べてしまいます。 _____

4. ～おく

The auxiliary verb おく follows a verb in the te-form and it expresses that the action denoted by the verb is done for future convenience.

Following the example, form a sentence stating what you would prepare for each event.

Example: たいふうが来ます。 ⟶ 食べ物を買っておきます。

1. お客さんが来ます。 ⟶ _____

2. 来月日本に行きます。 ⟶ _____

3. 来週の水曜日は友達のたんじょう日です。 ⟶ _____

4. 来週めんせつがあります。 ⟶ _____

5. 明日はテストがあります。 ⟶ _____

5. ～ある

The verb ある means *to exist*. For example, ドアがあります means *There is a door*. If we add a transitive verb in the te-form before the verb ある, the sentence expresses how something exists. For example, ドアが開けてあります literally means *a door exists after being opened*, which actually means *The door has been opened*, or *The door is open*.

Look at the illustration and describe the room by paying attention to the state of the things in the room.

_____
_____
_____
_____
_____
_____
_____

Conversation and Usage

お別れ会

For organizing a party or an event with your friends or colleagues, you can make suggestions using the phrase ませんか or ましょうか. You can also recommend something using 方がいいです. The latter follows a verb in the affirmative plain past form, as in ビールを買った方がいいです (*It is better to buy beer.*) To suggest someone not to do something, use the plain present negative form, as in ビールは買わない方がいいです (*It is better not to buy beer.*)

Ms. Takahashi (高橋) is suggesting to the manager to have a farewell party (お別れ会) for Ms. Kato (加藤), who is quitting her job as she is getting married. Listen to their conversation carefully and answer the questions that follow.

高橋 ： 課長、来週、加藤さんの送別会をしませんか？

課長 ： 今、私もそれを考えていたところです。どこでしましょうか。

高橋 ： ジンジャー・ハウスはどうですか？

課長 ： ああ、いいですね。

高橋 ： じゃあ、私が予約しておきます。

課長 ： ああ、ありがとう。それから、何かプレゼントを買った方がいいでしょう。

高橋 ： そうですね。みんなから500円ぐらいずつ集めましょうか。[*1]

課長 ： ちょっと少なすぎませんか？1,000円ずつ集めてもいいと思いますよ。

高橋 ： じゃあ、全部で10人いますから、1万円ですね。

課長 ： ええ。プレゼントは何がいいでしょう。

高橋 ： ネックレスか、さいふがいいと思います。

課長 ： そうですね。

[*Unfamiliar words:* 課長 *manager (section head)*, 送別会 *farewell party*, 考える *to think*]

Note: (*1) The suffix ずつ always follows a quantity phrase (such as 3人 and 2本) and it means *each*.

1. Where are they going to have a farewell party for Ms. Kato? _____

2. How many people are contributing to the gift for Ms. Kato? _____

3. How much would the present be? _____

4. What would the present be? _____

Listening Comprehension

テレビでショッピング

🔊 Listen to the TV commercial promoting a leather handbag (ハンドバッグ), and answer the following questions.

1. How many pockets (ポケット) are there in front of the handbag? _____

2. What colors are available? _____

3. How much is the bag? _____

Reading Comprehension

私のたんじょう日

Below is an essay written by Momoko Yamada about her 誕生日 (birthday). Let's read it aloud and answer the questions (in English) that follow. You may need to use a dictionary.

私の誕生日

山田もも子

　私の誕生日は4月1日です。4月1日はエープリル・フールズ・デイです。害のないいたずらをしてもいいという日ですから、私への誕生日のプレゼンは99％びっくり箱です。きれいな包装紙で包んだ箱の中から、バネのついた蛇や蛙の人形が飛び出します。それで、びっくり箱のコレクションができました。最近は誕生日のプレゼントはたぶんびっくり箱だろうと思うので、ぜんぜんびっくりしません。びっくり箱じゃない時に、とてもびっくりします。友達からのバースデーカードにも嘘ばかり書いてあります。

　悔しいので、私も家族や、友達や、会社の同僚にいたずらをします。去年は、妹のハンドバッグの中に祖母のかつらを入れておきました。妹がハンドバッグの中に手を入れた時、かつらに触ったので、「キャー」と悲鳴をあげました。それから、父の座布団の下にブーブークッションを入れておきました。父が座った時に、「ブー」と大きい音がして、父はびっくりしてお茶をこぼしてしまいました。いつもカメラをこっそり用意しておいて、みんながびっくりした瞬間を撮って、写真集を作っています。

　私の誕生日は毎年いたずらばかりですが、とても楽しいです。

---

1. When is Momoko's birthday? _____

2. What kind of birthday presents is a surprise for her? _____

3. What trick did she play on her sister last year? _____

4. What do you think ブーブークッション is? _____

5. Does Momoko like her birthday? _____

Writing

たんじょう日

Write about your birthday.

_____

_____

_____

_____

_____

_____

_____

New Vocabulary Reference List

NOUN

え (絵) *painting, drawing, illustration*

かびん (花瓶) *vase*

かべ (壁) *wall*

ぎゅうにゅう (牛乳) *milk*

ぎょうざ (餃子) *(Chinese-style) dumpling*

けんきゅうしつ (研究室) *university faculty's office, laboratory*

ごみ (ゴミ・ごみ) *trash, garbage*

たいふう (台風) *typhoon*

てんじょう (天井) *ceiling*

にんぎょう (人形) *doll*

ひしょ (秘書) *secretary*

ゆか (床) *floor*

ADJECTIVE

おもい (重い) *heavy*

くるしい (苦しい) *distressful, uncomfortable*

VERB (Ru-verb)

あける (開ける) *to open* (ドアを開ける *to open the door*)

いれる (入れる) *to put* (かばんに本を入れる *to put a book in the bag*)

こわれる (壊れる) *to break* (カメラが壊れた *The camera broke.*)

しめる (閉める) *to close* (ドアを閉める *to close the door*)

すてる (捨てる) *to throw away* (ゴミを捨てる *to throw away the garbage*)

ためる *to save up* (お金をためる *to save money*)

つける *to turn on* (テレビをつける *to turn on the TV*)

つづける (続ける) *to continue* (日本語の勉強(べんきょう)を続ける *to continue the study of Japanese*)

はじめる (始める) *to start* (クラスを始める *to start the class*)

わすれる (忘れる) *to forget* (宿題(しゅくだい)を忘れる *to forget one's homework*)

VERB (U-verb)

うごく（動く）*to move*

おく（置く）*to put, to place*（テーブルの上にかびんを置く *to put a vase on the table*）

けす（消す）*to turn off*（テレビを消す *to turn off the TV*）

こわす（壊す）*to break*（カメラを壊す *to break a camera*）

しまう *to store, to put away*（おもちゃをしまう *to put away the toys*）

はらう（払う）*to pay*（授業料を払う *to pay for the tuition*）

はる（貼る）*to post, to paste*（かべにポスターを貼る *to put up a poster on the wall*）

まつ（待つ）*to wait*（ガールフレンドを待つ *to wait for one's girlfriend*）

もつ（持つ）*to hold or carry by hand*（かばんを持つ *to carry a bag*）

IRREGULAR VERB

よやくする（予約する）*to make a reservation, to make an appointment*（ホテルを予約する *to make a reservation at a hotel*）

COUNTER

〜こ（〜個）a counter for medium-sized inanimate objects

PARTICLE

〜ずつ *each, at a time, by* (2つずつ食べる *eat two pieces at a time*)

OTHERS

〜ある *to have been ...ed*（ドアが開けてある *The door is left opened.*）

〜おく *to do ... in advance*（本を読んでおく *to read a book in advance*）

〜おわる（〜終わる）*to finish ...ing*（食べ終わる *to finish eating*）

〜しまう *to complete ...ing*（食べてしまう *to complete eating something*）

〜すぎる（〜過ぎる）*to overdo ...ing*（食べ過ぎる *to eat too much*）

〜つづける（〜続ける）*to continue ...ing*（食べ続ける *to continue eating*）

〜にくい *to be difficult to ...*（食べにくい *to be difficult to eat*）

〜はじめる（〜始める）*to start ...ing*（食べ始める *to start eating*）

〜ほうがいい（〜方がいい）*It is better to ...*（ねた方がいい *to be better to sleep*）

〜やすい *to be easy to ...*（食べやすい *to be easy to eat*）

くせになる（癖になる）*to become a habit*

もっている（持っている）*to have, to possess*（車を持っている *to have a car*）

CHAPTER TWENTY

Giving and Receiving

Objectives:

- to use the verbs of giving and receiving
- to use the auxiliaries made from the verbs of giving and receiving
- to name gift items
- to use the phrases for requesting and thanking

Kanji and Vocabulary

1. Reading and Writing Kanji Characters

A) Let's read each of the following kanji words or phrases aloud several times.

花 *flower*
友達 *friend*
よう子 *Yoko* (given name)
時計 *clock, watch*
泣く *to cry*

送る *to send*
祖父 *one's own grandfather*
祖母 *one's own grandmother*
住所 *address*

B) In the boxes provided, write each kanji character following the correct stroke order.

| 花 はな・カ *flower* | 一 十 艹 芢 花 花 花 [7] |
| | 花 花 |

- 艹 (plants) + 化 (to change) = 花 (flower)

The bud of a "plant" ultimately "changes" to a FLOWER.

Example: 花瓶 *vase,* 花火 *fireworks,* 花見 *blossom viewing*

| 友 とも・ユウ *friend* | 一 ナ 方 友 [4] |
| | 友 友 |

- ナ + 又 (again) = 友 (friend)

derived from the pictograph of a "handshake" between FRIENDS or partners

⺍→发→友

Example: 友達 *friend,* 友人 *friend,* 友情 *friendship*

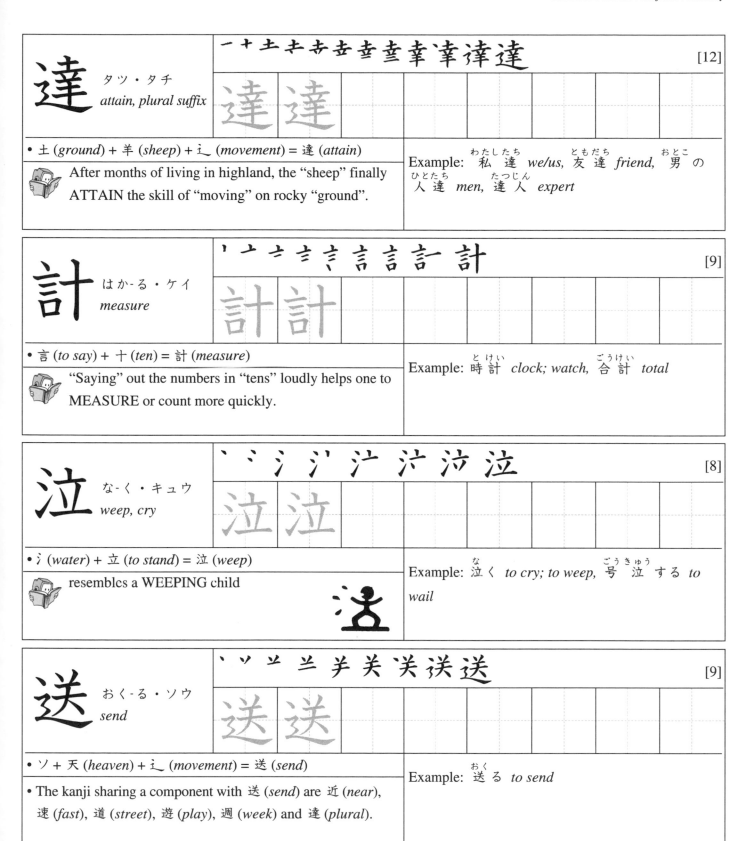

達 タツ・タチ
attain, plural suffix

一 十 士 击 吉 壵 查 查 幸 幸 幸 達 達 [12]

- 土 (ground) + 羊 (sheep) + 辶 (movement) = 達 (attain)

After months of living in highland, the "sheep" finally ATTAIN the skill of "moving" on rocky "ground".

Example: 私達 we/us, 友達 friend, 男の人達 men, 達人 expert

計 はか-る・ケイ
measure

丶 亠 さ 言 言 言 言 計 [9]

- 言 (to say) + 十 (ten) = 計 (measure)

"Saying" out the numbers in "tens" loudly helps one to MEASURE or count more quickly.

Example: 時計 clock; watch, 合計 total

泣 な-く・キュウ
weep, cry

丶 冫 氵 氵 汁 汁 汸 泣 [8]

- 氵 (water) + 立 (to stand) = 泣 (weep)

resembles a WEEPING child

Example: 泣く to cry; to weep, 号泣する to wail

送 おく-る・ソウ
send

丶 ソ 丷 关 关 关 送 送 [9]

- ソ + 天 (heaven) + 辶 (movement) = 送 (send)
- The kanji sharing a component with 送 (send) are 近 (near), 速 (fast), 道 (street), 遊 (play), 週 (week) and 達 (plural).

Example: 送る to send

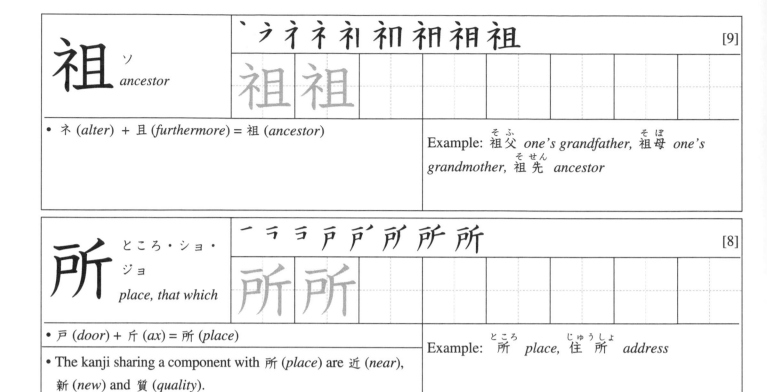

祖 ソ ancestor

` ラ ネ ネ ネ 初 初 初 祖 祖 [9]

祖 祖

- ネ (alter) + 且 (furthermore) = 祖 (ancestor)

Example: 祖父 (そふ) one's grandfather, 祖母 (そほ) one's grandmother, 祖先 (そせん) ancestor

所 ところ・ショ・ジョ place, that which

一 ラ ヨ 戸 戸 所 所 所 [8]

所 所

- 戸 (door) + 斤 (ax) = 所 (place)
- The kanji sharing a component with 所 (place) are 近 (near), 新 (new) and 質 (quality).

Example: 所 (ところ) place, 住所 (じゅうしょ) address

C) Let's read aloud to check how well you've mastered the kanji you've learned.

1. 祖父と祖母は入学のおいわいに時計をくれました。
2. ぼくはガールフレンドに花をあげました。友達にはティーシャツをあげました。
3. すいせんじょうを送りますから、住所を教えて下さい。
4. 母は映画を見てよく泣きます。

D) Fill in the correct kanji characters in the boxes provided.

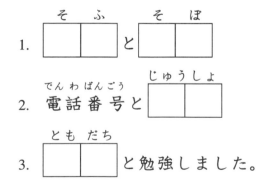

1. [そ ふ] と [そ ほ]

2. 電話番号 (でんわばんごう) と [じゅうしょ]

3. [とも だち] と勉強しました。

2. Identifying Common Gifts

Draw lines to match.

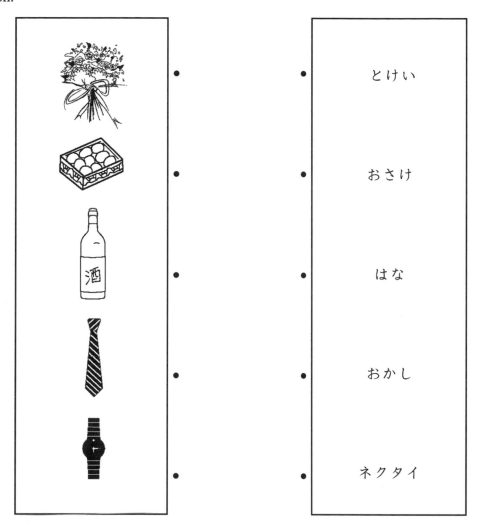

とけい

おさけ

はな

おかし

ネクタイ

3. Requesting a Letter of Recommendation

Fill in the blanks by selecting appropriate words from the following list.

しめきり・じゅうしょ・ようし・りゅうがく・すいせんじょう

1.　日本に＿＿＿＿＿＿＿＿＿＿＿したいと思います。

2.　＿＿＿＿＿＿＿＿＿＿＿を書いて 頂_{いただ}けないでしょうか。

3.　＿＿＿＿＿＿＿＿＿＿＿はこの 封筒_{ふうとう}に入っています。

4.　＿＿＿＿＿＿＿＿＿＿＿は 封筒_{ふうとう}に書いてあります。

5.　＿＿＿＿＿＿＿＿＿＿＿は来月のはじめです。

Grammar

1. あげる and くれる

Both あげる and くれる mean *to give*. くれる is the verb used only when the recipient is the speaker or his/her insider who is closer to the speaker than the giver. In all other contexts, the verb あげる is used. The recipient is marked by the particle に.

Underline the correct option in the parentheses.

1. 私は田中さんに本を（あげました・くれました）。
2. 田中さんは私にペンを（あげました・くれました）。
3. 田中さんは母に花を（あげました・くれました）。
4. 田中さんはマイクさんにおかしを（あげました・くれました）。
5. 父は母にネックレスを（あげました・くれました）。

2. さしあげる, くださる and やる

The verb あげる (*to give*) must be replaced by さしあげる (*to modestly give*) when the receiver is socially superior to, and/or distant from, the giver. Similarly, the verb くれる (*to give*) must be replaced by くださる (*to kindly give*) when the giver is socially superior to, and/or distant from, the receiver. The verb あげる (*to give*) can be optionally replaced by やる (*to give*) when the receiver is socially lower than the giver.

Underline the correct option in the parentheses.

1. 私は社長（しゃちょう）にお酒（さけ）を（あげました・さしあげました）。
2. 私は父におかしを（あげました・さしあげました）。
3. 私はよう子ちゃんにTシャツを（あげました・さしあげました）。
4. 社長は私にかばんを（くれました・くださいました）。
5. 父は私に時計を（くれました・くださいました）。
6. 犬（いぬ）にステーキを（あげました・やりました・くれました）。

Note:

- The verb くださる is an u-verb, but its stem form is ください, not くださり.
- 〜ちゃん is the respectful title that can be used for both male and female children.

3. もらう **and** いただく

The verb もらう (*to receive*) must be replaced by いただく (*to modestly receive*) when the giver is socially superior to, and/or distant from, the receiver. The particle に or から marks the receiver.

Underline the correct option in the parentheses.

1. 社長にチョコレートを（もらいました・いただきました）。
2. 友達のおばさんから手紙を（もらいました・いただきました）。
3. 入学のお祝いに祖父から時計を（もらいました・いただきました）
4. 姉はたんじょう日にボーイフレンドから花を（もらいました・いただきました）。
5. 母は父からネックレスを（もらいました・いただきました）。

4. ～あげる, ～くれる **and** ～もらう

To make a sentence that states someone does something for someone else, use the verb in the te-form followed by the verbs of giving and receiving such as あげる and もらう—the latter is functioning as an auxiliary verb that clarifies who is offering help and who is receiving it. For example, 私は弟とあそんであげました means *I played with my little brother (for him)*.

Fill in the blanks using the verbs of giving and receiving as auxiliaries.

1. 私は妹に本を＿＿＿＿＿＿＿＿＿＿＿＿＿＿＿＿＿＿。 *I read a book to my sister.*
2. 先生は私に漢字を＿＿＿＿＿＿＿＿＿＿＿＿＿＿＿＿。 *The teacher taught me kanji.*
3. 私は先生に漢字を＿＿＿＿＿＿＿＿＿＿＿＿＿＿＿。 *The teacher taught me kanji.*
4. 私は犬にセーターを＿＿＿＿＿＿＿＿＿＿＿＿＿＿＿。 *I made a sweater for my dog.*
5. 私は妹に買い物に＿＿＿＿＿＿＿＿＿＿＿＿＿＿。 *I had my sister go shopping for me.*

5. ～ていただきたいんですが

Phrases such as ～いただく, ～もらう, ～くださる and ～くれる are commonly used in sentences for asking a favor from others very politely, as in すいせんじょうを書いていただきたいんですが *Would you please write a letter of recommendation (for me)?*

Following the example, rephrase each sentence with いただきたいんですが.

Example: うちに来て下さい。　　➝　　うちに来ていただきたいんですが。

1. お金をかして下さい。　➝　＿＿＿＿＿＿＿＿＿＿＿＿＿＿＿＿＿＿

2. 父に会って下さい。　➝　＿＿＿＿＿＿＿＿＿＿＿＿＿＿＿＿＿＿

3. メールアドレスを教<ruby>教<rt>おし</rt></ruby>えて下さい。　　→　　_____

4. タバコをすわないで下さい。　　→　　_____

5. この<ruby>仕事<rt>しごと</rt></ruby>をてつだって下さい。　　→　　_____

Conversation and Usage

おみやげ

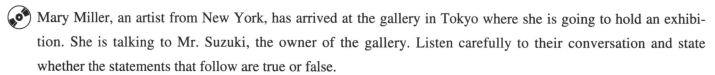 Mary Miller, an artist from New York, has arrived at the gallery in Tokyo where she is going to hold an exhibition. She is talking to Mr. Suzuki, the owner of the gallery. Listen carefully to their conversation and state whether the statements that follow are true or false.

ミラー： ああ、<ruby>鈴木<rt>すずき</rt></ruby>さん。

<ruby>鈴木<rt>すずき</rt></ruby>　： ああ、ミラーさん。お<ruby>久<rt>ひさ</rt></ruby>しぶりです。お<ruby>元気<rt>げんき</rt></ruby>ですか。

ミラー： はい。元気です。<ruby>鈴木<rt>すずき</rt></ruby>さんは？

鈴木　： ええ、おかげさまで。まだ38<ruby>才<rt>さい</rt></ruby>なのに、<ruby>今年<rt>ことし</rt></ruby>おじいちゃんになってしまいました。*1

ミラー： えっ？お<ruby>孫<rt>まご</rt></ruby>さんが<ruby>生<rt>う</rt></ruby>まれたんですか？

鈴木　： ええ。3月に女の子が。

ミラー： ああ、おめでとうございます。

鈴木　： ああ、どうも。

ミラー： じゃあ、<ruby>奥<rt>おく</rt></ruby>さんはお<ruby>忙<rt>いそが</rt></ruby>しいでしょう。

鈴木　： ええ。でも、<ruby>家内<rt>かない</rt></ruby>は<ruby>仕事<rt>しごと</rt></ruby>をやめたので、<ruby>孫<rt>まご</rt></ruby>の<ruby>世話<rt>せわ</rt></ruby>を<ruby>楽<rt>たの</rt></ruby>しんでいますよ。*2

ミラー： ああ、そうですか。

鈴木　： ミラーさんはお<ruby>忙<rt>いそが</rt></ruby>しいですか？

ミラー： ええ。今年は<ruby>海外<rt>かいがい</rt></ruby>での<ruby>展覧会<rt>てんらんかい</rt></ruby>も<ruby>多<rt>おお</rt></ruby>いし、大学でも<ruby>教<rt>おし</rt></ruby>えているし。*3

鈴木　： ああ、そうですか。すばらしいですね。

ミラー： いいえ、ぜんぜん。忙しいだけですよ。(Ms. Miller takes out something from her bag.) あのう、これ、つまらないものですが、どうぞ。

鈴木　： ああ、ご<ruby>丁寧<rt>ていねい</rt></ruby>にありがとうございます。

ミラー： いいえ。

鈴木　： あ、これはフランスのワインですね。

ミラー：ええ、今年はフランスに2度<ruby>行<rt>ど</rt></ruby>ったんですよ。

鈴木　：いいですね。<ruby>結構<rt>けっこう</rt></ruby>なもの、ありがとうございます。

ミラー：いいえ。

[*Unfamiliar words:* お<ruby>久<rt>ひさ</rt></ruby>しぶりです *It has been a long time,* <ruby>孫<rt>まご</rt></ruby> *grandchild,* おめでとうございます *Congratulations!,* <ruby>楽<rt>たの</rt></ruby>しむ *to enjoy,* <ruby>海外<rt>かいがい</rt></ruby> *overseas,* <ruby>展覧会<rt>てんらんかい</rt></ruby> *exhibition,* すばらしい *wonderful,* ご<ruby>丁寧<rt>ていねい</rt></ruby>に *politely,* <ruby>結構<rt>けっこう</rt></ruby>な *good; wonderful*]

Note:

(*1) The clause connective のに relates two sentences that are in conflict or in contradiction. It usually follows plain form verbs and adjectives. But だ at the end of a copula and na-type adjective changes to な when it precedes のに or ので.

(*2) The clause connective ので relates two sentences that are in a cause-and-result relationship. It also follows plain form verbs and adjectives. But だ at the end of a copula and na-type adjective changes to な when it precedes のに or ので.

(*3) For listing actions and properties emphatically, use plain form verbs and adjectives and add し after each of them. The last verb or adjective in the sentence may be in regular form.

1. Ms. Miller met Mr. Suzuki for the first time. 　　　　(True • False)
2. Mr. Suzuki's child is 38 years old. 　　　　(True • False)
3. Mrs. Suzuki has quit the job. 　　　　(True • False)
4. Ms. Miller teaches at a high school. 　　　　(True • False)
5. Ms. Miller went to France twice this year. 　　　　(True • False)

Listening Comprehension

あげました・さしあげました

 Listen to the CD and match the correct illustrations to the verbs read out to you.

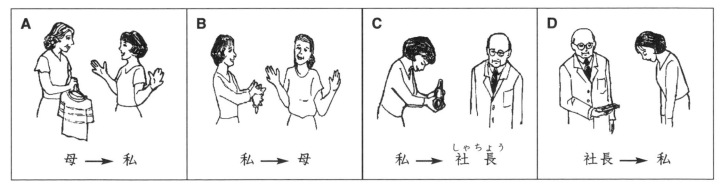

1. _____ 2. _____ 3. _____ 4. _____ 5. _____

Reading Comprehension

お礼状

Yoko received a package, delivered to her house. It was a birthday present for her from Kazuo (一男), her friend in Osaka. To thank him, Yoko prepared the following thank you card (お礼状). Let's read what's on the card and answer the questions that follow.

一男さん

毎日さむいですが、お元気ですか。

誕生日のプレゼントをおくって下さって、ありがとうございました。私の誕生日を覚えていて下さったんですね。びっくりしました。とてもかわいいハンドバッグなので、毎日会社に行く時に使います。また東京に来た時には、うちに遊びに来て下さいね。

では、お元気で。

まずは、お礼まで。

よう子

[*Unfamiliar words:* びっくりする *to be surprised,* まずは、お礼まで。*Just to show my appreciation*]

1. What was Yoko's present? _____
2. Is Yoko studying or working? _____
3. Where does Yoko live? _____

Writing

お礼状

Write a thank you letter to a friend who has given you a birthday present.

New Vocabulary Reference List

NOUN

おいわい（御祝い）*celebration*
おじ・おじさん（叔父／伯父・叔父さん／伯父さん）
 uncle
おせいぼ（お歳暮）*year-end present*
おねがい（お願い）*favor*
おば・おばさん（叔母／伯母・叔母さん／伯母さん）
 aunt
おわり（終わり）*ending*
かし・おかし（菓子・お菓子）*sweet, confectionery*
しめきり（締め切り）*deadline*
じゅうしょ（住所）*address*
しんせき（親戚）*relative*
すいせんじょう（推薦状）*recommendation letter*
はじめ（始め・初め）*beginning*
はな・おはな（花・お花）*flower*
ようし（用紙）*form, sheet*
りゅうがく（留学）*studying abroad*

ADVERB

ちょくせつ（直接）*directly*

VERB (Ru-verb)

あげる *to give*
くれる *to give*
さしあげる（差し上げる）*to give* (the humble form of あげる)
つれる（連れる）*to take (someone) with*（弟を学校に連れて行く *to take one's brother to his school*）

VERB (U-verb)

いただく（頂く）*to receive* (the humble form of もらう)
おくる（送る）*to send*
くださる（下さる）*to give* (the honorific form of くれる)

たのむ（頼む）*to ask, to request*（兄に頼む *to ask my brother (to do something)*）
てつだう（手伝う）*to assist, to help*（弟の宿題を手伝う *to assist one's brother's homework*）
なおす（直す）*to repair, to fix, to correct*
やる *to give (to one's subordinate)*

CONJUNCTION

～ので *because* ...（日本人なので、日本語が話せます。*He can speak Japanese because he is Japanese.*）
～のに *although* ...（日本人なのに、日本語が話せません。*Although he is Japanese, he cannot speak Japanese.*）

OTHERS

～あげる *to do something for someone*（本を読んであげる *to read a book for someone*）
～いただく（～頂く）*to have someone do* ... (the humble form of ～もらう)
～か（～課）... *section, ... division, Lesson* ...
～くださる（下さる）*to do something for me or for one of us* (the honorific form of ～くれる)
～くれる *to do something for me or for one of us*（本を読んでくれる *to read a book for me or for one of us*）
～さしあげる（～差し上げる）*to do something for someone* (the humble form of ～あげる)
～ちゃん *the respectful title for young children*（よう子ちゃん）
～みる *to try ...ing*
～もらう *to have someone do* ...（本を読んでもらう *to have someone read a book*）
～やる *to do something for one's subordinate*

CHAPTER TWENTY-ONE

Describing Changes

Objectives:

- to express changes with 〜ようにする and 〜ようになる
- to express decisions using 〜ようにする and 〜ようになる
- to express consequences using clauses with と
- to use health-related words
- to write a letter to a friend

Kanji and Vocabulary

1. Reading and Writing Kanji Characters

A) Let's read each of the following kanji words or phrases aloud several times.

<table>
<tr><td>

じぶん
自分 *self*
じてんしゃ
自転車 *bicycle*
うんどう
運動する *to exercise*
はこ
運ぶ *to transport, to carry*
さいきん
最近 *recently*
と
取る *to take*

</td><td>

もう
申す *to say* (humble form of いう)
おんがく
音楽 *music*
おと
音 *sound*
すうがく
数学 *mathematics*
ねが
お願いする *to ask a favor*
とり
鳥 *bird*

</td></tr>
</table>

B) In the boxes provided, write each kanji character following the correct stroke order.

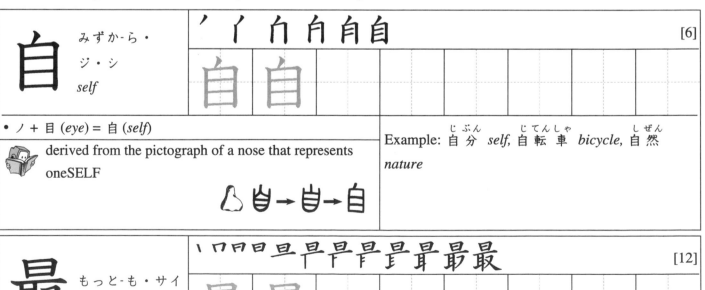

自 みずか-ら・ジ・シ self	ノ イ 冇 白 自 自　[6]

- ノ + 目 (*eye*) = 自 (*self*)

　derived from the pictograph of a nose that represents oneSELF

Example: じぶん 自分 *self*, じてんしゃ 自転車 *bicycle*, しぜん 自然 *nature*

最 もっと-も・サイ most	一 冂 曰 日 旦 早 昌 昌 冣 冣 最 最　[12]

- 日 (*sun*) + 取 (*to take*) = 最 (*most*)

　One of the MOST challenging shots "to take" is a photo of the "sun".

Example: さいきん 最近 *recently*, さいご 最後 *last*, さいだい 最大の〜 *the greatest ...*

取　と-る・シュ　take, get, hold, acquire

一 丁 丆 丆 耳 耳 取 取　[8]

取 取

• 耳 (*ear*) + 又 (*again*) = 取 (*take*)

derived from the pictograph of a hand pulling on the ear to mean "TAKE hold of"

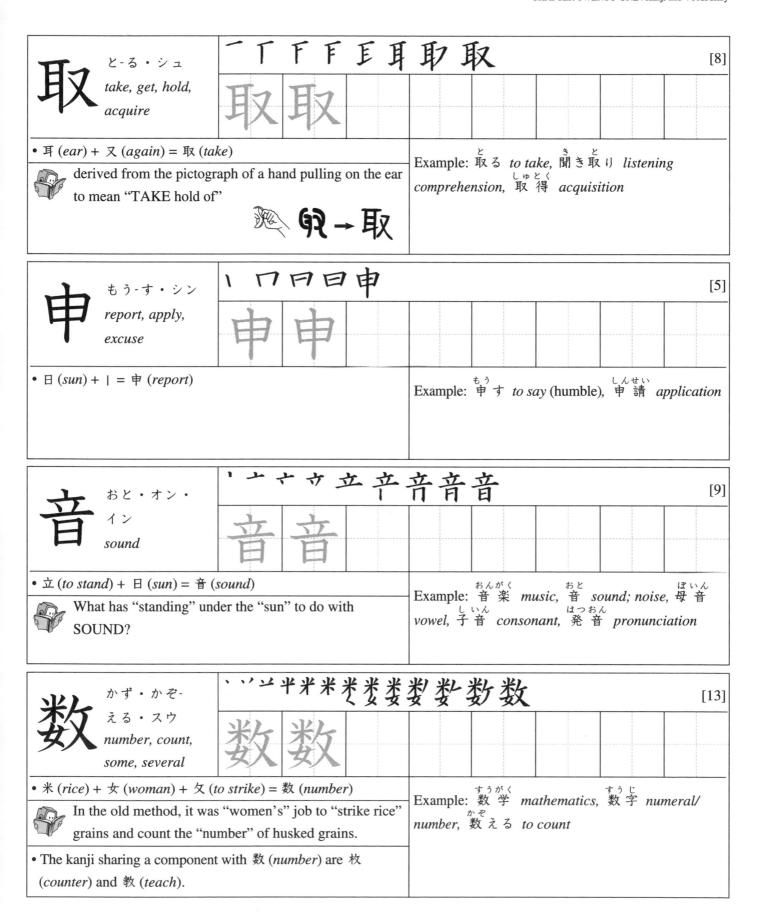

Example: 取る *to take*, 聞き取り *listening comprehension*, 取得 *acquisition*

申　もう-す・シン　report, apply, excuse

丶 冂 冋 曰 申　[5]

申 申

• 日 (*sun*) + | = 申 (*report*)

Example: 申す *to say* (humble), 申請 *application*

音　おと・オン・イン　sound

丶 亠 立 立 产 产 音 音 音　[9]

音 音

• 立 (*to stand*) + 日 (*sun*) = 音 (*sound*)

What has "standing" under the "sun" to do with SOUND?

Example: 音楽 *music*, 音 *sound; noise*, 母音 *vowel*, 子音 *consonant*, 発音 *pronunciation*

数　かず・かぞ-える・スウ　number, count, some, several

丶 丷 丷 半 米 米 粆 娄 娄 数 数 数 数　[13]

数 数

• 米 (*rice*) + 女 (*woman*) + 攵 (*to strike*) = 数 (*number*)

In the old method, it was "women's" job to "strike rice" grains and count the "number" of husked grains.

• The kanji sharing a component with 数 (*number*) are 枚 (*counter*) and 教 (*teach*).

Example: 数学 *mathematics*, 数字 *numeral/ number*, 数える *to count*

願 ねが-う・ガン pray, beg	一丆𠃋𠂆𠂆厉𠩄厉原原原 原 原 願 願 願 願 願 願 [19]					
	願 願					

- 原 (*field*) + 頁 (*big shell, head*) = 願 (*pray*)
- The kanji sharing a component with 願 (*pray*) is 題 (*theme*).

Example: 願う *to pray*, お願いする *to request*, 志願者 *applicant*

鳥 とり・チョウ bird	ノ𠂆𠂉𠂊𠂊自鳥鳥鳥鳥鳥 [11]					
	鳥 鳥					

derived from the pictograph of a long tailed bird

鳥 → 鳥 → 鳥

Example: 鳥 *bird*

C) Let's read aloud to check how well you've mastered the kanji you've learned.

1. せんたくと、りょうりと、そうじは自分でして下さい。そのはこは自分で部屋に運んで下さい。
2. 最近ジムで運動をしはじめました。ウエイトリフティングを30分しています。それから、自転車で会社まで行っています。会社の後はヨガのクラスに行きます。
3. 小学校の音楽のクラスでバイオリンをひきました。いい音が出なくて、とてもたいへんでした。
4. せんこうは文学でしたが、数学も好きだったので、大学でも数学のクラスを2つ取りました。
5. 森田まことと申します。よろしくお願いします。
6. 私は犬と、ねこは好きですが、鳥はきらいです。友達のうちに鳥がいるんですが、あたまの上に乗るんです。とてもいやです。

D) Fill in the correct kanji characters in the boxes provided.

1. ［さい］［きん］　よく勉強します。
2. ［すう］［がく］を［と］っています。
3. 犬と、ねこと、［とり］。
4. ［じ］［てん］［しゃ］に乗ります。

2. Planning for Health

Fill in the blanks by selecting suitable words from the following list.

かいだん・けんこう・たまご・運動（うんどう）・なっとう・たばこ

　父はいつも＿＿＿＿＿＿＿＿＿にいいことをしています。朝はジムで30分＿＿＿＿＿＿＿＿＿します。エレベーターを使わないで、＿＿＿＿＿＿＿＿＿を使います。＿＿＿＿＿＿＿＿＿はすいません。お酒も飲みません。肉や＿＿＿＿＿＿＿＿＿はあまり食べません。やさいや、＿＿＿＿＿＿＿＿＿を食べます。

Grammar

1. 〜ようにする and 〜ようになる

The phrase with a plain form verb plus ように means *in a way that ...* . 〜ようにする expresses what change one tries to make. For example, 野菜（やさい）を食べるようにしました means *I tried to eat vegetables.* 〜ようになる expresses the change that takes place. For example, 私は野菜（やさい）を食べるようになりました means *I started to eat vegetables.* Both express a change, but 〜ようにする implies that the change was made consciously while 〜ようになる does not.

Form a sentence following the example.

Example: 泳（およ）げる・なる ⟶ 泳げるようになりました。

1. 自分で宿題（しゅくだい）をする・なる ⟶ ＿＿＿＿＿＿＿＿＿＿
2. 電気（でんき）をせつやくする・する ⟶ ＿＿＿＿＿＿＿＿＿＿
3. クラスを休む・なる ⟶ ＿＿＿＿＿＿＿＿＿＿
4. 漢字が書ける・なる ⟶ ＿＿＿＿＿＿＿＿＿＿
5. たまごを食べない・する ⟶ ＿＿＿＿＿＿＿＿＿＿
6. なまけない・なる ⟶ ＿＿＿＿＿＿＿＿＿＿

Note: 〜ないようになる is often contracted to 〜なくなる.

2. 〜ことにする and 〜ことになる

〜ことにする means *to dicide to ...* and 〜ことになる means *to be decided to ...* . Although both follow a plain form verb and express a decision, 〜ことにする implies that the decision was made by the person denoted by the subject noun while 〜ことになる does not. For example, 私が行くことにしました means *I decided to go (there)*, and 私が行くことになりました means *it was decided that I will go (there)*.

Form a sentence following the example.

Example: 日本に行く・する ⟶ 日本に行くことにしました。

1. 私がそうじをする・なる ⟶ _____

2. 香港で働く・する ⟶ _____

3. 今日からここで働く・なる ⟶ _____

4. オーストラリアにりゅうがくする・する ⟶ _____

5. 来月けっこんする・なる ⟶ _____

6. ここでタバコをすってはいけない・なる ⟶ _____

3. 〜と、〜する and 〜と、〜した

〜と、〜する expresses an automatic consequence or something that always happens after some action. For example, ここにお金を入れると、きっぷが出ます means *If you put some money here, a ticket will come out.* By contrast, its past tense counter part, 〜と、〜した, expresses what happened after a specific event. For example, 本屋に行くと、マイクさんに会いました means *When I went to the bookstore, I met Mike.*

State what the following sentences mean.

1. 春になると、あたたかくなります。
_____

2. 女の人だと、ワインが安くなります。
_____

3. ドアをあけると、警察官が立っていました。
_____

4. このローションを使うと、肌がきれいになりますよ。(肌 *skin*)
_____

5. うちに帰ると、ご飯が作ってありました。
_____

Note: When an adverb such as 高<ruby>高<rt>たか</rt></ruby>く or きれいに is followed by the verb なる (*to become*), it indicates a higher degree of the property or feature expressed by the adverb was reached. For example, 高くなる means *to become more expensive*, and きれいになる means *to become prettier*.

Conversation and Usage

小学校の時の友達

Takako has run into Kenta, her old friend from elementary school (<ruby>小学校<rt>しょうがっこう</rt></ruby>の<ruby>時<rt>とき</rt></ruby>の<ruby>友達<rt>ともだち</rt></ruby>), on the street. Listen to their conversation on the CD and answer the questions that follow.

たか子: あれ？けんた<ruby>君<rt>くん</rt></ruby>？

けんた: えっ？

たか子: 私よ。たか子。<ruby>石山小学校<rt>いしやましょうがっこう</rt></ruby>でいっしょのクラスだったでしょう。

けんた: ああ、たか子ちゃん！ぜんぜんわからなかった。<ruby>元気<rt>げんき</rt></ruby>？

たか子: うん。

けんた: 今どこの<ruby>高校<rt>こうこう</rt></ruby>に行ってるの？

たか子: <ruby>東<rt>ひがし</rt></ruby>高校。

けんた: ああ、そう。いい<ruby>高校<rt>こうこう</rt></ruby>に<ruby>入<rt>はい</rt></ruby>れたんだね。

たか子: でも、<ruby>勉強<rt>べんきょう</rt></ruby>しないで、フィギュアスケートばかりしてるの。[*1]

けんた: へえ。<ruby>何年<rt>なんねん</rt></ruby>ぐらいやってるの？

たか子: 6<ruby>才<rt>さい</rt></ruby>から<ruby>始<rt>はじ</rt></ruby>めたから、<ruby>今年<rt>ことし</rt></ruby>で10年になるんだ。[*2]

けんた: そう。オリンピックに<ruby>出<rt>で</rt></ruby>るの？

たか子: さあ。でも、出られるように<ruby>毎日努力<rt>まいにちどりょく</rt></ruby>してる。

けんた: きっと出られるよ。たか子ちゃんには<ruby>有名<rt>ゆうめい</rt></ruby>になってほしいな。[*3] がんばってね。

たか子: ありがとう。けんた君はどう？

けんた: ぼくは今年オーストラリアに<ruby>留学<rt>りゅうがく</rt></ruby>することにしたんだ。

たか子: わあ、すごい！

けんた: おじさんがオーストラリアにいるんだ。

たか子: いいわね。

Note:

(*1) ～ないで means *without ... ing*.

(*2) The particle で specifies the time or the age at which some period ends or some state changes.

(*3) Xに～ほしい means *to want X to do ...*

1. Which high school does Takako go to?　　　　_____

2. How many years has Takako been practicing figure skating?　　_____

3. Which country is Kenta going this year?　　_____

Listening Comprehension

自己紹介

Today is Sean Brown's first day of work at a trading company in Japan. His boss has just introduced him to his colleagues. Listen to Sean's self introduction (自己 紹 介) and then answer the questions.

1. Where did Sean come from?

_____

2. What was his major in college?

_____

3. How many Japanese courses did Sean take when he was a college student in the US?

_____

4. Which city did he stay when he was studying abroad in Japan?

_____

5. What courses did he take when he was studying abroad in Japan? Give examples.

_____

Reading Comprehension

手紙

David Wilson is currently living in Mr. Morita's house in Japan. The following is a letter (手紙) from him to his friend Yuko. Let's read it and answer the questions that follow.

ゆう子さん

暑い夏も終わって、秋になってしまいましたね。ゆう子さんはお元気ですか。大阪の新しいお仕事はどうですか？

今、僕は東京の森田さんのお宅にホームステイをしています。森田さんは英語をぜんぜん話さないので、僕は毎日日本語で話しています。日本語が前よりうまく話せるようになりました。とてもうれしいです。森田さんはとてもやさしくて、いろいろなことを教えてくれます。毎日いっしょに晩御飯を作って、食べます。先月はいっしょに富士山に登りました。ジェニーさんもいっしょでした。とても楽しかったです。

来月からは中山大学で日本語のコースをとることにしました。漢字をたくさん勉強しようと思います。

ゆう子さんも、元気で、がんばって下さいね。

九月二十一日

デイヴィッド・ウイルソン

[*Unfamiliar words:* お宅＝うち (*polite*)]

1. Where does Yuko work?　　_____
2. Where is Mr. Morita's house located?　_____
3. Does Mr. Morita speak English?　_____
4. Who was with David when he climbed Mt. Fuji?　_____
5. What is David's plan for next month?　_____

Writing

手紙

Write a letter to one of your friends or relatives to let him/her know your current situations.

New Vocabulary Reference List

NOUN

あいさつ（挨拶）*greeting*（挨拶をする *to greet*）

イーメール *electric mail*（*cf. E*メール・メール）

かいだん（階段）*stair, stairway*

けいけん（経験）*experience*

けんこう（健康）*health*

じぶん（自分）*self*（自分で *by oneself*）

しゅうしかてい（修士課程）*master's program*

たまご（卵・玉子）*egg*

とり（鳥）*bird*

どりょく（努力）*effort*

なっとう（納豆）*fermented soybeans*

はかせかてい（博士課程）*doctoral program*

はこ（箱）*box*

ふうとう（封筒）*envelop*

ボタン *button*

みなさん（皆さん）*everyone, all of you*

もんく（文句）*complaint*（文句をいう *to complain*）

QUESTION WORD

いかが *how*（*polite form of* どう）

VERB (U-verb)

はこぶ（運ぶ）*to transport, to carry*

こぼす *to spill*

もうす（申す）*to say*（humble form of 言う）

おす（押す）*to press*

もどる（戻る）*to return*

ちらかる（散らかる）*to become messy*

IRREGULAR VERB

うんどうする（運動する）*to exercise*

せつやくする（節約する）*to save, to economize*

びっくりする *to be surprised*

ADVERB

いろいろ（色々）*for all sorts of things*

さいきん（最近）*recently*

できるだけ *as much as one can*

やっと *finally*（やっとおわりました *It finally ended.*）

やっぱり *expectedly*（*c.f.* やはり）

CONJUNCTION

しかし *but*（*c.f.* でも）

そして *and then, and*（*c.f.* それから）

OTHERS

〜ほしい *to want someone to do ...*

CHAPTER TWENTY-TWO

Describing How Things and People Appear to Be

Objectives:

- to learn and use common phrases that describe people's personality
- to describe using ～そう(な), ～らしい, ～よう(な) and ～みたい(な)
- to list activities or events using たり

Kanji and Vocabulary

1. Reading and Writing Kanji Characters

A) Let's read each of the following kanji words or phrases aloud several times.

き　つよ
気が強い *strong-willed, hardheaded*

き　よわ
気が弱い *coward, timid*

てんし
天使 *angel*

おとな
大人 *adult*

おや
親 *parent*

ちちおや
父親 *father*

ははおや
母親 *mother*

しんせつ
親切だ *kind*

きって
切手 *stamp*

むし
虫 *insect, bug*

にんげん
人間 *human being*

B) In the boxes provided, write each kanji character following the correct stroke order.

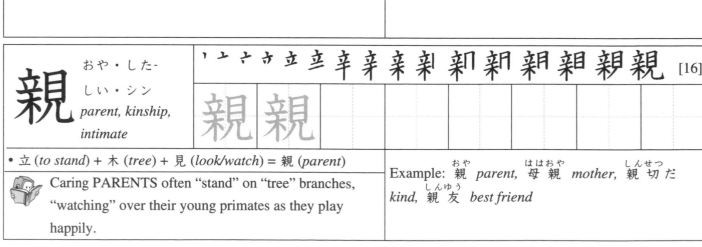

弱	よわ-い・よわ-る・ジャク *weak*	｀ ｀ 弓 弓 弓' 弓' 弱 弱 弱 [10]

- 弓 (*bow*) + ン + 弓 (*bow*) + ン = 弱 (*weak*)

Example: 弱い *weak*, 弱点 *weak point*

親	おや・した-しい・シン *parent, kinship, intimate*	｀ 一 ナ 古 立 立 辛 辛 亲 亲 新 新 新 親 親 親 [16]

- 立 (*to stand*) + 木 (*tree*) + 見 (*look/watch*) = 親 (*parent*)

Caring PARENTS often "stand" on "tree" branches, "watching" over their young primates as they play happily.

Example: 親 *parent*, 母親 *mother*, 親切だ *kind*, 親友 *best friend*

– 84 –

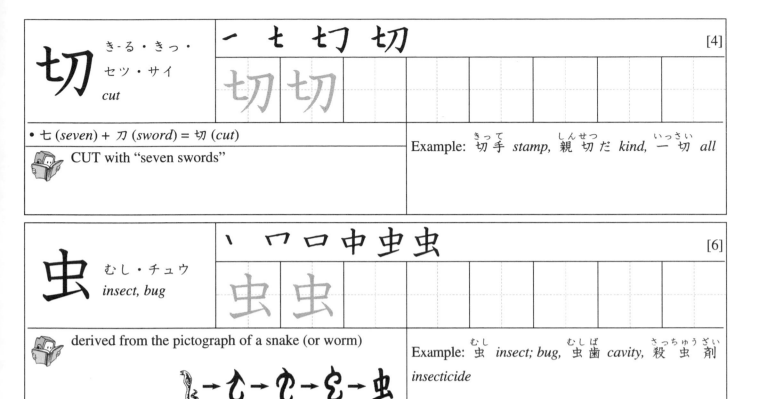

切　き-る・きっ・セツ・サイ　cut

一　七　切　切　[4]

切　切

• 七 (seven) + 刀 (sword) = 切 (cut)

CUT with "seven swords"

Example: 切手 *stamp*, 親切だ *kind*, 一切 *all*

虫　むし・チュウ　insect, bug

丶　丆　口　中　虫　虫　[6]

虫　虫

derived from the pictograph of a snake (or worm)

Example: 虫 *insect; bug*, 虫歯 *cavity*, 殺虫剤 *insecticide*

C) Let's read aloud to check how well you've mastered the kanji you've learned.

1. ようこさんはとても親切で、やさしくて、天使のような人です。たかこさんは気が強くて、ちょっとこわいです。としおさんは気が弱くて、しずかですが、とてもいい人です。虫も殺さないやさしい人です。(殺す *to kill*)

2. 子供には父親と母親はとても大切です。(大切です *important*)

3. 私の子供も大人になって、親になりました。

D) Fill in the correct kanji characters in the boxes provided.

1.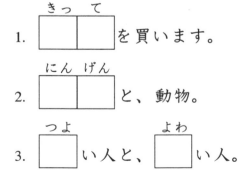
　　きって
　　□□ を買います。

2. にんげん
　　□□ と、動物。

3. つよ　　　よわ
　　□い人と、□い人。

2. Describing People

A) The following are items often used to describe people in simile. Draw lines to match.

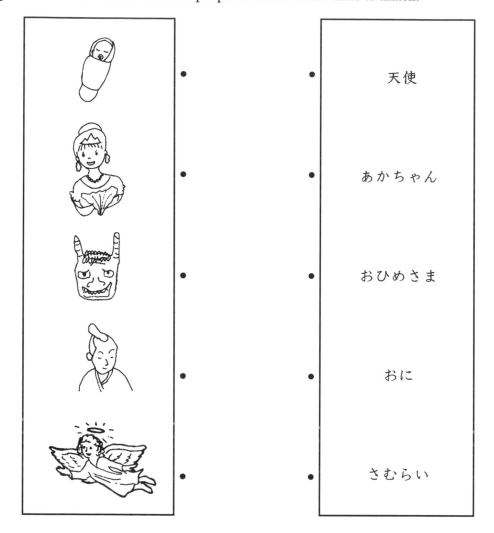

天使

あかちゃん

おひめさま

おに

さむらい

B) Fill in the blanks by selecting appropriate words and phrases from the following list.

ゆうき・せきにんかん・気が強い・こわい・気が弱い・やさしい

1. 父はとても＿＿＿＿＿＿＿＿＿＿です。よく子供をたたきます。(たたく *to hit*)

2. 母はとても＿＿＿＿＿＿＿＿＿＿です。天使のようです。

3. 姉はちょっと＿＿＿＿＿＿＿＿＿＿です。父の言うことを聞きません。

4. 兄は＿＿＿＿＿＿＿＿＿＿があります。約束は忘れません。(約束 *appointment*)

5. 弟は＿＿＿＿＿＿＿＿＿＿があります。何もこわくありません。

6. 妹はちょっと＿＿＿＿＿＿＿＿＿＿です。はっきり意見を言えません。(はっきり *clearly*, 意見 *opinion*)

Grammar

1. ～そう(な)

～そう(な) follows an adjective or a verb in the stem form, and it forms the adjective which expresses a speaker's conjecture about the person or thing he/she is looking at. For example, あの人はこわそうです means *That person over there looks scary*, and ボタンがおちそうですよ means *Your button is about to fall off*.

Following the example, complete the sentences by selecting appropriate words from the list below, and conjugating them as required.

難しい・高い・やさしい・こわれる・泣く

Example: この本は 難し そうですから、買いません。

1. あの人は新しいマネージャーですね。まあまあ＿＿＿＿＿＿＿＿＿＿そうですね。

2. この車は＿＿＿＿＿＿＿＿＿＿そうです。へんな音がします。

3. 映画を見て、＿＿＿＿＿＿＿＿＿＿そうになりましたが、泣きませんでした。

4. このきものはとてもきれいですが、＿＿＿＿＿＿＿＿＿＿そうですね。

Note:
- The adjective いい becomes よさそうな when followed by そう(な).
- For a negative adjective, ～さそう(な) is added after dropping the final い, as in まじめじゃなさそう(な) and やさしくなさそう(な).

2. ～のよう(な) and ～みたい(な)

～のよう(な) and ～みたい(な) follow a noun, and both form the adjectives that describe things and people in terms of their similarities and resemblances. For example, 天使のような人 means *A person who is just like an angel*.

Fill in the blanks by selecting appropriate words from the list below.

子供・天使・おに・母親・犬

1. 山田さんはとてもやさしいです。＿＿＿＿＿のような人です。

2. 兄は遊んでばかりいて、せきにんかんがありません。大学生ですが、＿＿＿＿＿みたいです。

3. 私は母がいません。姉は私のせわをよくしてくれました。姉は私の＿＿＿＿＿のような人です。

4. あき子さんはいじわるで、こわいです。＿＿＿＿＿＿のような人です。

5. ＿＿＿＿＿＿のような食べ方はいけませんよ。ちゃんとスプーンで食べて！

Note: When 方 follows a stem form verb, it denotes *the way of ... ing*. For example, 食べ方 means *the way of eating*.

3. ～らしい

～らしい follows a noun, and it forms the adjective that denotes *like the ideal model of* ... or *stereotypical* .... For example, 男らしい男の人 means *a manly man*. Do not confuse it with ～のよう(な) or ～みたい(な), which denotes *just like ...* .

Underline the appropriate option in the parentheses.

1. 私のボーイフレンドは（男・女）らしい人です。

2. 私のボーイフレンドは（男・女）のような人です。

3. 先生は（かみさま・先生）みたいな人です。

4. 父は（父親・先生）のような人です。

5. 母はとても（母親・父親）らしい人です。

4. ～たり

In a sentence, you can list several activities or events randomly by using the verbs in the ～たり form. The verb する is placed at the very end of the sentence, following the verbs in the ～たり form, and its tense represents the tense of all the verbs in the ～たり form. For example, ピザを食べたり、コーヒーを飲んだり、テレビを見たりしました means *I ate pizza, drank coffee, watched TV, (and so on)*. The ～たり form can be created simply by adding り at the end of the plain past form, even though the たり form does not denote "past".

 Form a sentence following the example.

Example: 昨日・食べる・テレビを見る ⟶ 昨日は食べたり、テレビを見たりしました。

1. 昨日・おんがくを聞く・えいがを見る

　＿＿＿＿＿＿＿＿＿＿＿＿＿＿＿＿＿＿＿＿＿＿＿＿＿＿＿＿＿＿＿＿＿＿＿＿

2. 明日・りょうりをする・そうじをする

　＿＿＿＿＿＿＿＿＿＿＿＿＿＿＿＿＿＿＿＿＿＿＿＿＿＿＿＿＿＿＿＿＿＿＿＿

3. しゅうまつ・新聞を読む・テニスをする・買いものをする

　＿＿＿＿＿＿＿＿＿＿＿＿＿＿＿＿＿＿＿＿＿＿＿＿＿＿＿＿＿＿＿＿＿＿＿＿

4. 夏休み・アルバイトをする・りょこうをする

　＿＿＿＿＿＿＿＿＿＿＿＿＿＿＿＿＿＿＿＿＿＿＿＿＿＿＿＿＿＿＿＿＿＿＿＿

Conversation and Usage

ドレス

Tomiko would like to buy a dress for an upcoming dinner party. She is at a lady's clothing store with her friend Atsuko. Listen carefully to their conversation and then state whether the following statements are true or false.

あつ子：このドレスはどう？

とみ子：ええ？リボンが多すぎるわよ。お姫様みたい。

あつ子：じゃあ、これは？

とみ子：ああ、すごく上品！でも、高そうね。

あつ子：うんん。高くないよ。9,800円。

とみ子：本当？安い！それにとても女らしくて、すてき！ちょっと着てみる。(Tomiko goes into the fitting room and comes out a few minutes later.)

あつ子：どうだった？

とみ子：ちょっと小さかった。大きいのはない？

あつ子：(Atsuko looks for a bigger one.) ピンクはたくさんあるけど、黒はそれしかない。[1]

とみ子：ああ、そう。このデザイン好きなんだけど、ピンクはちょっと。

あつ子：ピンクもいいよ。

とみ子：えっ？ピンク？やだ。

あつ子：どうして？

とみ子：ピンクはちょっと派手すぎるわよ。

あつ子：ぜんぜん。

とみ子：でも、ピンクは着たことないし。

あつ子：はずかしがらないでよ。[2]

とみ子：でも。

あつ子：すごく似合うよ。

あつ子：そう？

とみ子：うん。

あつ子：じゃあ、ピンクにする。

[**Unfamiliar words:** ドレス *dress*, リボン *ribbon*, 上品 *elegant; refined*, すてき *wonderful*, やだ *No way!*, はずかしい *embarrassed*, 派手 *gaudy; showy*, すごく *very much*, 似合う *to look good on (someone)*]

Note:

(*1) The particle 〜しか is used with a negative predicate and it denotes *only*.

(*2) The adjective that describes a psychological or physiological state such as ほしい (*want*), はずかしい (*embarrassed*) and 寒い (*cold*) can be followed by the suffix がる to mean *to show signs of...* . がる must be used when the adjective applies to the third person.

1. The black dress was too big for Tomiko.   (True • False)
2. Atsuko thinks Tomiko looks good in pink.   (True • False)
3. Tomiko decided to buy a pink dress.   (True • False)

Listening Comprehension

機内アナウンス

Listen carefully to the announcement on an airplane (機内アナウンス) and then answer the questions that follow.

1. What is the name of the airline?   _____
2. What is the current time in Tokyo?   _____
3. What time will the plane arrive at Tokyo International Airport?   _____
4. What is the current temperature in Tokyo?   _____

Reading Comprehension

ももたろう

Let's read the Japanese folktale about 桃太郎 (Momotaro)—a child who was born from a gigantic 桃 (*peach*), and circle the meaning of the underlined words.

むかしむかし、あるところに、おじいさんと、おばあさんが住んでいました。ある日、おじいさんは山柴刈りに、おばあさんは川に洗濯に行きました。おばあさんが川で洗濯をしていると、大きな桃がドンブラコ、ドンブラコと流れてきました。おばあさんはその桃をうちに持って帰りました。おじいさんは山から帰ると、大きな桃を見てびっくりしました。おじいさんとおばあさんは食べてみることにしました。おばあさんが (1)包丁を持って来て、桃にあてると、その時、桃がゴゾゴゾと動きました。おじいさんとおばあさんは桃が動いたので、びっくり。そうすると、桃が割れて、中からとても元気な男の子が出てきました。おじいさんと、おばあさんは子供がいなかったので、

とても 喜びました。桃から生まれたので、男の子を桃太郎と名づけました。桃太郎は
たくさん食べて、大きくなりました。

　そのころ、(2)村には悪い鬼がいて、(3)盗みや、人さらいなどをして、村の人を苦し
めていました。力の強い桃太郎は鬼退治に行くことにしました。おじいさんとおばあ
さんは心配しましたが、晴れ着ときびだんごをそろえてあげました。桃太郎はその晴
れ着を着て、きびだんごを腰につけ、家を出て、鬼ヶ島に向かいました。

　途中、犬が1匹来て、桃太郎に言いました。

「桃太郎さん、桃太郎さん、お腰につけたきびだんご、1つ私に下さい。あなたの(4)家来
になりますよ。」

桃太郎は犬にきびだんごを1つあげて、犬は桃太郎の家来になりました。しばらくすると、
さるが出てきました。さるも桃太郎からきびだんごを1つもらって、桃太郎の家来にな
りました。しばらくすると、今度はきじが出てきて、きじも桃太郎からきびだんごを1つ
もらって、桃太郎の家来になりました。

　桃太郎と、犬と、さると、きじは野をこえ、山をこえ、船にのって、鬼ヶ島に着
きました。まず、きじが鬼たちの様子を見に飛んで行きました。きじは桃太郎のところ
に帰ってきて、鬼たちはお酒を飲んでいるようだと言いました。次に、さるが門をの
りこえて、門の扉をあけました。そして、桃太郎と犬は、門を通って、中に入り
ました。鬼たちはびっくり。犬と、さると、きじが鬼たちに飛びかかって、ひっかいた
り、かみついたり、つっついたりしました。そして、力の強い桃太郎が鬼たちをた
たきました。鬼たちは(5)負けてしまって、盗んだ宝物を全部返しました。桃太郎は
その宝物を村の人たちに返して、おじいさんとおばあさんのうちに無事に帰りま
した。

1. 包丁　　　　　　　a. brush　　　　　b. knife　　　　　c. ladle
2. 村　　　　　　　　a. village　　　　b. house　　　　　c. school
3. 盗みや、人さらい　a. stealing and kidnapping, etc.

　　　　　　　　　　b. drawing and painting, etc.

　　　　　　　　　　c. drinking and singing, etc.

4. 家来　　　　　　　a. teacher　　　　b. follower　　　　c. cook
5. 負けて　　　　　　a. lost　　　　　　b. won　　　　　　c. died

Writing

物語を作ろう

Write a short story (物 語 ^{ものがたり}) about an elderly couple with their animals.

New Vocabulary Reference List

NOUN

あかちゃん (赤ちゃん) *baby*

おとな (大人) *adult*

おに (鬼) *ogre*

おひめさま (お姫様) *princess*

おや (親) *parent*

かみさま (神様) *god*

がくしゃ (学者) *scholar*

じょせい (女性) *woman*

せきにんかん (責任感) *a sense of responsibility*

だんせい (男性) *man*

ちちおや (父親) *father*

てんし (天使) *angel*

にんげん (人間) *human being*

ははおや (母親) *mother*

むし (虫) *bug, insect*

ゆうき (勇気) *courage*

ADJECTIVE

こわい (怖い) *scary*

しんけいしつな (神経質な) *nervous, temperamental*

だめな (駄目な) *not good, hopeless*

つよい (強い) *strong*

よわい (弱い) *weak*

VERB (Ru-verb)

おちる (落ちる) *to fall* (川に落ちる *to fall into a river*)

たすける (助ける) *to rescue, to help, to save* (困っている人を助ける *to help the people who are in trouble*)

ADVERB

つまり *that is to say, in other words*

まるで *just like, so to speak*

PARTICLE

～しか (～ない) *only*

OTHERS

～かた (～方) *the way of ... , the manner of ...* (食べ方 *the way of eating*)

～がる *to show the signs of ...* (兄はお金をほしがっている *My brother wants money.*)

きがつよい (気が強い) *strong-willed, hardheaded*

きがよわい (気が弱い) *coward, timid*

そういえば (そう言えば) *if you say so, it reminds me of that ...*

～そう (な) *to look like ...*

～のよう (な) *just like ...*

～みたい (な) *just like ...*

～らしい *to be a typical ...* (男らしい人 *a manly man*)

CHAPTER TWENTY-THREE

Evaluating Facts

Objectives:

- to familiarize with the use of polite commands and plain commands
- to express one's opinion using べき
- to express objective analyses and predictions using はず
- to create an embedded question
- to familiarize with the use of different terms for spouses

Kanji and Vocabulary

1. Reading and Writing Kanji Characters

A) Let's read each of the following kanji words or phrases aloud several times.

部長 *division head*

～部 (ぶ) *... division, ... club*

仕方 *method, way*

正しい *correct*

悪い *bad*

着く *to arrive*

東京 *Tokyo*

大阪 *Osaka*

奥さん *someone else's wife*

妻 *one's own wife*

家内 *one's own wife*

家 *house*

夫 *one's own husband*

決める *to decide*

考える *to consider, to think*

違う *to differ*

専攻 *major*

専門 *specialty*

B) In the boxes provided, write each kanji character following the correct stroke order.

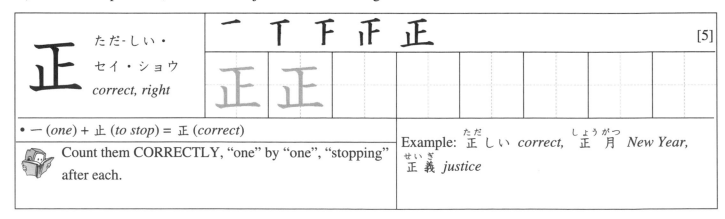

正　ただ-しい・セイ・ショウ　*correct, right*

一　丁　下　正　正　[5]

正　正

- 一 (*one*) + 止 (*to stop*) = 正 (*correct*)

Count them CORRECTLY, "one" by "one", "stopping" after each.

Example: 正しい *correct*, 正月 *New Year*, 正義 *justice*

悪 わる-い・アク・オ bad, ill

一 丆 丆 亓 币 亜 亜 悪 悪 悪 [11]

悪 悪

- 亜 (sub) + 心 (heart) = 悪 (bad)

Perhaps there's a link between a "sub" standard "heart" with one's BAD characters.

- The kanji sharing a component with 悪 (bad) are 思 (think) and 忘 (forget).

Example: 悪い bad, 悪魔 devil

京 キョウ・ケイ capital

' 亠 亠 亠 古 古 京 京 京 [8]

京 京

- 亠 (lid) + 口 (mouth) + 小 (small) = 京 (capital)

derived from the pictograph of a noble's house on top of a hill which eventually associated with the CAPITAL

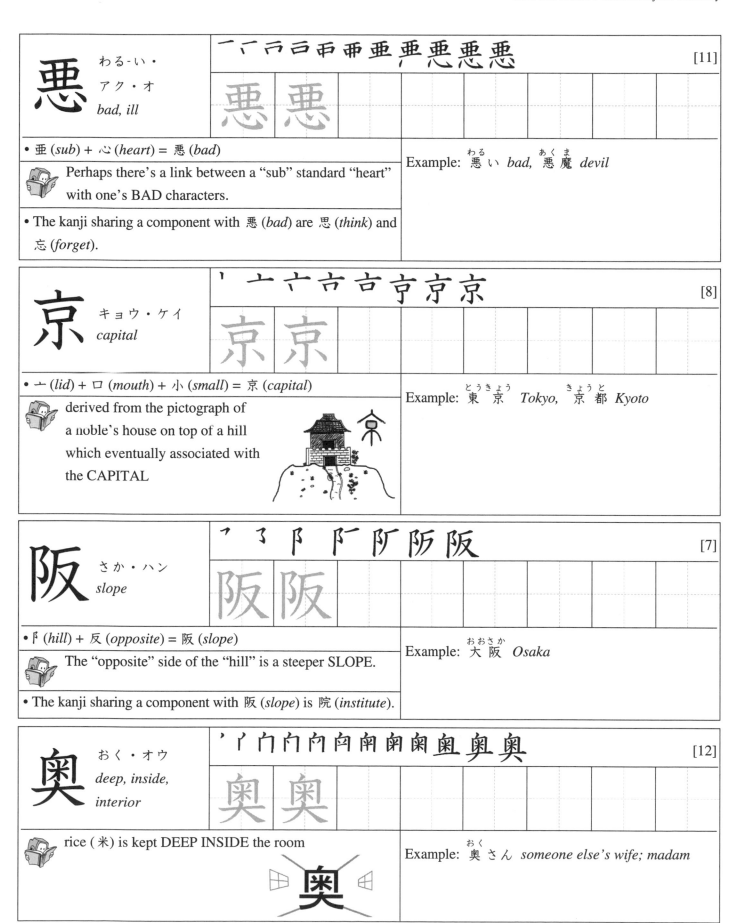

Example: 東京 Tokyo, 京都 Kyoto

阪 さか・ハン slope

' 了 阝 阝 阞 阪 阪 [7]

阪 阪

- 阝 (hill) + 反 (opposite) = 阪 (slope)

The "opposite" side of the "hill" is a steeper SLOPE.

- The kanji sharing a component with 阪 (slope) is 院 (institute).

Example: 大阪 Osaka

奥 おく・オウ deep, inside, interior

' 丿 冂 冂 冋 甪 甪 奥 奥 奥 奥 [12]

奥 奥

rice (米) is kept DEEP INSIDE the room

奥

Example: 奥さん someone else's wife; madam

妻 つま・サイ *wife*	一 ラ ヲ ヨ 聿 妻 妻 妻							[8]
	妻	妻						

- 一 (*one*) + ヨ (*hand*) + | + 女 (*woman*) = 妻 (*wife*)

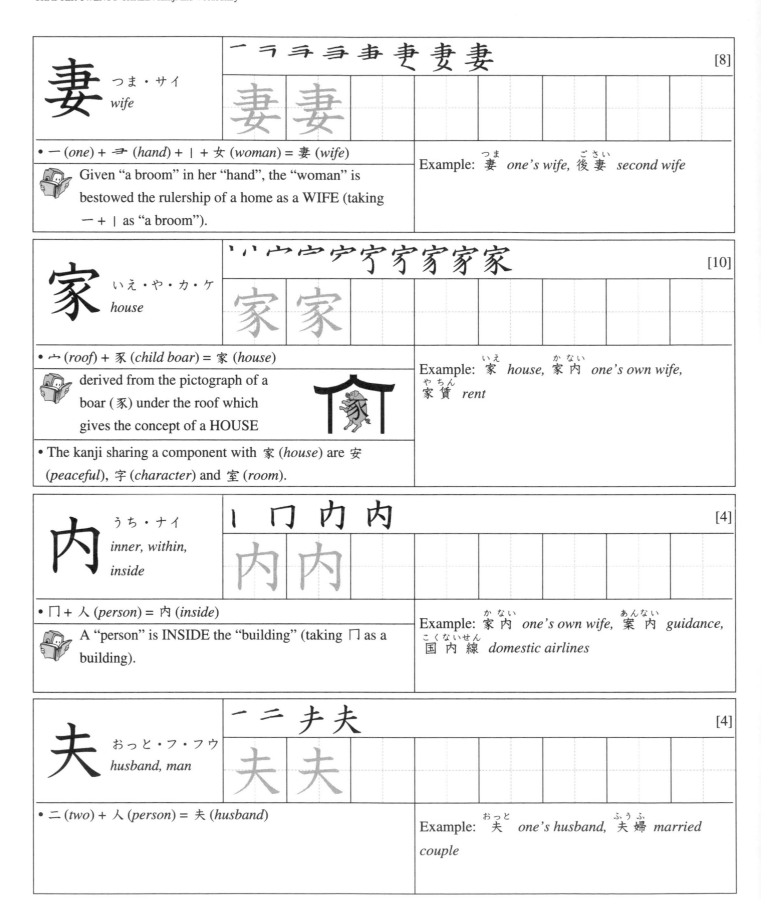 Given "a broom" in her "hand", the "woman" is bestowed the rulership of a home as a WIFE (taking 一 + | as "a broom").

Example: 妻 *one's wife*, 後妻 *second wife*

家 いえ・や・カ・ケ *house*	ﾉ ハ ウ 宀 宇 宇 宇 家 家 家							[10]
	家	家						

- 宀 (*roof*) + 豕 (*child boar*) = 家 (*house*)

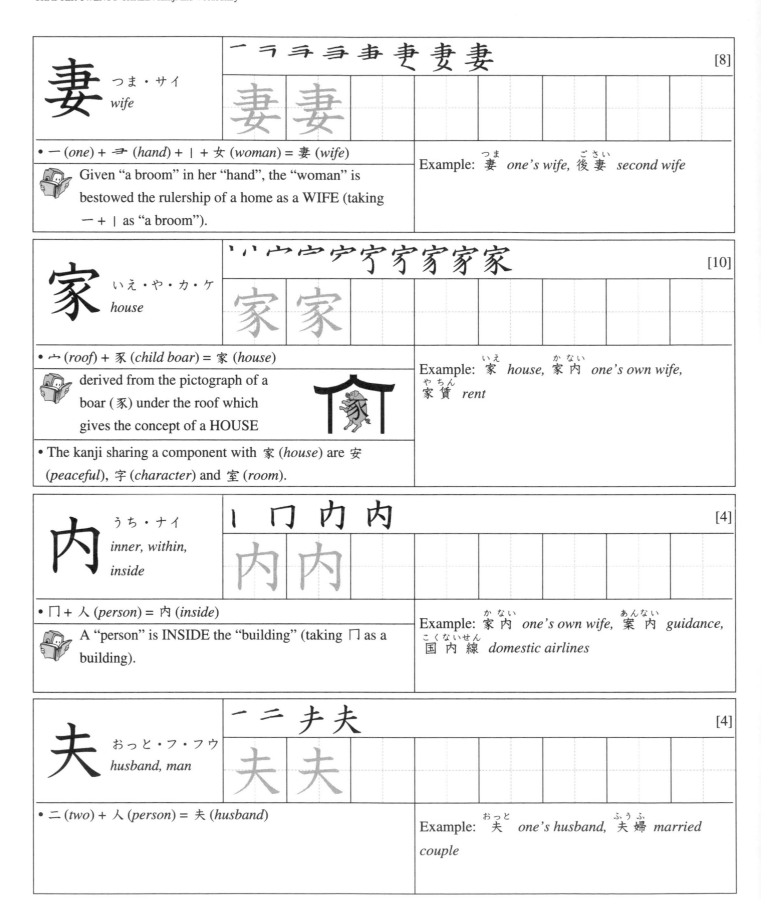 derived from the pictograph of a boar (豕) under the roof which gives the concept of a HOUSE

Example: 家 *house*, 家内 *one's own wife*, 家賃 *rent*

- The kanji sharing a component with 家 (*house*) are 安 (*peaceful*), 字 (*character*) and 室 (*room*).

内 うち・ナイ *inner, within, inside*		口 内 内						[4]
	内	内						

- 冂 + 人 (*person*) = 内 (*inside*)

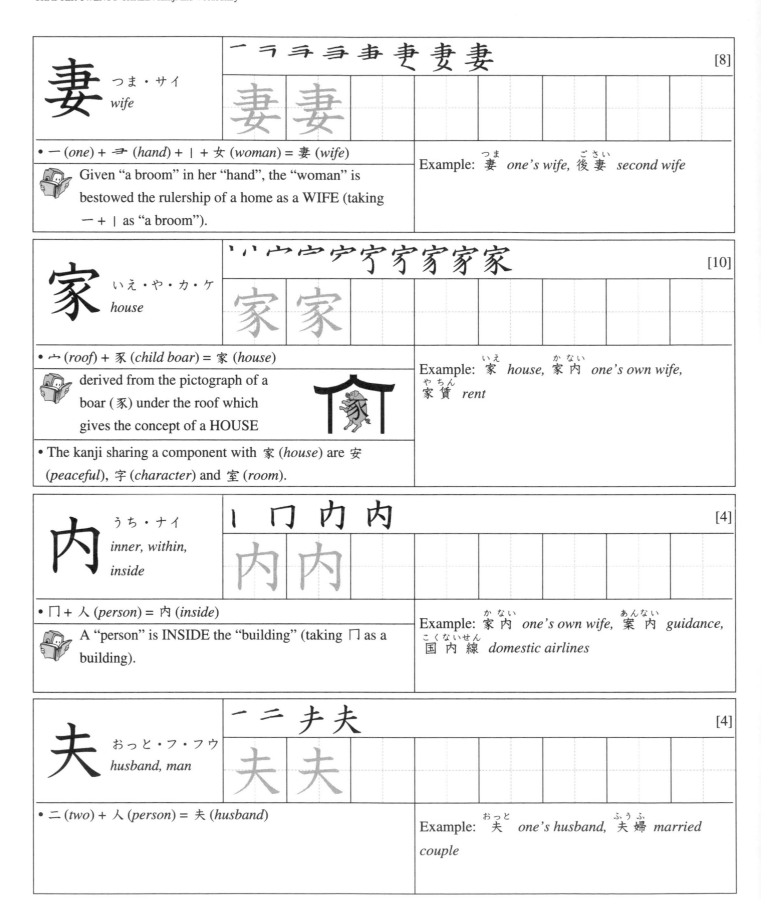 A "person" is INSIDE the "building" (taking 冂 as a building).

Example: 家内 *one's own wife*, 案内 *guidance*, 国内線 *domestic airlines*

夫 おっと・フ・フウ *husband, man*	一 二 ヺ 夫							[4]
	夫	夫						

- 二 (*two*) + 人 (*person*) = 夫 (*husband*)

Example: 夫 *one's husband*, 夫婦 *married couple*

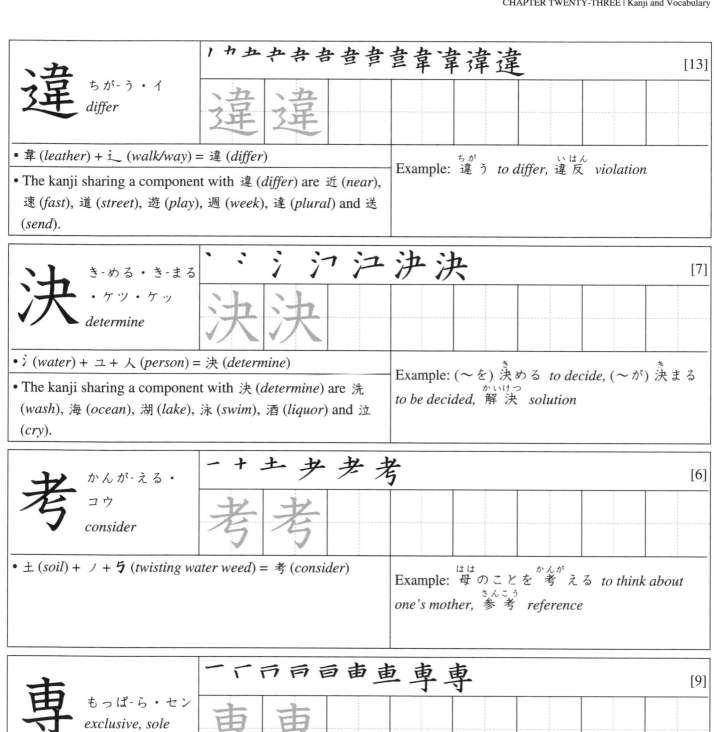

違　ちが-う・イ　differ

ノ カ 五 サ 吾 吾 查 查 查 章 章 違 違　[13]

違 違

• 韋 (leather) + 辶 (walk/way) = 違 (differ)
• The kanji sharing a component with 違 (differ) are 近 (near), 速 (fast), 道 (street), 遊 (play), 週 (week), 達 (plural) and 送 (send).

Example: 違(ちが)う to differ, 違反(いはん) violation

決　き-める・き-まる・ケツ・ケツ　determine

丶 冫 氵 沪 沪 決 決　[7]

決 決

• 氵 (water) + ユ + 人 (person) = 決 (determine)
• The kanji sharing a component with 決 (determine) are 洗 (wash), 海 (ocean), 湖 (lake), 泳 (swim), 酒 (liquor) and 泣 (cry).

Example: (～を) 決(き)める to decide, (～が) 決(き)まる to be decided, 解決(かいけつ) solution

考　かんが-える・コウ　consider

一 十 土 耂 考 考　[6]

考 考

• 土 (soil) + ノ + 丂 (twisting water weed) = 考 (consider)

Example: 母(はは)のことを 考(かんが)える to think about one's mother, 参考(さんこう) reference

専　もっぱ-ら・セン　exclusive, sole

一 厂 戸 戸 百 申 亩 専 専　[9]

専 専

• 一 (one) + 日 (sun) + 丨 + 寸 (measure/inch) = 専 (exclusive)

Example: 専門(せんもん) specialty, 専攻(せんこう) academic major

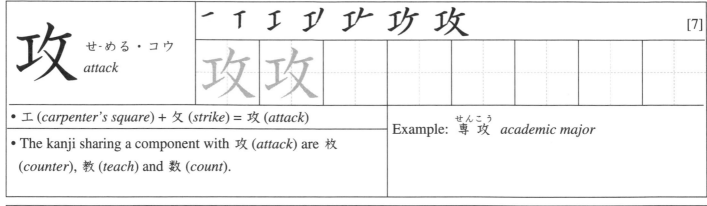

攻 せ-める・コウ attack	一 丁 工 エ 攷 攻 攻									[7]
	攻 攻									

- 工 (*carpenter's square*) + 攵 (*strike*) = 攻 (*attack*)
- The kanji sharing a component with 攻 (*attack*) are 枚 (*counter*), 教 (*teach*) and 数 (*count*).

Example: 専攻 *academic major* せんこう

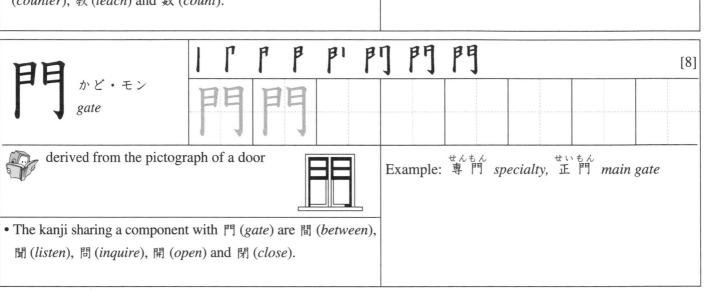

門 かど・モン gate	丨 冂 冂 冂 冂 門 門 門									[8]
	門 門									

 derived from the pictograph of a door

Example: 専門 *specialty*, 正門 *main gate* せんもん せいもん

- The kanji sharing a component with 門 (*gate*) are 間 (*between*), 聞 (*listen*), 問 (*inquire*), 開 (*open*) and 閉 (*close*).

C) Let's read aloud to check how well you've mastered the kanji you've learned.

1. 東京を3時に出たので、大阪には6時に着きます。
2. 今の仕事の専門はコンピューターです。大学では数学を専攻しました。
3. 部長の奥さんはとてもいい方です。
4. うちの家内は大阪で生まれました。
5. 妻と夫はよく話しをするべきです。
6. テニス部の部長は気が強いです。でも、いい人です。正しいことは正しい、悪いことは悪いと言います。
7. 夫とは考えがいつも違います。でも、家のことを決める時は、よく話し合いますから、だいじょうぶです。
8. もう少し勉強の仕方を考えた方がいいですよ。

D) Fill in the correct kanji characters in the boxes provided.

1. つま　おっと
　[　] と [　]

2. とうきょう　おお さか
　[　][　] と [　][　]

3. ただ　　　　わる
　[　] しいことと、[　] いこと

2. Using the Terms for Spouses

In Japanese, different terms for spouses—奥さん, 家内, ご主人 and 主人—are used depending on the context. 夫 and 妻 are also used in conversation, even though they are more for written forms.

Fill in the blanks with appropriate terms for spouses. You may not use the same item more than once.

1. 私の＿＿＿＿＿＿はゴルフばかりしていて、子供_{こども}のめんどうをぜんぜんみません。

2. マリアさんの＿＿＿＿＿＿は今どこにいらっしゃいますか？

3. うちの＿＿＿＿＿＿は母親^{ははおや}なのに、りょうりも、そうじもしないんです。

4. マイクさんの＿＿＿＿＿＿は働^{はたら}いていらっしゃいますか。

3. Figuring Out Where to Eat on Yoko's Birthday

Fill in the blanks by selecting appropriate words from the following list and conjugating them if necessary.

> 決める・考える・もっと・たしか・ちゃんと

たけし：ようこさんのたんじょう日は＿＿＿＿＿＿5月31日だよね。

ようこ：ええ。

たけし：いっしょに食事^{しょくじ}をしませんか。

ようこ：いいんですか。

たけし：ええ。どこがいいか＿＿＿＿＿＿おいて下さい。

ようこ：私が＿＿＿＿＿＿もいいんですか。

たけし：もちろん。

ようこ：じゃあ、ピザハット。

たけし：＿＿＿＿＿＿いいところにして下さいよ。

ようこ：いいんですか。

たけし：もちろん。

ようこ：じゃあ、ラ・ベル・ヴィは？

たけし：ああ、いいですよ。

ようこ：本当に？＿＿＿＿＿＿さいふを持^もって来^きて下さいよ。

Grammar

1. ～なさい and ～ろ

The polite command form, such as 食べなさい and 飲みなさい, is created simply by adding なさい at the end of a verb in the stem form. The plain command form, such as 食べろ and 飲め, is created by adding "ro" or "e" at the end of a verb in the root form ("ro" for ru-verbs and "e" for u-verbs). The plain command forms of する and くる are しろ and こい respectively. The plain command form sounds extremely blunt and rough when used independently.

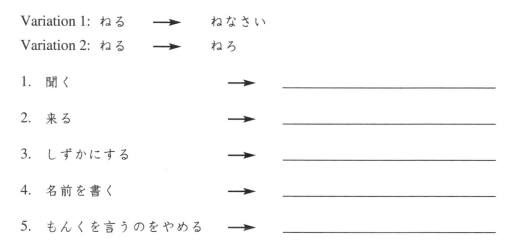 Convert the sentences following the example.

Variation 1: ねる ⟶ ねなさい

Variation 2: ねる ⟶ ねろ

1. 聞く ⟶ _____

2. 来る ⟶ _____

3. しずかにする ⟶ _____

4. 名前を書く ⟶ _____

5. もんくを言うのをやめる ⟶ _____

Note: The plain negative command form is created by adding な at the end of a verb in the dictionary form, as in 食べるな (*Don't eat!*) and 飲むな (*Don't drink!*). There is no specific polite negative command form.

2. ～はずだ and ～べきだ

～はずだ follows a verb or an adjective in the pre-nominal form, and it expresses the situation that is supposed to hold or to have held judging from the circumstantial facts related to time, place, regulations, actions, etc. ～べきだ follows a verb in the plain present affirmative form and it expresses the speaker's strong subjective opinion about what should be the case.

Select はず or べき in each of the following sentences.

1. 子供は早くねる（はず・べき）です。

2. ひこうきは3時に着く（はず・べき）ですから、4時にはここに来るでしょう。

3. 大学生は勉強する（はず・べき）です。なまけてはいけませんよ。

4. 田中さんは今日来ない（はず・べき）ですから、うちに電話して下さい。

5. たばこはすう（はず・べき）じゃありません。

3. ～か（どうか）

Verbs like しる (*to know*) and わかる (*to understand*) can take an embedded question followed by か. The verbs and adjectives in an embedded question must be in the plain form, and だ at the end of a na-type adjective and a copula is usually deleted. If the embedded question does not contain a question word such as だれ, か may be replaced by かどうか.

Convert the sentences following the example.

Example: あの方はどなたですか。　→　あの方はどなたかしっていますか。

1. 山田さんの専攻は何ですか。　→　_____

2. これはいくらですか。　→　_____

3. 昨日のパーティーにだれが来ましたか。　→　_____

4. スミスさんは今何をしていますか。　→　_____

5. 明日はしけんがありますか。　→　_____

Conversation and Usage

1. ボーイフレンドとガールフレンド？

You will hear the conversation between a man and a woman. Listen carefully and state why the woman thinks the man should go to Boston.

男 の 人 ： 実はアメリカの大学の数学の教授が僕を誘ってくれたんだ。

女 の 人 ： 大学院に？

男の人 ： うん。奨学金も出してくれるんだ。

女の人 ： へえ。すごい。数学はアメリカがいいの？

男の人 ： 大学によって違うけど、その大学は、すごくいいんだ。[1]

女の人 ： アメリカのどこ？

男の人 ： ボストン。

女の人 ： ああ、そう。

男の人 ： うん。でも、行くべきかどうか迷っているんだ。

女の人 ： 行きなさいよ。若いうちに、がんばるべきよ。[2]

男の人 ： でも、君は寂しくないの？

女の人 　：ぜんぜん。

男の人 　：本当<ruby>本当<rt>ほんとう</rt></ruby>に？

女の人 　：うん。

男の人 　：そんなはずはないでしょう！僕<ruby><rt>ぼく</rt></ruby>がいなくても寂<ruby><rt>さび</rt></ruby>しくないということは、どういうこと？*3

女の人 　：何<ruby>何<rt>なに</rt></ruby>か勘違<ruby>勘違<rt>かんちが</rt></ruby>いしてるの？

[*Unfamiliar words:* 誘<ruby><rt>さそ</rt></ruby>う *to invite,* 奨学金<ruby>奨学金<rt>しょうがくきん</rt></ruby> *scholarship,* すごい *great,* 〜けど *although ...,* すごく *very much,* 迷<ruby><rt>まよ</rt></ruby>う 若<ruby><rt>わか</rt></ruby>い *young,* 君<ruby><rt>きみ</rt></ruby> *you,* そんなはずはない *It cannot be the case.,* 何<ruby>何<rt>なに</rt></ruby>か勘違<ruby>勘違<rt>かんちが</rt></ruby>いしてるの？ *Are you misunderstanding something?*]

Note:

(*1) 〜によって means *depending on ...*

(*2) 〜うちに forms a time adverbial clause that denotes *while ...* or *before ...,* but it implies that failing to perform the action during/before the specified time may cause some negative circumstance.

(*3) XということはYということです denotes *X means Y.* In this case, X and Y must be a sentence and the predicate must be in the plain form.

_____

_____

_____

2. 母とむすめ

You will hear the conversation between a mother and her daughter, Michiko, over dinner. Listen carefully and answer the questions that follow.

娘<ruby>娘<rt>むすめ</rt></ruby> 　：お母さん、それ、とって。

母 　：どれ？

娘 　：それ。

母 　：野菜<ruby>野菜<rt>やさい</rt></ruby>？

娘 　：ううんん。

母 　：肉<ruby>肉<rt>にく</rt></ruby>？

娘 　：うん。

母 　：肉ばかり食べないで、野菜<ruby>野菜<rt>やさい</rt></ruby>も食べなさいよ。

娘 　：はい、はい。

母 　：「はい」は一回<ruby>一回<rt>いっかい</rt></ruby>でいいの。

娘　　：はい。

母　　：今日は学校どうだった？

娘　　：大阪から転校生が来たの。

母　　：女の子？

娘　　：うん。田中みどりさん。お父さんが銀行員だから、よく引越しするんだって。

母　　：ああ、そう。それは大変ね。仲良くしてあげなさいよ。

娘　　：うん。明日、うちに連れて来てもいい？

母　　：いいわよ。でも、何時ごろ？

娘　　：明日は部活がないから、3時半ごろ。

母　　：お母さんはいるかどうかわからないわよ。

娘　　：どうして。・

母　　：明日の午後はおばあちゃんを病院に連れて行かないといけないのよ。

娘　　：ああ、そう。

[*Unfamiliar words:* 一回 *once,* 転校生 *transferred student,* 銀行員 *bank employee,* 引越し *moving,* 仲良くする *to be friendly with,* 部活 *club activities*]

1. What is the name of the transferred student?　＿＿＿＿＿＿＿＿＿＿＿＿＿＿＿＿＿＿＿
2. Where is she from?　＿＿＿＿＿＿＿＿＿＿＿＿＿＿＿＿＿＿＿
3. What does her father do?　＿＿＿＿＿＿＿＿＿＿＿＿＿＿＿＿＿＿＿
4. What time will Michiko come home tomorrow?　＿＿＿＿＿＿＿＿＿＿＿＿＿＿＿＿＿
5. What will Michiko's mother do tomorrow afternoon?　＿＿＿＿＿＿＿＿＿＿＿＿＿＿

Listening Comprehension

メッセージ

Listen carefully to the voice messages for Yuki on the CD, then answer the following questions.

1. Who is having dinner with Sean this Friday?　＿＿＿＿＿＿＿＿＿＿＿＿＿＿＿＿＿＿＿
2. What is Sean's phone number?　＿＿＿＿＿＿＿＿＿＿＿＿＿＿＿＿＿＿＿
3. What did Yuki's mother ask?　＿＿＿＿＿＿＿＿＿＿＿＿＿＿＿＿＿＿＿
4. What was Mika's question to Yuki?　＿＿＿＿＿＿＿＿＿＿＿＿＿＿＿＿＿＿＿
5. What is Mika's phone number?　＿＿＿＿＿＿＿＿＿＿＿＿＿＿＿＿＿＿＿

Reading Comprehension

地球温暖化

Let's read the following passage about what three Japanese middle school students think of (地球温暖化) (*global warming*), then answer the questions that follow.

1. 田中健一　14歳

　私達は地球を守ることをもっと真剣に考えるべきです。しかし、ほとんどの人はそれをしません。ゴミをどこにでも捨てたり、戦争を続けたり、排気ガスを出し続けたりしています。このままだと、地球が滅びてしまいます。もっと地球を守ることを考えた方がいいと思います。

2. 山口恵子　13歳

　地球温暖化は私達が防げるものだと思います。私たちは日常生活の中で、電気や、ガソリンの節約をして、ものを捨てないようにするべきです。地球温暖化は私達の努力で防げるはずです。

3. 石川恵美　13歳

　このまま地球温暖化が続くと、地球はなくなってしまうかもしれない。人にこうするべきだとか、ああするべきだとか言う前に、自分から何か実行したい。私はまずゴミを捨てないようにする。

[*Unfamiliar words:* 地球 *earth*, 守る *to protect*, 真剣に *seriously*, ほとんどの〜 *most ...,* どこにでも *anywhere*, 戦争 *war*, 排気ガス *exhaust gas*, このまま *as it is,* 滅びる *perish*, 防ぐ *to prevent*, 日常生活 *daily life*, 節約 *saving*, 努力 *effort*, こう *this way*, ああ *that way*, 実行する *to execute*]

1. What are three examples of bad things that people do according to Kenichi Tanaka?

_____

_____

2. What does Keiko Yamaguchi claim that people should do?

_____

3. What is unique about Emi Ishikawa's attitude to preventing global warming?

_____

Writing

ちきゅうおんだんか
地球 温暖化

What should or shouldn't we do to protect the earth? Give as many suggestions as possible.

Example: 車を運転しないで、自転車に乗るようにするべきです。

* _____
* _____
* _____
* _____

New Vocabulary Reference List

NOUN

おくさん (奥さん) *someone else's wife*

おっと (夫) *one's own husband*

かない (家内) *one's own wife*

しかた (仕方) *method, way* (勉強の仕方 *the way of studying*)

せいせき (成績) *grade, score, performance*

つま (妻) *one's own wife*

ぶちょう (部長) *the head of a department, division, or club*

みんな *everyone, everything*

やくそく (約束) *personal appointment, promise* (c.f. 予約 *reservation/business appointment*)

ADJECTIVE

ただしい (正しい) *correct, precise* (正しいこたえ *correct answers*)

ADVERB

たしか (確か) *if I remember correctly, I suppose*

ちゃんと *tidily, properly, perfectly, correctly*

とにかく *anyway, in any case*

まず *first of all* (まず朝ごはんを食べる *to eat breakfast first*)

もっと *more, some more* (もっと食べてください *Please eat some more.*)

VERB (Ru-verb)

かたづける (片付ける) *to put things in order, to tidy up* (へやを片付ける *to tidy up the room*, おもちゃを片付ける *to put the toys in order*)

かんがえる (考える) *to consider, to think* (山田さんのこ

とを考える *to think about Ms. Yamada*)

きめる (決める) *to decide* (専攻を決める *to decide on one's major*)

VERB (U-verb)

つく (着く) *to arrive* (ニューヨークに着く *to arrive at New York*)

IRREGULAR VERB

しっかりする *to become reliable* (しっかりしている *to be reliable*)

OTHERS

〜うちに *while ..., before ...* (子供がねているうちに *while the children are sleeping*, 子供がねないうちに *before the children fall asleep*)

〜か (どうか) *whether or not ...* (いいかどうか考える *to consider whether (it) is good or not*)

〜ということは〜ということだ *The fact that ... means ... .*

〜なさい *Do ... .* (かたづけなさい *Tidy up!*)

〜によって *depending on ...* (人によって違う *to differ depending on the person*)

〜はずだ *I suppose that ...*

〜ぶ (〜部) *... division, ... club*

〜べきだ *It should be the case that ... .* (学生は勉強するべきだ *Students should study.*)

めんどうをみる (面倒を見る) *to take care of or look after a person or an animal* (子供の面倒を見る *to take care of the children*)

CHAPTER TWENTY-FOUR

What Would You Do?

Objectives:

- to use various verbs that means "to take"
- to use the volitional form to express intention, attempt and effort making
- to express a variety of conditions using たら and なら
- to use the words related to sight-seeing

Kanji and Vocabulary

1. Reading and Writing Kanji Characters

A) Let's read each of the following kanji words or phrases aloud several times.

受ける *to receive, to take (an exam)*

申しこむ *to apply*

～級 *level ...*

試験 *exam, test*

金持ち *rich person*

若い *young*

図書館 *library*

映画館 *movie theater*

名古屋 *Nagoya*

京都 *Kyoto*

店 *store*

高級だ *high grade, high class, fancy*

～的 *typical ..., like ...*

B) In the boxes provided, write each kanji character following the correct stroke order.

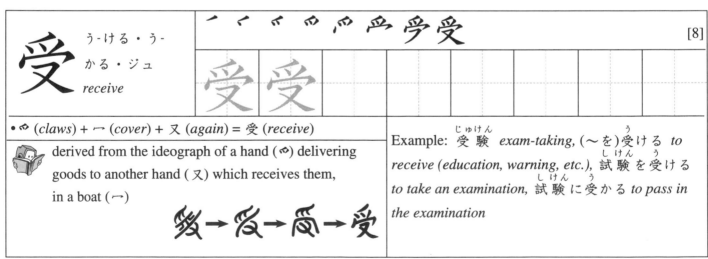

受　う-ける・う-かる・ジュ　receive

ノ　ハ　ヅ　ビ　ピ　ヅ　受　受 [8]

受　受

• ⺥ (claws) + ⺆ (cover) + 又 (again) = 受 (receive)

derived from the ideograph of a hand (⺥) delivering goods to another hand (又) which receives them, in a boat (⺆)

Example: 受験 *exam-taking*, (～を)受ける *to receive (education, warning, etc.)*, 試験を受ける *to take an examination*, 試験に受かる *to pass in the examination*

級 キュウ
level, rank, grade

ㄥ ㄠ ㄠ ㄠ ㄠ 糸 糸 紗 級 級 [9]

級 級

• 糸 (*thread*) + 及 (*reach*) = 級 (*level*)

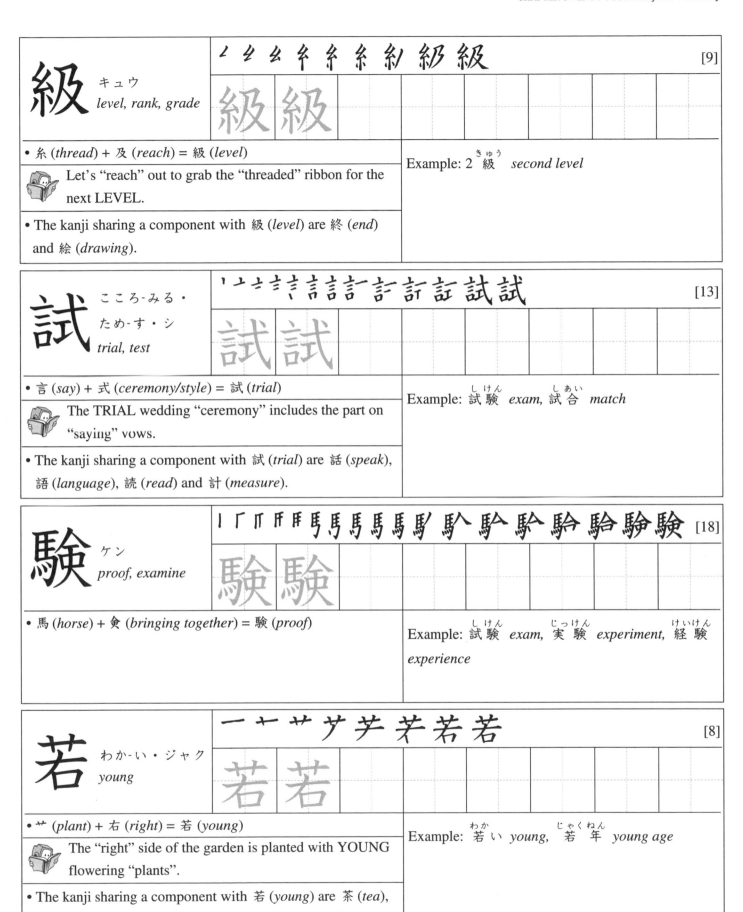

Let's "reach" out to grab the "threaded" ribbon for the next LEVEL.

• The kanji sharing a component with 級 (*level*) are 終 (*end*) and 絵 (*drawing*).

Example: 2 級 きゅう *second level*

試 こころ-みる・ ため-す・シ
trial, test

ノ 亠 亠 言 言 言 言 言 訂 訂 試 試 [13]

試 試

• 言 (*say*) + 式 (*ceremony/style*) = 試 (*trial*)

The TRIAL wedding "ceremony" includes the part on "saying" vows.

• The kanji sharing a component with 試 (*trial*) are 話 (*speak*), 語 (*language*), 読 (*read*) and 計 (*measure*).

Example: 試 験 しけん *exam*, 試 合 しあい *match*

験 ケン
proof, examine

l 厂 厂 巨 厓 馬 馬 馬 馬 馬 駇 駇 駇 験 験 験 [18]

験 験

• 馬 (*horse*) + 僉 (*bringing together*) = 験 (*proof*)

Example: 試 験 しけん *exam*, 実 験 じっけん *experiment*, 経 験 けいけん *experience*

若 わか-い・ジャク
young

一 ナ 十 サ サ 芊 若 若 [8]

若 若

• 艹 (*plant*) + 右 (*right*) = 若 (*young*)

The "right" side of the garden is planted with YOUNG flowering "plants".

• The kanji sharing a component with 若 (*young*) are 茶 (*tea*), 薬 (*medicine*), 英 (*superb/England*), 苦 (*bitter*) and 花 (*flower*).

Example: 若 い わか *young*, 若 年 じゃくねん *young age*

館 カン
large building, hall

ノ 人 ト 今 今 今 食 食 食' 食' 飠 飠 節 節 館 館 [16]

• 飠 (*eat*) + 官 (*official*) = 館 (*hall*)

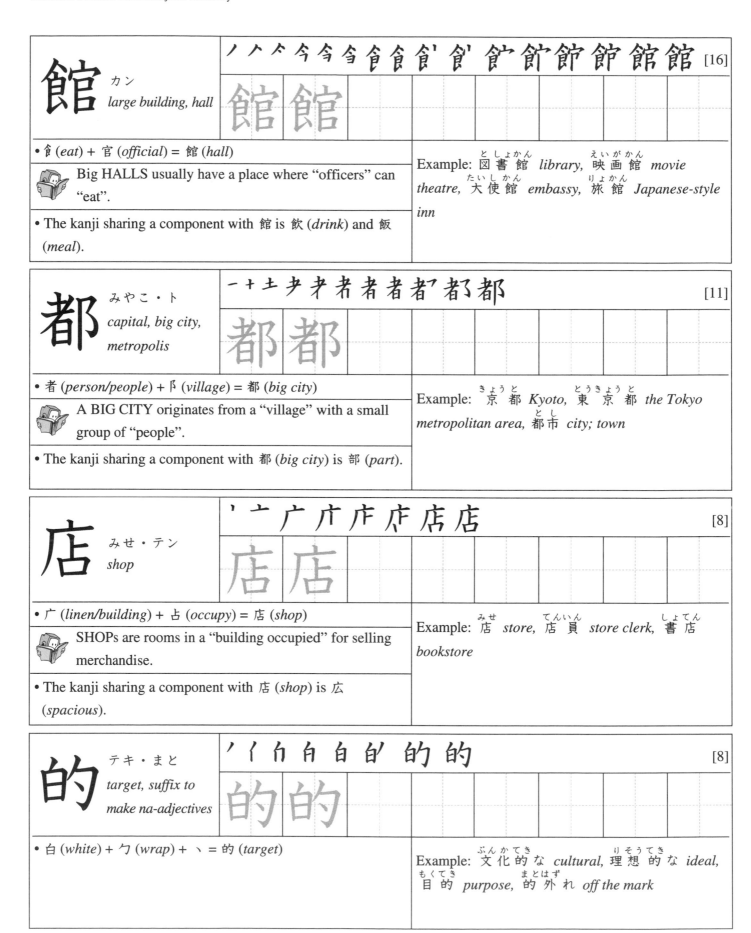 Big HALLS usually have a place where "officers" can "eat".

• The kanji sharing a component with 館 is 飲 (*drink*) and 飯 (*meal*).

Example: 図書館 *library*, 映画館 *movie theatre*, 大使館 *embassy*, 旅館 *Japanese-style inn*

都 みやこ・ト
capital, big city, metropolis

一 十 土 耂 耂 者 者 者 者' 都 都 [11]

• 者 (*person/people*) + 阝 (*village*) = 都 (*big city*)

A BIG CITY originates from a "village" with a small group of "people".

• The kanji sharing a component with 都 (*big city*) is 部 (*part*).

Example: 京都 *Kyoto*, 東京都 *the Tokyo metropolitan area*, 都市 *city; town*

店 みせ・テン
shop

' 亠 广 广 庁 庐 店 店 [8]

• 广 (*linen/building*) + 占 (*occupy*) = 店 (*shop*)

SHOPs are rooms in a "building occupied" for selling merchandise.

• The kanji sharing a component with 店 (*shop*) is 広 (*spacious*).

Example: 店 *store*, 店員 *store clerk*, 書店 *bookstore*

的 テキ・まと
target, suffix to make na-adjectives

ノ 亻 竹 白 白 白' 的 的 [8]

• 白 (*white*) + 勹 (*wrap*) + 丶 = 的 (*target*)

Example: 文化的な *cultural*, 理想的な *ideal*, 目的 *purpose*, 的外れ *off the mark*

C) Let's read aloud to check how well you've mastered the kanji you've learned.

1. この間、日本語能力^{のうりょく}試験の3級を受けようと思って申しこみました。3週間の間、毎日図書館で勉強しました。日本語の先生にもたすけていただきました。聞き取りの問題はまあまあかんたんでしたが、漢字の問題はちょっと難しかったです。

2. 私の祖母は名古屋で生まれました。22さいの時、若くて金持ちの男性^{だんせい}と結婚^{けっこん}しました。

3. 京都には古い日本的なたてものがたくさんあります。

4. 銀座^{ぎんざ}には高級なブティックや、レストランや、店がたくさんあります。

D) Fill in the correct kanji characters in the boxes provided.

1. し けん ｜｜｜｜を｜う｜けました。

3. な ご や ｜｜｜｜｜と きょう と ｜｜｜

2. と しょ かん ｜｜｜｜｜や えい が かん ｜｜｜｜｜

2. Using the Verbs "To Take"

Fill in each blank with the relevant verb that means "to take".

1. 薬^{くすり}を＿＿＿＿＿＿＿＿＿

2. 日本語^{にほんご}のコースを＿＿＿＿＿＿＿

3. 試験を＿＿＿＿＿＿＿＿＿

4. シャワーを＿＿＿＿＿＿＿＿＿

5. 電車^{でんしゃ}に＿＿＿＿＿＿＿＿＿

3. Sight-seeing

Below is an email from Yoko to her American friend in New York, advising him on his first visit to Japan. Complete the paragraph by selecting appropriate words from the list provided.

しんかんせん・でんとう・りょこうがいしゃ・店・りょかん・かんこう

＿＿＿＿＿＿＿＿なら、京都がいいでしょう。＿＿＿＿＿＿＿＿＿的なたてものがたくさんあります。JRパスを買^かうと、＿＿＿＿＿＿＿＿に安く乗^のれますよ。ニューヨークの＿＿＿＿＿＿＿＿で聞^きいてみて下さい。それから、＿＿＿＿＿＿＿＿に泊^とまって下さいね。ふとんで寝^ねられますよ。京都にはいろいろな＿＿＿＿＿＿＿＿がたくさんありますから、おみやげをたくさん買って下さいね。

Grammar

1. ～よう

The volitional form of a verb can be created by adding yō or ō at the end of a verb in the root form—yō for a ru-verb and ō for an u-verb. The volitional forms of する and くる are しよう and こよう, respectively.

Convert the following verbs into volitional forms.

Example: 受ける ⟶ 受けよう

1. にげる ⟶ _____
2. 飲む ⟶ _____
3. 歩く ⟶ _____
4. 取る ⟶ _____
5. 運ぶ ⟶ _____

6. 待つ ⟶ _____
7. 会う ⟶ _____
8. 行く ⟶ _____
9. する ⟶ _____

2. ～ようと思う

The verb in the volitional form (～よう) can be used with a verb that expresses thinking such as 思う (to think) and 考える (to consider), for expressing one's intention or will. For example, 行こうと思います means *I'm thinking of going*.

Complete the sentences below.

1. スペインは行ったことがないので、来月＿＿＿＿＿＿＿＿＿と思います。

   I have never been to Spain, so I am thinking of going there next month.

2. 前の試験は悪かったので、今度の試験は＿＿＿＿＿＿＿＿＿と考えています。

   The previous exam was bad, so I am thinking of trying my best for the next one.

3. 今年は日本語能力試験の３級を受けたいので、来月＿＿＿＿＿＿＿＿＿と思います。

   I would like to take the Japanese-Language Proficiency Test at level 3, so I am thinking of applying for it next month.

4. あまり好きじゃありませんが、＿＿＿＿＿＿＿＿＿と思います。

   I do not like (it) very much, but I am thinking of eating (it.)

5. 弟は日本にりゅう学＿＿＿＿＿＿＿＿＿と思っています。

   My brother is thinking of studying abroad in Japan.

3. ～ようとする

The volitional form (～よう) can be used with する for expressing a momentum act of attempt. For example, なっとうを食^たべようとしました means someone attempted or tried to eat fermented soybeans by bringing them to his/her mouth.

Form a sentence following the example.

Example: ねる　　⟶　　ねようとしましたが、ねられませんでした。

1. おきる　⟶　_____

2. にげる　⟶　_____

3. 言^いう　⟶　_____

4. 飲^のむ　⟶　_____

5. 乗^のる　⟶　_____

4. ～ようにする

The volitional form (～よう) can be used with the particle に and the verb する for expressing a long-term or continuous conscious effort. For example, 毎日^{まいにち}なっとうを食べるようにしました means *I tried to eat fermented soybeans everyday*.

Translate the following sentences.

1. できるだけ、くだものを食べるようにしています。

   _____

2. 出かけようとした時に、山田さんが来ました。

   _____

3. 来年は中国語を勉強しようと思います。

   _____

4. 食べようとしましたが、食べられませんでした。

   _____

5. たまごは食べないようにして下さい。

   _____

5. 〜たら

The 〜たら form is created by adding ら at the end of verbs, adjectives and copulas in their plain past tense. If the main clause is in the present tense, the 〜たら clause represents a condition (generic, temporal, hypothetical or counterfactual condition). If the main clause is in the past tense, the 〜たら clause expresses some situation where one's attention is caught by what happened after doing something.

Translate the following sentences.

1. 学位をもらったら、しゅうしょくしやすいですよ。

    _____

2. 仕事がきらいだったら、やめた方がいいですよ。

    _____

3. ものを使ったら、必ずかたづけて下さい。

    _____

4. このボタンをおしたら、きっぷが出ます。

    _____

5. 私が金持ちだったら、家を持っているでしょう。

    _____

6. 本屋に行ったら、テニス部のせんぱいに会いました。

    _____

6. 〜なら

The 〜なら clause defines the context or assumption on which the statement in a main clause is based, and it means *if...* or *if you are talking about ....* なら follows a verb and an adjective in the plain form, except that だ that appears at the end of a copula and a na-adjective must be dropped.

Following the examples, complete the sentences creatively.

Example: • 日本に行くなら、<u>京都に行って下さい。</u> *If you are going to Japan, please go to Kyoto.*
　　　　 • 日本の高校に行ったなら、<u>日本語が話せるでしょう。</u> *If (he) went to a Japanese high school, he is probably able to speak Japanese.*

1. 日本語を勉強するなら、日本_____。

2. 漢字を2,000しっているなら、新聞_____。

3. いいカメラを買いたいなら、_____。

4. お酒が好きなら、＿＿＿＿＿＿＿＿＿＿＿＿＿＿＿＿＿＿＿＿＿＿。

5. 新幹線を使うつもりなら、＿＿＿＿＿＿＿＿＿＿＿＿＿＿＿＿＿＿＿。

Conversation and Usage

北海道

Wei Ming (ウエイミン) is talking to his friend Akiko (明子) about his travel plan to Hokkaido (北海道) this winter. Listen to their conversation on the CD, and answer the questions.

ウエイミン ： この冬は北海道に行こうと思っているんだ。

明子 ： 冬に？

ウエイミン ： うん。雪を見たいんだ。

明子 ： 雪を見たことないの？

ウエイミン ： うん。僕は台湾で生まれて、台湾で育ったから、まだ一度も雪を見たことがないんだ。

明子 ： ああ、そう。北海道に行くなら、雪祭りも見た方がいいわよ。

ウエイミン ： ああ、そう、そう。北海道の雪祭りは有名だよね。

明子 ： ええ。

ウエイミン ： 明子さんは雪祭りを見たことがあるの？

明子 ： ええ、一度。5年ぐらい前に。とってもきれいよ。

ウエイミン ： ああ、そう。

明子 ： 北海道に行ったら、温泉にも入るといいわよ。

ウエイミン ： ああ、温泉もあるの？

明子 ： もちろん。

ウエイミン ： ああ、そう。

明子 ： それに、スキーもできるよね。

ウエイミン ： ああ、そうだね。僕は温泉にも入ったことないし、スキーもしたことないから、すごく楽しみ。

明子 ： それに、おいしいものもたくさんあるわよ。

ウエイミン ： ああ、そう。例えば？

明子　　　：　例えば、カニとか、魚とか。

ウエイミン　：　ああ、僕、カニ大好き。

[**Unfamiliar words:** 台湾 Taiwan, 育つ to grow up, 雪祭り Snow Festival, 温泉 hot spring, 楽しみだ to look forward to, カニ crab]

1. Why Wei Ming wants to go to Hokkaido this winter? _____
   _____

2. How many times has Akiko seen the Snow Festival? _____

3. How many times has Wei Ming tried a hot spring in his life? _____

4. What sport is Wei Ming going to try in Hokkaido? _____

5. What are the examples of delicious foods in Hokkaido? List two. _____
   _____

Listening Comprehension

デパートでの呼び出し

Customer paging (呼び出し) at a department store uses a lot of polite expressions. For instance, the respectful title 様 is used instead of さん. お越し下さい is also used instead of 来て下さい, to mean *Please come.*

Listen carefully to three instances of customer paging on the CD, then answer the questions that follow.

1. What is the name of the person called in the first paging?

   _____

2. What is the description of the car mentioned in the second paging?

   _____

3. What is the description of the girl mentioned in the third paging?

   _____

Reading Comprehension

日記

Let's read the following 日記 (diary) written by Yoko, and then answer the questions that follow.

3月17日（金）晴れ

　今日はさち子と、真と、健二と、お昼を食べた。食べ終わって、払おうとしたら、健二がみんなにおごってくれると言った。ボーナスをもらったらしい。健二のようにいい会社で働けたら、いいと思う。

3月18日（土）雨

　今日九州からおじさんが遊びに来た。おみやげに焼酎を持って来てくれた。夜おそくまで、おじさんと焼酎を飲んだ。珍しい焼酎でとてもおいしかった。

3月19日（日）くもり

　今日さち子と料理教室に行った。思ったより勉強になるし、楽しかった。さち子が続けるなら、私も続けようと思う。

3月20日（月）晴れ

　今日はさち子と会社の昼休みにパチンコに行った。2,000円使ってしまった。もし、昼休みでなかったら、きっと1万円ぐらい使ったかもしれない。やっぱり、パチンコはやめようと思う。

1. On March 17, who treated Yoko to a lunch?　＿＿＿＿＿＿＿＿＿＿＿＿＿＿＿
2. On March 18, who came to visit Yoko?　＿＿＿＿＿＿＿＿＿＿＿＿＿＿＿
3. On March 19, where did Yoko go to?　＿＿＿＿＿＿＿＿＿＿＿＿＿＿＿
4. On March 20, how much did Yoko spent for pachinko?　＿＿＿＿＿＿＿＿＿＿＿

Writing

日記 (*diary*)

Keep a record of your experiences for three days starting today.

＿＿＿月＿＿＿日（　　）＿＿＿＿＿＿＿

＿＿＿

＿＿＿

＿＿＿

＿＿＿

＿＿＿

＿＿＿月＿＿＿日（　　）＿＿＿＿＿＿＿

＿＿＿

＿＿＿

＿＿＿

＿＿＿

＿＿＿

＿＿＿月＿＿＿日（　　　）＿＿＿＿＿＿

＿＿＿＿＿＿＿＿＿＿＿＿＿＿＿＿＿＿＿＿＿＿＿＿＿＿＿

＿＿＿＿＿＿＿＿＿＿＿＿＿＿＿＿＿＿＿＿＿＿＿＿＿＿＿

＿＿＿＿＿＿＿＿＿＿＿＿＿＿＿＿＿＿＿＿＿＿＿＿＿＿＿

＿＿＿＿＿＿＿＿＿＿＿＿＿＿＿＿＿＿＿＿＿＿＿＿＿＿＿

＿＿＿＿＿＿＿＿＿＿＿＿＿＿＿＿＿＿＿＿＿＿＿＿＿＿＿

New Vocabulary Reference List

NOUN

がくい（学位）*academic degree*

かねもち（金持ち）*rich person*

かんこう（観光）*sight-seeing*

こうはい（後輩）*one's junior*

しんかんせん（新幹線）*Shinkansen* (bullet train in Japan)

せんぱい（先輩）*one's senior*

でんとう（伝統）*tradition*

のうりょく（能力）*ability, capacity*

みせ・おみせ（店・お店）*store*

りょかん（旅館）*Japanese-style inn*

りょこうがいしゃ（旅行会社）*travel agency*

PROPER NOUN

あきはばら（秋葉原）*Akihabara* (place name)

なごや（名古屋）*Nagoya* (place name)

ADJECTIVE

こうきゅうな（高級な）*high grade, high class, fancy*

ざんねんな（残念な）*regrettable*

わかい（若い）*young*

VERB (Ru-verb)

うける（受ける）*to receive, to take (an exam)*

にげる（逃げる）*to escape*

VERB (U-verb)

もうしこむ（申し込む）*to apply*

IRREGULAR VERB

しゅうしょくする（就職する）*to find employment*

ADVERB

かならず（必ず）*certainly, without fail, by all means*

もし *if (by any chance)*

OTHERS

うそをつく（嘘をつく）*to tell a lie*

〜てき（な）（〜的な）*typical ..., like ...*（日本的だ *very Japanese*）

〜きゅう（〜級）*level ...*

〜なら *if...*

CHAPTER TWENTY-FIVE

Your Way of Thinking

Objectives:

- to create a conditional clause using れば
- to describe tastes and to name disasters
- to learn how to report what you heard
- to learn about expressions such as *even, even though, even if* and *no matter how*, using も
- to learn additional function of で

Kanji and Vocabulary

1. Reading and Writing Kanji Characters

A) Let's read each of the following kanji words or phrases aloud several times.

苦い *bitter*
太る *to gain weight*
空港 *airport*
結婚 *marriage*
間違える *to make a mistake, to mix up*
仕方がない *cannot be helped*
火事 *fire*
事故 *accident*

平均点 *average (score)*
中間試験 *mid-term exam*
期末試験 *final exam*
週末 *weekend*
人気 *popularity*
集まる *to gather*
死ぬ *to die*

B) In the boxes provided, write each kanji character following the correct stroke order.

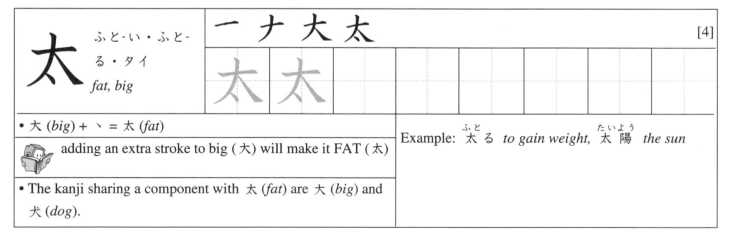

太 ふと-い・ふと-る・タイ *fat, big*	一 ナ 大 太 　　　　　　　　[4]
• 大 (*big*) + 丶 = 太 (*fat*) adding an extra stroke to big (大) will make it FAT (太) • The kanji sharing a component with 太 (*fat*) are 大 (*big*) and 犬 (*dog*).	Example: 太る *to gain weight*, 太陽 *the sun*

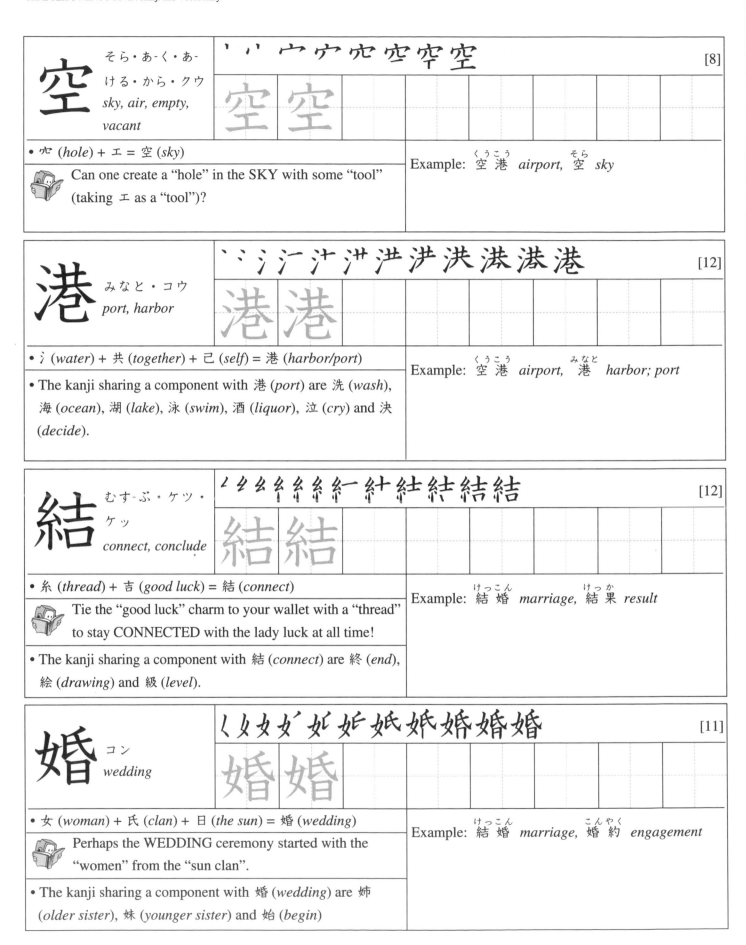

空 そら・あ-く・あ-ける・から・クウ
sky, air, empty, vacant

丶 丷 宀 灾 空 空 空 空 [8]

空 空

• 穴 (*hole*) + エ = 空 (*sky*)

Can one create a "hole" in the SKY with some "tool" (taking エ as a "tool")?

Example: 空港 くうこう *airport,* 空 そら *sky*

港 みなと・コウ
port, harbor

丶 丶 氵 汁 汁 洪 洪 洪 港 港 [12]

港 港

• 氵 (*water*) + 共 (*together*) + 己 (*self*) = 港 (*harbor/port*)
• The kanji sharing a component with 港 (*port*) are 洗 (*wash*), 海 (*ocean*), 湖 (*lake*), 泳 (*swim*), 酒 (*liquor*), 泣 (*cry*) and 決 (*decide*).

Example: 空港 くうこう *airport,* 港 みなと *harbor; port*

結 むす-ぶ・ケツ・ケッ
connect, conclude

幺 幺 幺 糸 糸 紀 紅 結 結 結 [12]

結 結

• 糸 (*thread*) + 吉 (*good luck*) = 結 (*connect*)

Tie the "good luck" charm to your wallet with a "thread" to stay CONNECTED with the lady luck at all time!

• The kanji sharing a component with 結 (*connect*) are 終 (*end*), 絵 (*drawing*) and 級 (*level*).

Example: 結婚 けっこん *marriage,* 結果 けっか *result*

婚 コン
wedding

く タ 女 女 妒 妒 妒 妒 婚 婚 婚 [11]

婚 婚

• 女 (*woman*) + 氏 (*clan*) + 日 (*the sun*) = 婚 (*wedding*)

Perhaps the WEDDING ceremony started with the "women" from the "sun clan".

• The kanji sharing a component with 婚 (*wedding*) are 姉 (*older sister*), 妹 (*younger sister*) and 始 (*begin*)

Example: 結婚 けっこん *marriage,* 婚約 こんやく *engagement*

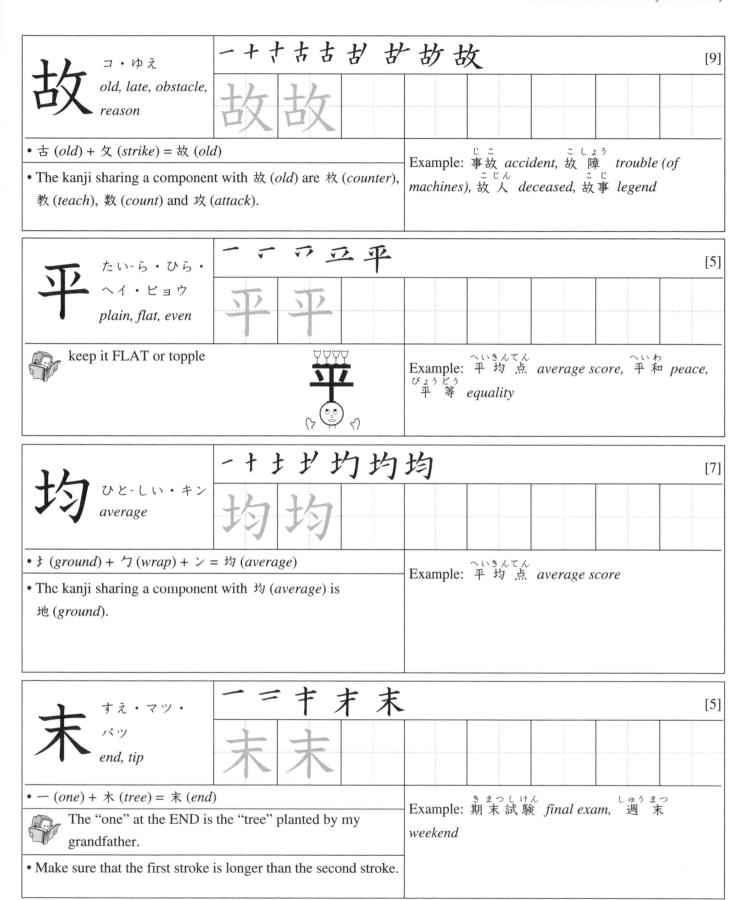

故　コ・ゆえ　old, late, obstacle, reason

一 十 十 古 古 苫 苫 故 故 [9]

故 故

• 古 (*old*) + 攵 (*strike*) = 故 (*old*)
• The kanji sharing a component with 故 (*old*) are 枚 (*counter*), 教 (*teach*), 数 (*count*) and 攻 (*attack*).

Example: 事故 *accident*, 故障 *trouble (of machines)*, 故人 *deceased*, 故事 *legend*

平　たい-ら・ひら・ヘイ・ビョウ　plain, flat, even

一 一 一 五 平 [5]

平 平

keep it FLAT or topple

Example: 平均点 *average score*, 平和 *peace*, 平等 *equality*

均　ひと-しい・キン　average

一 十 土 均 均 均 均 [7]

均 均

• 土 (*ground*) + 勹 (*wrap*) + ン = 均 (*average*)
• The kanji sharing a component with 均 (*average*) is 地 (*ground*).

Example: 平均点 *average score*

末　すえ・マツ・バツ　end, tip

一 二 チ 才 末 [5]

末 末

• 一 (*one*) + 木 (*tree*) = 末 (*end*)
• The "one" at the END is the "tree" planted by my grandfather.
• Make sure that the first stroke is longer than the second stroke.

Example: 期末試験 *final exam*, 週末 *weekend*

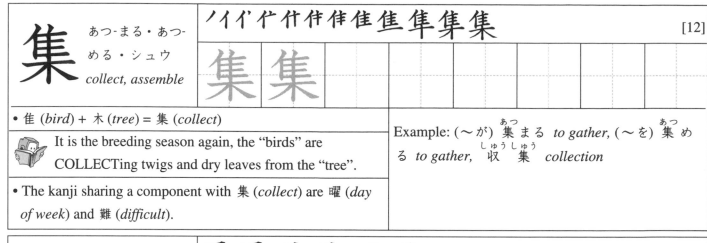

集　あつ-まる・あつ-める・シュウ　collect, assemble

ノイイ′イ′什什′佳佳隹隼隼集集　[12]

• 隹 (*bird*) + 木 (*tree*) = 集 (*collect*)

It is the breeding season again, the "birds" are COLLECTing twigs and dry leaves from the "tree".

• The kanji sharing a component with 集 (*collect*) are 曜 (*day of week*) and 難 (*difficult*).

Example: (～が) 集まる *to gather*, (～を) 集める *to gather*, 収集 *collection*

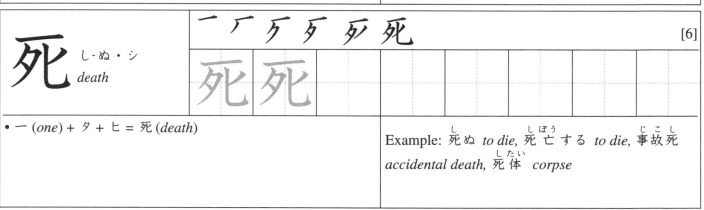

死　し-ぬ・シ　death

一 厂 歹 歹 歺 死　[6]

• 一 (*one*) + 夕 + ヒ = 死 (*death*)

Example: 死ぬ *to die*, 死亡する *to die*, 事故死 *accidental death*, 死体 *corpse*

C) Let's read aloud to check how well you've mastered the kanji you've learned.

1. 空港を間違えて、ひこうきに乗れませんでした。仕方がなかったので、うちに帰りました。

2. 結婚した後に太ってしまいました。子供が生まれた後はもっと太りました。中国のやせる薬をもらいましたが、苦いのでぜんぜん飲んでいません。

3. 去年は火事や事故でたくさんの人が死にました。

4. 中間試験の平均点は期末試験の平均点より高かったです。

5. ジンジャーハウスは東京で一番人気があるいざかやです。週末は友達とよくジンジャーハウスに行きます。安くて、おいしいです。

6. 外国の切手が769枚集まりました。

D) Fill in the correct kanji characters in the boxes provided.

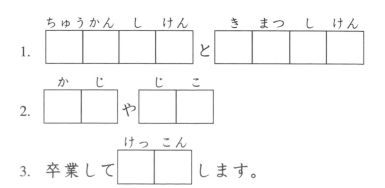

1. ちゅうかん　し　けん 〔　　　〕と き　まつ　し　けん 〔　　　〕

2. か　じ 〔　〕や じ　こ 〔　〕

3. 卒業して けっ　こん 〔　〕します。

2. Describing Tastes

Draw lines to match.

しお (*salt*) •	• すっぱい
さとう (*sugar*) •	• にがい
レモン (*lemon*) •	• あまい
キムチ (*kimchi*) •	• しょっぱい
コーヒー (*coffee*) •	• からい

3. Identifying Disasters

Draw lines to match.

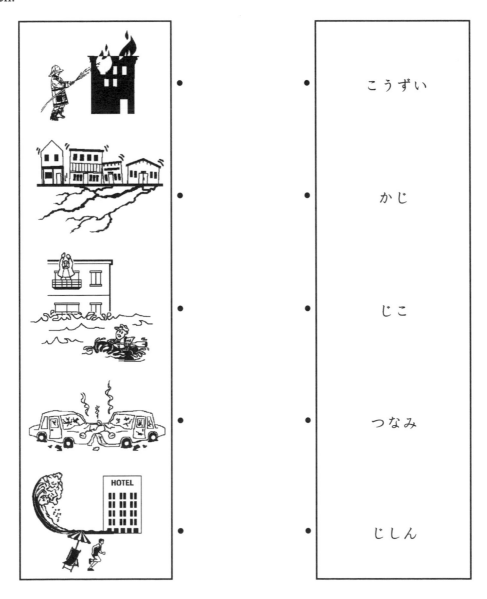

•	• こうずい
•	• かじ
•	• じこ
•	• つなみ
•	• じしん

Grammar

1. 〜でも

The particle 〜でも follows a noun and it means *even*. For example, こんな簡単な問題は子供でもできます means *Even a child can solve such an easy problem*. Note that the particles が and を must not occur with 〜でも. When 〜でも is combined with a question word, it means *any item*. For example, だれでもできます means *Anyone can do it*.

Fill in the blanks with appropriate words.

1. 私の兄は＿＿＿＿＿＿＿＿＿でも食べます。からいものも、あまいものも食べます。姉は肉は食べませんが、魚なら、＿＿＿＿＿＿＿＿＿でも食べます。

2. しょうがくきんがもらえるなら、＿＿＿＿＿＿＿＿＿大学にでも行きます。

3. 東京なら、ATM は＿＿＿＿＿＿＿＿＿にでもありますよ。

4. ＿＿＿＿＿＿＿＿＿でもいいですよ。1万円でも、2万円でも、いいですよ。

5. わからないことがあったら、＿＿＿＿＿＿＿＿＿でも私に聞いて下さい。

2. 〜ても／〜でも

A clause that ends in a verb or an adjective in the te-form plus the particle も means *even if...* or *even though...* . For example, いっしょうけんめい勉強しても、100点は取れませんでした means *I couldn't get 100 points even though I studied very hard*. When it is combined with a question word, it means *no matter...* . For example, 何を食べても太りません means *I do not gain weight no matter what I eat*.

Fill in the blanks with appropriate words.

1. どのじしょを＿＿＿＿＿＿＿＿＿ても、この漢字はありませんでした。

2. ＿＿＿＿＿＿＿＿＿に行っても、安いホテルにとまります。

3. 父に＿＿＿＿＿＿＿＿＿を言っても、わかってくれません。

4. いくら勉強＿＿＿＿＿＿＿＿＿も、ぜんぜんわかりません。

5. ぜんぜん勉強＿＿＿＿＿＿＿＿＿も、わかります。

3. 〜れば 1

The conditional form with れば for verbs is created by adding "reba" or "eba" at the end of a verb in the root form: reba for a ru-verb and eba for a u-verb (たべる ➔ たべれば, かく ➔ かけば). The irregular verbs する and くる become すれば and くれば, respectively. For i-type adjectives, add "kereba" at the end of the stem (たかい ➔ たかければ). いい is irregular, and it becomes よければ. The simple れば form is unavailable for na-type adjectives and copulas. Its equivalent form is 〜であれば, as in しずかであれば and 学生であれば.

Practice forming the れば forms following the example.

Example: 食^たべる ⟶ 食べれば

高^{たか}い ⟶ 高ければ

1. 待^まつ ⟶ _____
2. 歩^{ある}く ⟶ _____
3. 太る ⟶ _____
4. やせる ⟶ _____
5. 集まる ⟶ _____
6. くさっている ⟶ _____

7. する ⟶ _____
8. しない ⟶ _____
9. 安^{やす}い ⟶ _____
10. あまい ⟶ _____
11. おいしくない ⟶ _____

4. ～れば 2

The れば clause expresses generic, temporal, hypothetical or counterfactual conditions. For example, 薬^{くすり}をのめば、なおりますよ means *If you take the medication, you will get better.*

Following the example, join the two phrases in each set to form a sentence.

Example: 書^かく・覚^{おぼ}えられます ⟶ 書けば、覚えられます。

1. れいぞうこに入^いれない・くさります

⟶ _____

2. 早^{はや}くよやくする・いいホテルがとれたはずです

⟶ _____

3. クレジットカードで買^かう・安^{やす}かったと思^{おも}います

⟶ _____

4. パチンコをしない・よかったと思います

⟶ _____

5. 苦い・飲みません

⟶ _____

5. 〜そうだ

〜そうです (or 〜そうだ in the plain form) is added at the end of a statement that denotes a report of what the speaker heard or read. For example, 雨^{あめ}がふるそうです means *I heard that it will rain* or *they say that it will rain*. The verb and adjective that precede 〜そうです must be in the plain form.

Following the example, add 〜そうです at the end of each sentence and make the necessary changes.

Example: 山田さんはオーストラリアに行きます。　　⟶　　山田さんはオーストラリアに行くそうです。

1. メアリーさんはダンスが上手です。

　⟶　_____

2. 林^{はやし}さんの車はトラックにぶつかりました。

　⟶　_____

3. 石田^{いしだ}さんのねこは死にました。

　⟶　_____

4. 森田^{もりた}さんはけがをしました。

　⟶　_____

5. リーさんは中国人じゃありません。

　⟶　_____

6. 〜ようだ and 〜らしい

To express a conjecture, add 〜ようです or 〜らしいです at the end of the sentence. For example, スミスさんはガールフレンドがいるようです or スミスさんはガールフレンドがいるらしいです means *Mr. Smith appears to have a girlfriend*. 〜ようです can be used in almost all contexts, but 〜らしいです is mainly used for non-intuitive relatively careful conjectures. 〜ようです follows the verb and adjective in pre-nominal form. 〜らしいです follows the verb and adjective in plain form, except that だ that appears at the end of a copula or a na-type adjective must be deleted.

Convert the sentences following the example.

Example: 明日はテストがあります。　　⟶　　(a) 明日はテストがあるようです。
　　　　　　　　　　　　　　　　　⟶　　(b) 明日はテストがあるらしいです。

1. 昨日サンフランシスコでじしんがありました。　⟶

　(a) _____ ようです。
　(b) _____ らしいです。

2. スミスさんはからいものは食べません。 ⟶

   (a) _____ようです。

   (b) _____らしいです。

3. 東京はぶっかが高いです。 ⟶

   (a) _____ようです。

   (b) _____らしいです。

4. マイクさんはようこさんが好きです。 ⟶

   (a) _____ようです。

   (b) _____らしいです。

5. チェンさんのうちにきゅうきゅうしゃが来ました。 ⟶

   (a) _____ようです。

   (b) _____らしいです。

7. Particle で

The verb ある can express what event or incident takes place or took place. In this case, the location of the event or incident is marked by the particle で.

Fill in the blanks with で or に.

1. 東京_____ジョブ・フェアーがあります。
2. 明日スミスさんと京都_____行きます。
3. 月曜日はカフェテリア_____働きます。
4. 大阪_____大きい地震がありました。
5. としょかん_____コンピューターが30台あります。

Conversation and Usage

てんぷら

Takeshi and Kate are chatting about Japanese foods. Listen to their conversation carefully and then answer the questions that follow.

たけし ：ケイトさん、すしは好き？

ケイト ：すしは、ちょっと。生の魚はなかなか好きになれないの。[*1]

たけし ：ああ。じゃあ、日本料理では何が一番好き？

ケイト ：てんぷら。

たけし　：ああ、そう。これ知ってた？てんぷらはスペインやポルトガルの宣教師が日本に伝えたんだよ。

ケイト　：え？本当？いつごろ？

たけし　：16世紀ごろ。

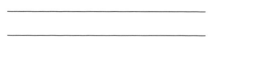

ケイト　：てんぷらって日本語じゃないの？

たけし　：もともとスペイン語かポルトガル語みたい。

ケイト　：ああ、そう。知らなかった。日本語だと思ってた。ところで、徳川家康はてんぷらを食べて死んだって、本当？

たけし　：さあ、わからない。胃癌っていう説もあるから。

ケイト　：ああ、そう。でも、てんぷらはおいしいから、家康も食べすぎて、おなかをこわしたんでしょう。

たけし　：そうかもね。僕もおいしいものはつい食べすぎて、よくおなかをこわしちゃうんだ。

ケイト　：まあ、しょうがないわね。*2

たけし　：ケイトさんは？

ケイト　：私はいくら食べても、おなかはこわさないの。

たけし　：へえ。いいね

[**Unfamiliar words:** 生 *raw*, 宣教師 *missionary*, 伝える *to pass down; to introduce*, 16世紀 *16th century*, ところで *by the way*, 徳川家康 *Ieyasu Tokugawa (1542-1616)—the founder and first shogun of the Tokugawa Shogunate of Japan*, 胃癌 *stomach cancer*, っていう＝という, 説 *theory*, おなかをこわす *to get a digestion problem*, そうかもね=そうかもしれませんね, つい *without thinking; carelessly*]

Note:

(*1)　When the adverb なかなか is used with a negative verb, it means *(not) easily*.

(*2)　しかたがない or しょうがない literally means *there is no method*, and it expresses one's reconciliation or disappointment.

1. Does Kate like sushi?　　　　　　　　　_____
2. Who brought てんぷら to Japan and when?　_____
3. Does Takeshi often get a digestion problem?　_____
4. Does Kate often get a digestion problem?　_____

Listening Comprehension

ラジオのニュース

Listen to the news on the radio and select the correct answer to the following questions.

1. What time did the accident happen?   a. 11:35 a.m.   b. 10:35 a.m.   c. 10:35 p.m.
2. What is the name of the taxi driver?   a. たかた　たろう   b. たかだ　たろう   c. あかだ　たろう
3. How old was the taxi driver?   a. 40   b. 41   c. 42
4. Why did the taxi applied a sudden brake?   a. to avoid the truck
   b. to avoid the elementary school student
   c. to avoid the middle school student
5. Who got injured?   a. taxi driver   b. pedestrian   c. truck driver

Reading Comprehension

折鶴と禎子

Let's read the story about folded paper cranes (折鶴) and Sadako Sasaki, and then answer the questions that follow.

折鶴を作ったことがありますか？日本ではだれかが病気になると、よく千羽鶴を作ります。その人の病気がよくなることを願って、鶴を千羽折り、糸でつないで、贈ります。

広島の佐々木禎子ちゃんと折鶴の物語はとても有名です。1945年8月6日に原爆が広島に投下されました。その時、禎子ちゃんは爆心地から1.7キロの自宅にいました。2歳でした。その直後は禎子ちゃんには何も異常はありませんでした。そして、禎子ちゃんは運動がよくできるとても元気な小学生になりました。しかし、1955年、小学校6年生の時に、白血病になってしまいました。2歳の時に原爆で放射線をあびたのが原因だったようです。禎子ちゃんは友達から千羽鶴を作れば自分の病気がよくなると聞き、病院に入院している間、いっしょうけんめい鶴を折りました。しかし、同じ年に、12歳で亡くなってしまいました。

その後、禎子ちゃんの同級生の活動もあり、日本、世界のいろいろなところから寄付金が集まり、原爆で亡くなった子供たちのために、1958年、広島平和記念公園に禎子ちゃんと折鶴をモデルにした原爆の子の像ができました。それから、折鶴は世界の平和のシンボルになりました。

[**Unfamiliar words:** 折鶴 or 折り鶴 *folded paper crane,* 千羽鶴 *threaded one thousand paper cranes,* 願う *to wish; to pray,* 鶴 *crane,* 千羽 *one thousand (birds),* 折る *to fold,* 糸 *thread,* つなぐ *to connect; to tie,* 贈る *to present (a person with something),* 物語 *story,* 原爆 (= 原子爆弾) *atomic bomb,* 投下されました *was dropped,* 爆心地 *ground zero,* 1.7キロ *1.7 kilometer,* 自宅 *one's house,* 直後 *right after,* 異常 *abnormality; trouble,* 白血病 *leukemia,* 原爆で放射線をあびる *to get exposed to radiation at the time of an atomic bombing,* 原因 *cause,* 入院する *to be hospitalized,* 年 *year,* 亡くなる *to pass away,* 同級生 *classmates,* 活動 *action; movement,* 寄付金 *donation (money),* 広島平和記念公園 *Hiroshima Peace Memorial Park,* 原爆の子の像 *Statue of the A-Bomb Children,* 平和 *peace*]

1. How old was Sadako when the atomic bomb was dropped in Hiroshima? _____

2. Did she get leukemia right after the atomic bombing? _____

3. What did Sadako do at the hospital? _____

4. How old was Sadako when she died? _____

5. When was the Statue of the A-Bomb Children built? _____

Writing

ノン・フィクション

Write a story you have heard of.

_____
_____
_____
_____
_____
_____
_____
_____
_____
_____
_____
_____
_____
_____

New Vocabulary Reference List

NOUN

うわさ (噂) *rumor*

かじ (火事) *fire*

きまつしけん (期末試験) *final exam*

きゅうきゅうしゃ (救急車) *ambulance*

くうこう (空港) *airport*

けが (怪我) *injury* (けがをする *to get injured*)

こうずい (洪水) *flood*

さとう (砂糖) *sugar*

しお (塩) *salt*

じこ (事故) *accident*

じしん (地震) *earthquake*

じゅうたい (渋滞) *traffic jam*

ちゅうかんしけん (中間試験) *mid-term exam*

つなみ (津波) *tsunami, big wave*

どろぼう (泥棒) *thief*

にんき (人気) *popularity* (人気がある *to be popular*)

へいきんてん (平均点) *average score*

ADJECTIVE

あまい (甘い) *sweet*

からい (辛い) *(hot) spicy*

しょっぱい *salty*

にがい (苦い) *bitter*

すっぱい (酸っぱい) *sour*

ADVERB

いっしょうけんめい(に) (一生懸命(に)) *hard*

なかなか (〜ない) *(not) easily ...* (なかなか漢字が覚えられない *cannot easily memorize kanji*)

VERB (Ru-verb)

やせる (痩せる) *to lose weight*

VERB (U-verb)

あつまる (集まる) *to gather*

くさる (腐る) *to spoil, to rot*

しぬ (死ぬ) *to die*

ぶつかる *to collide* (車にぶつかる *to crash into a car*, 車とぶつかる *to collide with a car*)

ふとる (太る) *to gain weight*

まちがえる (間違える) *to mix up, to make a mistake*

PARTICLE

〜でも *even ...*

OTHERS

ギリギリになる *to become close to the last minute*

こんな〜 *this kind of ..., such ...* (*cf.* どんな〜)

しかたがない (仕方がない) *cannot be helped*

〜そうだ *I heard that ..., they say that ...*

〜によると *according to ...*

〜ようだ *it seems to be ...*

〜らしい *it seems to be ...*

やきもちをやく *to be jealous*

CHAPTER TWENTY-SIX

Perspective

Objectives:

- to learn about passive, causative and passive-causative constructions
- to seek permission very politely
- to name the actions that are applied to people

Kanji and Vocabulary

1. Reading and Writing Kanji Characters

A) Let's read each of the following kanji words or phrases aloud several times.

字 *letter, character*

客 *guest, customer*

知っている *to know*

悲しい *sad*

家出をする *to run away*

先に *in advance*

悪口 *slander, gossip*

降る *to fall (rain/snow)*

降りる *to get off*

手紙 *letter*

受験 *exam-taking*

習字 *calligraphy*

長電話 *long telephone conversation*

練習する *to practice*

校長室 *principal's office*

空手 *karate*

B) In the boxes provided, write each kanji character following the correct stroke order.

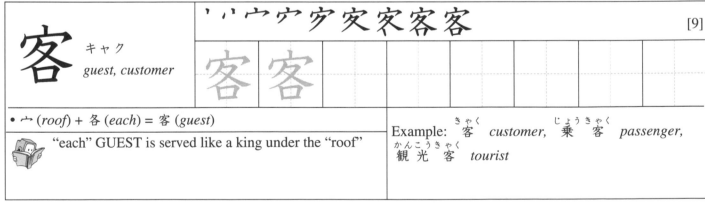

客 キャク
guest, customer

`ヽ ソ 宀 宀 灾 灾 客 客` [9]

- 宀 (*roof*) + 各 (*each*) = 客 (*guest*)

"each" GUEST is served like a king under the "roof"

Example: 客 *customer*, 乗客 *passenger*, 観光客 *tourist*

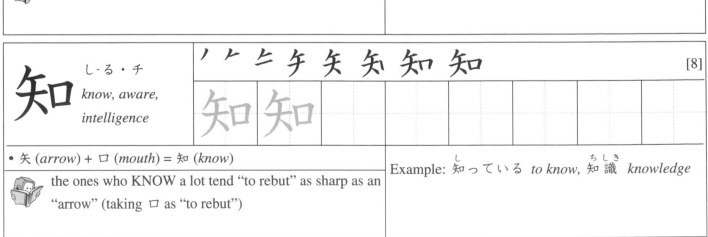

知 し-る・チ
know, aware, intelligence

`ノ 匸 匸 午 矢 矢 知 知` [8]

- 矢 (*arrow*) + 口 (*mouth*) = 知 (*know*)

the ones who KNOW a lot tend "to rebut" as sharp as an "arrow" (taking 口 as "to rebut")

Example: 知っている *to know*, 知識 *knowledge*

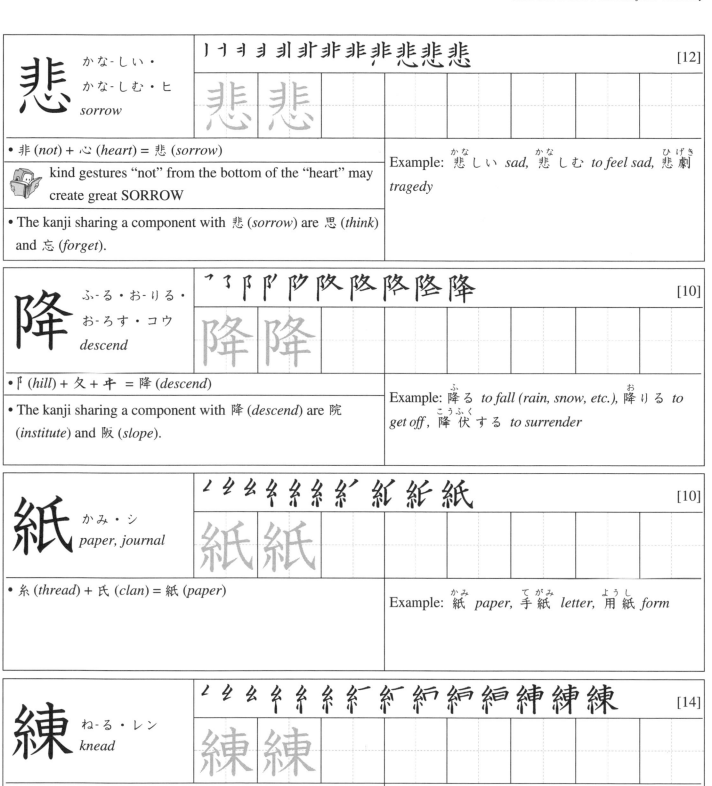

悲 かな-しい・かな-しむ・ヒ sorrow

｜ � ｊ ｊ 非 非 非 非 非 悲 悲 悲 [12]

悲 悲

• 非 (not) + 心 (heart) = 悲 (sorrow)

kind gestures "not" from the bottom of the "heart" may create great SORROW

• The kanji sharing a component with 悲 (sorrow) are 思 (think) and 忘 (forget).

Example: 悲しい sad, 悲しむ to feel sad, 悲劇 tragedy

降 ふ-る・お-りる・お-ろす・コウ descend

｀ ｊ ｐ ｐ 阝 降 降 降 降 降 [10]

降 降

• 阝 (hill) + 夂 + ヰ = 降 (descend)

• The kanji sharing a component with 降 (descend) are 院 (institute) and 阪 (slope).

Example: 降る to fall (rain, snow, etc.), 降りる to get off, 降伏する to surrender

紙 かみ・シ paper, journal

｀ ｌ ｌ ｌ 幺 糸 糸 糸 紅 紙 紙 [10]

紙 紙

• 糸 (thread) + 氏 (clan) = 紙 (paper)

Example: 紙 paper, 手紙 letter, 用紙 form

練 ね-る・レン knead

｀ ｌ ｌ ｌ 幺 糸 糸 糸 紅 紅 紅 絅 練 練 [14]

練 練

• 糸 (thread) + 東 (east) = 練 (knead)

• The kanji sharing a component with 練 (knead) are 終 (end), 絵 (drawing), 級 (level), 結 (connect) and 紙 (paper).

Example: 練習する to practice

C) Let's read aloud to check how well you've mastered the kanji you've learned.

1. 今週は雨や雪が降って、いやな天気でした。

2. 東京からしんかんせんに乗って、名古屋で降りました。それから、またしんかんせんに乗って、京都と大阪に行きました。

3. 小さい時に習字を習ったので、字を書くのがとくいです。手紙を書く時に字がきれいだと、とてもいいです。

4. 日本の高校生は受験勉強でたいへんです。私の兄は勉強がきらいで、家出をしてしまいました。ですから、私の方が先に高校を卒業して、大学に入学しました。兄は今もどこにいるのかわかりません。とても悲しいです。

5. 私の友達は空手を習っています。毎日2時間練習します。空手の先生はとてもきびしいです。

6. ジェイソンという学生を知っていますか？いつも悪いことをして校長室に行かせられていた学生です。みんなはジェイソンの悪口ばかり言っています。

7. この間レストランでお客さんがけいたいで長電話をしていました。

D) Fill in the correct kanji characters in the boxes provided.

1. から　て　　　れんしゅう
　　☐☐ の ☐☐

2. じゅ　けん
　　☐☐ の勉強

3. 子供が ☐☐ をした
　　いえ　で

2. What Can One Do to Others?

Fill in the blanks by selecting suitable verbs from the list below, and conjugating them if necessary.

からかう・しかる・だます・ほめる・ひはんする

1. 弟（おとうと）が悪（わる）いことをしたので、父は弟を＿＿＿＿＿＿＿＿＿ました。

2. 100点（てん）をとったので、母は私を＿＿＿＿＿＿＿＿＿くれました。うれしかったです。

3. 友達（ともだち）はいつも私を＿＿＿＿＿＿＿＿＿て、わらいます。とてもはらがたちます。

4. エープリル・フールの日はうそをついて、妹を＿＿＿＿＿＿＿＿＿ます。おもしろいです。

5. 社長がひどいので、みんなは社長を＿＿＿＿＿＿＿＿＿しました。

Grammar

1. 〜られる 1

The same situation can be expressed differently depending on the speaker's perspective. For example, when your father scolded your brother, you can either say 父が 弟 をしかりました (*My father scolded my brother*) or 弟 が父にしかられました (*My brother was scolded by my father*), depending on which person is your major concern. The former is an active sentence and the latter is a passive sentence, or more precisely, a direct passive sentence. You can create a passive verb by adding "(r)are-ru" at the end of the verb in the root form: "rare-ru" for a ru-verb; "are-ru" for an u-verb. For example, ほめる becomes ほめられる and しかる becomes しかられる. The passive form of two major irregular verbs, する and くる are される and こられる respectively.

 Convert each of the verbs below to a passive verb following the example.

Example: たべる ⟶ たべられる

1. ほめる ⟶ _____
2. たたく ⟶ _____
3. からかう ⟶ _____
4. しかる ⟶ _____
5. だます ⟶ _____
6. しょうたいする ⟶ _____
7. ひはんする ⟶ _____

2. 〜られる 2

To form a direct passive sentence, make the direct object a subject, mark the original subject with the particle に and change the verb into a passive verb.

 Convert each sentence below into a passive sentence following the example.

Example: 父が 弟 をしかりました。 ⟶ 弟が父にしかられました。

1. 母が 妹 をほめました。 ⟶ _____
2. てんいんが客をだましました。 ⟶ _____
3. 先生が学生をたたきました。 ⟶ _____
4. どろぼうがネックレスをぬすみました。 ⟶ _____
5. 兄が私の部屋を使いました。 ⟶ _____

3. 〜られる3

The passive verbs are used not only for altering the speaker's perspective, but also for expressing a situation where one is annoyed by some incident. Such sentences are called "indirect passive." In indirect passive, the direct object remains the direct object, marked by the particle を, and the person who is annoyed becomes the subject. The performer of the action, the annoyer, is marked by the particle に in indirect passive. For example, 田中さんはお母さんに日記を読まれました means *Mr. Tanaka was annoyed by his mother's reading his diary.*

Let's read each sentence below and write what it means and implies, considering who's what action displeased whom.

1. 私は弟に先に卒業されました。

   _____

2. 田中さんは昨日ガールフレンドに泣かれました。

   _____

3. 私は電車の中でとなりの人にけいたいで長電話をされました。

   _____

4. 石田さんは息子さんに家出をされました。

   _____

5. 林さんは子供さんに死なれました。

   _____

4. 〜させる1

You can create a causative verb (to make/let someone do something) by adding the causative suffix "(s)ase-ru" at the end of the verb root: the suffix is "sase-ru" for ru-verbs and "ase-ru" for u-verbs. For example, たべる becomes たべさせる and かく becomes かかせる. The causative forms of the two irregular verbs する and くる are させる and こさせる respectively.

Following the example, convert each verb below into a causative verb.

Example: 食べる ⟶ 食べさせる

1. 読む ⟶ _____

2. 勉強する ⟶ _____

3. 運動する ⟶ _____

4. 話す ⟶ _____

5. 習う ⟶ _____

6. 待つ　　　→ _____

7. ふく　　　→ _____

8. そうじする　→ _____

9. 持って来る　→ _____

5. 〜させる 2

A causative verb makes someone do something (make-causative) or to let someone do something (let-causative), depending on the context. For example, 子供に野菜を食べさせます is very likely to mean *I make my child eat vegetables*, but 子供にチョコレートを食べさせます is very likely to mean *I let my child eat chocolate*. The action performer is usually marked by に. Note that if the causative verb is originally a transitive verb, the action performer must be marked by に. If it is a intransitive verb, the action performer is marked by を although に can be used in some cases.

Convert the sentences below following the example.

Example: 子供がやさいを食べました。

　　　→ 母は子供にやさいを食べさせました。

1. 弟がさらを洗いました。

　　　→ 母は_____

2. 姉が車の運転を練習しました。

　　　→ 母は_____

3. 妹がテーブルをふきました。

　　　→ 母は_____

4. 兄が習字を習いました。

　　　→ 母は_____

6. 〜させていただきたいんですが

Let-causative is often used for seeking permission in a very polite context. All of the following sentences mean *Could I take a rest?* Or *Please let me take a rest*.

ちょっと休ませていただきたいんですが。

ちょっと休ませていただけませんか。

ちょっと休ませて下さいませんか。

ちょっと休ませて下さい。

Following the example, form a sentence to seek the permission for doing the action provided.

Example: 休む ⟶ 休ませていただきたいんですが。

1. 帰る ⟶ _____

2. 食事をする ⟶ _____

3. とまる ⟶ _____

4. 会社の車を使う ⟶ _____

5. レポートを読む ⟶ _____

7. 〜させられる

The combination of a causative suffix and a passive suffix, found in the ending "(s)ase-rare-ru", expresses the situation where one is made to do something. For example, 私は父に勉強させられました means *I was made to study by my father*. The person who is made to do something is the subject, and the person who makes him/her do it is marked by に.

Give the translation of each sentence.

1. マイクさんは田中さんにお酒を飲ませられました。

_____

2. 兄は父に庭をそうじさせられました。

_____

3. おばあさんに重いかばんを持たせられました。

_____

4. ガールフレンドに3時間待たせられました。

_____

Note: The causative-passive suffix "ase-rare" often contracts to "asare" for u-verbs whose dictionary forms do not end in す. For example, 待たせられる is contracted to 待たされる.

Conversation and Usage

書道

Kenta is talking with Inhee about the calligraphy (書道) lesson she took before. Listen to their conversation carefully and then answer the question that follows.

けんた　：インヒーさんは字がうまいですね。

インヒー：そうですか？

けんた　　　：書道は習いましたか？

インヒー　：ええ。韓国で。でも、大嫌いでした。

けんた　　　：どうして？

インヒー　：最初の一年は横線と、縦線と、丸ばかり描かせられたんです。

けんた　　　：へえ。

インヒー　：レッスンの前には座って墨をすらせられて、最後にはそうじもさせられました。

けんた　　　：それで、何年習ったんですか。

インヒー　：母がやめさせてくれなかったので、10年習いました。

けんた　　　：わあ。すごい。

インヒー　：ええ。書道よりも、忍耐を学びました。

[*Unfamiliar words:* 書道 *calligraphy,* 大嫌い(な) *to hate very much,* 最初の一年 *the first year,* 横線 *horizontal line,* 縦線 *vertical line,* 丸 *circle,* 描く *to draw,* 墨をする *to make ink (by rubbing the ink stick against the inkstone with a small amount of water),* 最後 *at the end,* すごい *amazing,* 忍耐 *patience,* 学ぶ *to learn*]

List what Inhee had to do in her calligraphy lesson during the first year.

1. _____

2. _____

3. _____

Listening Comprehension

お別れのことば

Mike Wilson is an exchange student from the United States, and has studied in Ishiyama High School in Japan for a year. He is returning to the United States soon. Listen carefully to his farewell speech (お別れのことば) to the class and answer the questions that follow.

1. When did Mike come to Ishiyama High School?　_____

2. When is Mike returning to the US?　_____

3. What is the name of the Japanese teacher who helped Mike's Japanese?　_____

4. What sport did he learn in Ishiyama High School?　_____

5. Where is Mike's house located in the US?　_____

Reading Comprehension

作文コンテスト

Below is an announcement of an essay competition (作文コンテスト) organized by Nakayama University in Tokyo. Contestants were required to write an essay on international exchange and their vision of the future. Let's study it carefully and answer the questions that follow. You may encounter many unfamiliar kanji without furigana, but you should be able to answer the questions.

作文コンテスト
あなたにとって国際文化交流とは何ですか？

外国人と友達になりたいですか？外国に行ってみたいと思いますか？どうしてですか？
自分の経験や、将来の展望をもとに国際文化交流について作文を書いて下さい。

---

1. **募集期間**
   平成18年9月1日～平成19年2月10日

2. **応募資格**
   高校生

3. **応募規定**
   • 1,000字以内
   • オリジナルと、複写3部を下記の住所宛に平成19年2月10日までに送付すること。

     〒160-1234
     東京都新宿区石川町15番地
     中山大学国際学部
     作文コンテスト実行委員会

   • 住所・氏名・年齢・電話番号・Eメールアドレスを明記

4. **審査員**
   田中哲也氏（ジャーナリスト）
   山田洋子氏（中山大学国際学部教授）
   川口まこと氏（ジャパンクラブ理事）
   石田まり子氏（東京国際文化交流クラブ理事）

5. **賞金**
   最優秀作品　　1点　　100,000円
   優秀作品　　　3点　　50,000円

6. **発表**
   受賞者には、平成19年3月31日までにEメールにて連絡。
   平成19年4月25日に中山大学国際ホールにて表彰式を開催。

7. **その他**
   作品は自作・未発表のものに限る。
   受賞作品の著作権は中山大学国際学部に帰属する。

---

1. Who were eligible for the competition?   _____
2. What was the required length of the essay?   _____
3. When was the deadline?   _____
4. How many judges were there?   _____
5. How much was the highest cash prize?   _____

Writing

日本についての作文

Write an essay about Japan, discussing one or more aspects (history, traditional culture, pop culture, art, philosophy, value, society, family, industry, technology, business, economics, etc.) you could relate to.

New Vocabulary Reference List

NOUN

うでたてふせ (腕立伏せ) *push-up*

こうちょうしつ (校長室) *principal's office*

ことば (言葉) *word*

さら (皿) *plate, dish*

じ (字) *character, letter*

しゅうじ (習字) *calligraphy*

じゅく (塾) *supplementary private school, cram school*

じゅけん (受験) *exam-taking*

そろばん (算盤) *abacus*

ながでんわ (長電話) *long telephone conversation*

にわ (庭) *yard, garden*

ろうか (廊下) *hallway*

ろんぶん (論文) *academic paper, thesis*

ADJECTIVE

いやな (嫌な) *unpleasant*

かなしい (悲しい) *sad*

かわいそうな *poor, pitiable*

ADVERB

さきに (先に) *in advance*

また *again*

むりやりに (無理やりに) *forcefully*

VERB (Ru-verb)

ほめる (褒める) *to praise*

VERB (U-verb)

からかう *to tease, to make fun of*

さく (咲く) *to bloom, to blossom*

しかる (叱る) *to scold*

たたく *to hit, to spank*

だます *to deceive, to trick*

とまる (泊まる) *to stay, to lodge* (ホテルに泊まる *to stay at a hotel*)

ぬすむ (盗む) *to steal*

ふく (拭く) *to wipe*

ふむ (踏む) *to step on*

IRREGULAR VERB

いえで(を)する (家出(を)する) *to run away from home*

しょうたいする (招待する) *to invite*

ひはんする (批判する) *to criticize*

OTHERS

(～の)せいで *due to ...*

(～の)おかげで *thanks to ...*

かえりに (帰りに) *on the way home*

はらがたつ (腹が立つ) *to become upset*

わるぐちをいう (悪口を言う) *to say bad things about a person behind his back*

Answers and Translations

Chapter Fifteen

Kanji and Vocabulary

1. Reading and Writing Kanji Characters

C) 1. <u>あした</u>の<u>てんき</u>はあまりよくないと<u>おも</u>います。<u>あめ</u>がふるかもしれません。それか、<u>ゆき</u>がふるかもしれません。<u>やまだ</u>さんと、<u>たなか</u>さんに<u>でんわ</u>をして、ピクニックはキャンセルします。

2. <u>きのう</u>はせきがでて、<u>あたま</u>が<u>いたくて</u>、<u>くすり</u>をのみました。それから、<u>びょういん</u>に<u>いき</u>ました。ごごは<u>らく</u>になりました。<u>きょう</u>はとても<u>げんき</u>になりました。

3. <u>げんごがく</u>のクラスは<u>しゅくだい</u>が<u>おおくて</u>、テストの<u>もんだい</u>が<u>むずかしくて</u>、たいへんです。でも、とてもおもしろくて、<u>だいすき</u>です。クラスではいつも<u>せんせい</u>に<u>しつもん</u>します。

4. いつも<u>でんしゃ</u>や、<u>くるま</u>や、バスを<u>つかい</u>ます。

5. <u>にほん</u>の<u>ぶんか</u>とアメリカの<u>ぶんか</u>は<u>ほんとう</u>にちがいます。

D) 1. <u>電車</u>で<u>病院</u>に行きます。
2. <u>宿題</u>をします。
3. <u>雪</u>がふります。
4. 日本の<u>文化</u>が好きです。

2. Naming and Describing

A) 1. けいようし 2. めいし 3. じょし 4. どうし

B) 1. あたたかい   2. あつい   3. すずしい

C) 私の大学は<u>じゅぎょうりょう</u>が高いです。でも、とてもゆうめいな<u>きょうじゅ</u>がたくさんいます。今とっている文学の<u>じゅぎょう</u>はとてもおもしろいです。<u>宿題</u>はあまりありませんが、テストは難しいです。

D) あたまが<u>痛い</u>です。のども少し<u>痛い</u>です。くしゃみと、せきが<u>出</u>ます。ねつも<u>あり</u>ます。

Grammar

1. The Plain Forms and ～と思います

1. あの人は<u>てんいんだ</u>と思います。
2. 父は7時に<u>帰る</u>と思います。
3. チェンさんは中国に<u>帰った</u>と思います。
4. 昨日のパーティーは<u>おもしろかった</u>と思います。

2. ～かもしれません and ～でしょう

1. 今晩は雨が<u>ふる</u>かもしれません。でも、明日は<u>はれる</u>でしょう。
2. <u>かぜ</u>でしょう。でも、<u>はいえん</u>かもしれません。
3. あの人はたぶん<u>けっこんしている</u>でしょう。

4. たけしくんは<u>べんごしになる</u>かもしれません。

3. ～と思います, ～かもしれません and ～でしょう

1. さむくないと思います。
   さむくないかもしれません。
   さむくないでしょう。
2. 帰ったと思います。
   帰ったかもしれません。
   帰ったでしょう。
3. 難しかったと思います。
   難しかったかもしれません。
   難しかったでしょう。
4. かぜだと思います。
   かぜかもしれません。
   かぜでしょう。
5. うそだったと思います。
   うそだったかもしれません。
   うそだったでしょう。

4. どうして～んですか and ～からです

1. A: どうして<u>薬をのんだ</u>んですか。
   B: <u>あたまが痛かった</u>からです。
2. A: どうして<u>会社をやめた</u>んですか。
   B: <u>きゅうりょうが安かった</u>からです。
3. A: どうして<u>そうじをしている</u>んですか。
   B: <u>おきゃくさんが来る</u>からです。
4. A: どうして<u>たけしさんが好きな</u>んですか。
   B: <u>やさしい人だ</u>からです。

Conversation and Usage

1. 成田空港からホテルまで

1. limousine bus   2. Narita Express
3. because the limousine bus stops at the hotel he wants to go to

<Translation>

Justin   : Excuse me.

Woman : Yes.

Justin   : I want to go to Tokyo, but how much does it cost approximately?

Woman : ¥2,940 by the Narita Express and 3,000 by a limousine bus.

Justin   : Oh, really. How long does it take?

Woman : About one hour by the Narita Express, and about one and a half hour by a limousine bus.

Justin   : Actually, I want to go to Takanawa Prince Hotel.

Woman : Then, the limousine bus is more convenient because it stops at Takanawa Prince Hotel.

Justin   : Oh, really. Then, I will take a limousine bus. Where can I buy the ticket?

Woman : You can buy it here.

Justin : Oh, really. Then, one adult please.

2. 宅配便

1. the man   2. tomorrow morning   3. 1,920 yen

<Translation>

Susan : Excuse me. This one, please. (Susan gives the suitcase to the man at the counter.)

Man : Sure. Thank you very much. Okay then, please write the name, address, and telephone number of the recipient, here.

Susan : I'm sorry, but could you write them by looking at this? (Susan shows her address book to the clerk.)

Man : Yes. Certainly. (The man writes the name, address, and telephone number of the recipient.)

Susan : Will it be delivered by tomorrow?

Man : Yes. It will probably be delivered tomorrow morning.

Susan : Oh, great! How much?

Man : ¥1,920.

Listening Comprehension

天気

1. clear   2. clear   3. clear

CD recording:

東京は午前中はくもりですが、午後ははれるでしょう。名古屋は午前中ははれますが、午後は雨がふるでしょう。大阪は一日はれでしょう。

Reading Comprehension

薬のふくろ

1. three times   2. two capsules   3. 28 days

Chapter Sixteen

Kanji and Vocabulary

1. Reading and Writing Kanji Characters

C) 1. まいにちたんごをななつおぼえます。クラスでまいにちたんごクイズがあります。

2. このじしょはちいさくてべんりです。まいにちつかっています。きょうしつにももっていきます。でも、あのじしょはおおきくてふべんです。いつもへやでつかっていますが、きょうしつにはもっていきません。まいしゅう、かんじテストがあります。とてもむずかしくて、こまっています。いま、いいかんじのテキストをさがしています。

3. まいつき、しごとでがいこくにいきます。かんこくや、ちゅうごくや、シンガポールに行

きます。いつもべんりで、やすいホテルをさがします。たべものにはきをつけています。

4. まいとし、こどものなつやすみにはかぞくでハワイにいきます。シュノーケリングをします。おみやげにネックレスやマカデミアンナッツをかいます。

D) 1. 本屋に行きます。   3. かぎを探しています。

   2. 便利なアパート。   4. 毎日、仕事をします。

2. Naming Various Occupations

弟は毎週日曜日にレストランで働いています。さらあらいをしています。じきゅうは900円です。5時間働いて、一日に4,500円もらいます。兄は貿易会社で働いています。つうきんは便利です。地下鉄で15分です。毎日ざんぎょうがあるので、うちには10時ごろに帰ります。

3. Naming Different Parts of a House

私のうちのだいどころはとても広いです。トイレは2つあります。たたみの部屋が2つと、じゅうたんの部屋が1つあります。

Grammar

1. ～てもいい and ～てはいけない 1

1. Permission: タバコをすってもいいですよ。
   Prohibition: タバコをすってはいけませんよ。

2. Permission: じしょを見てもいいですよ。
   Prohibition: じしょを見てはいけませんよ。

3. Permission: 友達に言ってもいいですよ。
   Prohibition: 友達に言ってはいけませんよ。

4. Permission: 会社の車を使ってもいいですよ。
   Prohibition: 会社の車を使ってはいけませんよ。

2. ～てもいい and ～てはいけない 2

今、アパートを探しています。友達といっしょに住むつもりです。ですから、寝室(*bedroom*)が2つなくてはいけません。料理はしませんから、台所はなくてもいいです。あまりお金がありませんから、家賃は安くなくてはいけません。ちょっと不便でもいいです。あまりきれいじゃなくてもいいです。

3. ～なくてはいけない and ～なくてもいい

1. Obligation: 漢字を覚えなくてはいけません。
   Discretion: 漢字を覚えなくてもいいです。

2. Obligation: ざんぎょうをしなくてはいけません。
   Discretion: ざんぎょうをしなくてもいいです。

3. Obligation: だいどころは広くなくてはいけません。
   Discretion: だいどころは広くなくてもいいです。

4. Obligation: ワインは赤じゃなくてはいけません。
   Discretion: ワインは赤じゃなくてもいいです。

Conversation and Usage

アパート探し

1. April 1st   2. No.

3. It is an apartment with a Japanese-style room, a Western-style room, and an eat-in-kitchen. Its rent is 40,000 yen. It is 40 minutes from Sakura-machi by bus.

<Translation>

Lyn : Ummm, I would like to rent an apartment in Sakuramachi starting April.

Realtor : Are you going to live by yourself?

Lyn : Yes.

Realtor : (The realtor starts checking the information.) Well ... Sakuramachi, Sakuramachi ...

Lyn : I prefer one that's near the International Center Building.

Realtor : Oh, that tall building?

Lyn : Yes.

Realtor : How much rent are you talking about?

Lyn : 50,000 yen or less.

Realtor : Ummm, I think it is a bit difficult to find one at 50,000 yen or below.

Lyn : Really?

Realtor : Please take a look at this. (The realtor shows the layout of an apartment.) This one has a six-tatami-mat Japanese-style room, and a kitchen. It is a 10-minute walk from the International Center Building. But the rent is 90,000 yen.

Lyn : That's expensive, isn't it?

Realtor : (The realtor shows the layout of another apartment.) This one is 20 minutes from Sakuramachi by the subway. It has one Western-style room and an eat-in-kitchen, and (the rent) is 50,000 yen.

Lyn : Oh ...

Realtor : Oops, but this one will not be vacant until July!

Lyn : That's a problem (for me). I want to (move) in by April 1st.

Realtor : Then, how about this one? (The realtor shows the layout of another apartment.) This one is 40,000 yen.

Lyn : Oh, it's cheap! In addition, it has a Japanese-style room, a Western-style room, and an eat-in-kitchen! Is there a subway station near it?

Realtor : No.

Lyn : I thought so. How long does it take to Sakuramachi?

Realtor : 40 minutes by bus.

Lyn : Oh, 40 minutes by bus. Then, I wonder if I should buy a motorcycle or something.

Realtor : Oh, motorcycle? Be careful, please.

Lyn : Sure, I'll be fine. In that case, I will take this apartment.

Listening Comprehension

仕事のルール

1. working on Mondays and Tuesdays
   using the company's car

2. working on Saturdays and Sundays
   wearing a suit on weekdays

CD recording:

土曜日と日曜日は働かなくてはいけません。月曜日と火曜日は働いてはいけません。水曜日と、木曜日と、金曜日は働いてもいいです。会社の電話は使ってもいいです。でも、会社の車は使ってはいけません。土曜日と日曜日はスーツを着なくてもいいです。でも、他の日はスーツを着なくてはいけません。

Reading Comprehension

りれきしょ (Resume)

1. Heisei 16 (2004), March   3. tour conductor

2. English

Chapter Seventeen

Kanji and Vocabulary

1. Reading and Writing Kanji Characters

C) 1. にほんはとちがせまくて、じんこうがおおいです。たかいたてものがたくさんあります。ちかにもショッピングモールがたくさんあります。やちんはたかいです。たべものもたかいです。にほんのにくやさかなはたかいですが、とてもおいしいです。

    2. わたしはおよぐのがだいすきです。プールでおよぐより、うみや、かわや、みずうみでおよぐほうがすきです。みずうみでおよぐのはいちばんたのしいです。まいとし、カナダのともだちのうちにいきます。ちかくにみずうみがあります。ともだちといっしょにおよぎます。

D) 1. 森田さんと林さん。　　3. 海や、川や、湖。

    2. どの色が好きですか。4. 肉と魚が大好きです。

2. Grouping Items

1. やさい   3. 肉   5. きせつ

2. くだもの   4. 魚   6. 国

3. Naming Japanese Islands

→ ほっかいどう

→ ほんしゅう

→ しこく

→ きゅうしゅう

Grammar

1. ～より

1. 漢字はカタカナより難しいです。
2. 犬はねこよりかわいいです。
3. 魚は肉よりからだにいいです。
4. 母は父よりやさしいです。

2. どちら

1. 魚と、肉とでは、どちらの方が好きですか。
2. 犬と、ねことでは、どちらの方がかわいいですか。
3. ひこうきと、車とでは、どちらの方があんぜんですか。
4. 北海道と、九州とでは、どちらの方が広いですか。
5. 日本語と、中国語とでは、どちらの方が難しいですか。

3. ～と同じぐらい～ and ～ほど～ない

1. けい子さんはメアリーさんと同じぐらい背が高いです。
2. けい子さんはアンさんほど背が高くありません。
3. けい子さんはよう子さんより背が高いです。

4. ～の

Answers vary.

5. いちばん

1. としょかんと、りょうと、ラボの中では、(どれ・どこ・何)が一番しずかですか。
2. ねこと、犬と、さるの中では、(どれ・何・だれ)が一番好きですか。
3. どうぶつでは、(どれ・何・だれ)が一番好きですか。
4. ピザと、ハンバーガーと、すしの中では、(どれ・どちら・何)が一番好きですか。
5. 食べものの中では、(どれ・どちら・何)が一番好きですか。
6. 今、(どれ・何・だれ)が一番したいですか。

Conversation and Usage

日本への留学

1. The commodity price is expensive.
2. Kelly loves Japanese old (traditional) culture, and there are many temples and shrines in Kyoto.

3. Tokyo, Osaka and Nagoya.

4. two hours (one way)

<Translation>

Kelly : I want to go for a study abroad program in Japan.

Toshihiko : Really?

Kelly : Yeh. Tokyo, Osaka, Nagoya or Kyoto.

Toshihiko : Oh.

Kelly : But it is expensive living in Tokyo, right?

Toshihiko : Yes. It is most expensive (in Tokyo).

Kelly : Then it is not good. (Lit. Then, it is impossible.) Among Osaka, Nagoya and Kyoto, which is most interesting?

Toshihiko : Do you like Japanese old (traditional) culture?

Kelly : Yes, I love it. (I love) temples, shrines, etc. (I love) kimono, flower arranging, etc., too.

Toshihiko : If so, I think Kyoto is most interesting. It is because there are many temples and shrines (in Kyoto).

Kelly : How about Nagoya?

Toshihiko : Nagoya is the third largest city in Japan, after Tokyo and Osaka.

Kelly : Is it far from Tokyo?

Toshihiko : It's about 2 hours by Shinkansen from Tokyo.

Kelly : Oh, it's near.

Toshihiko : Yes. But it costs 10,000 yen one way.

Kelly : Then, it's far.

Listening Comprehension

家のサイズ

Answer: A

CD recording:

山田さんの家はとてもきれいです。石川町にあります。山田さんの家は田中さんの家よりちょっと大きいです。でも、川口さんの家ほど大きくありません。川口さんの家は石田さんの家と同じぐらい大きいです。

Reading Comprehension

長生きをした人

1. 120   3. Kin was 107 and Gin was 108.
2. Jeanne Calment   4. Kin

<Translation>

According to Guinness World Records 2005, the longest living man in the world is Shigechiyo Izumi, a Japanese person. He was born in 1865 and died in 1986, at the age of 120. The longest living woman in the world is Jeanne Calment, a French person. She was born in 1875 and died in 1997 at the age of 122. The longest living twin sisters in the world are Kin Narita and Gin Kanie. The two were born in 1892. Kin died in 2000 at the age of 107, and Gin died in 2001 at the age of 108. The two lived in the 19th, 20th and 21st centuries. Kin gave birth to 11 children, and had 11 grandchildren, seven great-grandchildren and one great-grand-grandchild. Gin gave birth to five children, and had four grandchildren and nine great-grandchildren.

Chapter Eighteen

Kanji and Vocabulary

1. Reading and Writing Kanji Characters

C) 1. ひこうきは ニューヨークを ごご11じに でて、かん<u>こく</u>のソウルに<u>つぎ</u>の<u>ひ</u>の<u>ごぜん</u>4<u>じ</u>に<u>つ</u>きました。ひこうきに<u>のる</u> <u>まえ</u>におさけを<u>か</u>いました。ひこうきの<u>なか</u>では<u>しんぶん</u>を<u>よ</u>んで、かん<u>こく</u>のえいがを<u>み</u>ました。<u>しょくじ</u>は かん<u>こく</u>のビビンバと、<u>ごはん</u>でした。とてもおいしかったです。<u>しょくじ</u>の<u>あと</u>に6<u>じ</u>かんねました。<u>わたし</u>の<u>うしろ</u>の<u>ひと</u>もよくねていました。ひこうきはあまりこんでいなかったので、よかったです。ソウルに<u>つい</u>た<u>とき</u>に、ソウルの<u>ちず</u>を<u>か</u>いました。ホテルに<u>つい</u>て、シャワーをあびた<u>あと</u>に、<u>ひとり</u>で<u>で</u>かけました。

2. <u>わたし</u>の<u>しゅじん</u>は<u>だいがく</u>に<u>にゅうがく</u>しましたが、<u>そつぎょう</u>しませんでした。<u>そつぎょう</u>する<u>まえ</u>に、とてもいい<u>かいしゃ</u>に<u>しゅうしょく</u>したからです。<u>しゅうしょく</u>した<u>あと</u>は、いそがしくて、ぜんぜん<u>べんきょう</u>できませんでした。

D) 1. <u>食事</u>の<u>前</u>と<u>後</u>
　　2. <u>入学</u>と<u>卒業</u>
　　3. <u>午前</u>9時から<u>午後</u>5時
　　4. <u>地図</u>を買いました。

2. Using Common Set Phrases and Action Verbs

A) 1. ごめんください。　　4. 行ってきます。
　　2. いただきます。　　5. ただいま。
　　3. ごちそうさま。

B) 　今年、高校を<u>卒業</u>して、大学に<u>入学</u>しました。今学期はよく<u>勉強</u>しました。クラスを5つ<u>とり</u>ました。先週文学のしけんを<u>うけ</u>ました。難しくて、たいへんでした。来週ほかのクラスのしけんが<u>おわり</u>ます。冬休みは<u>のんびり</u>したいです。

Grammar

1. ～時に 1

1. I paid right before I got on the bus.

2. I paid right after I got on the bus.
3. Please do not watch TV when eating.
4. I'll tell you during the meal.
5. I read when it is quiet.
6. I go to the park when I feel good.

2. ～時に 2

1. 出かける時に、「行ってきます」と言います。
2. 帰った時に、「ただいま」と言います。
3. ねる時に、「おやすみなさい」と言います。
4. だれかに会った時に、「こんにちは」と言います。
5. ノックをする時に、「ごめんください」と言います。
6. 何かをもらった時に、「ありがとう」と言います。

3. ～前に・～間に・～後に

1. 地図を見た後に、運転します。／運転する前に、地図を見ます。
2. 手を洗った後に、ご飯を食べます。／ご飯を食べる前に、手を洗います。
3. シャワーをあびた後に、出かけます。／出かける前に、シャワーをあびます。

4. ～ながら

Example answers:
1. 私は<u>食べ</u>ながら勉強します。
2. 弟は<u>テレビを見</u>ながら宿題をします。
3. 兄はラジオを聞きながら運転します。
4. 父は<u>ビールを飲み</u>ながらテレビを見ます。
5. 母は<u>うたい</u>ながらりょうりをします。

Conversation and Usage

なまけものの奥さん

Answer:

父 ： ただいま。

妻 ： おかえりなさい。あのう、晩ご飯、まだ、できて(い)ないの。ごめんね。

夫 ： え？もう、7時だよ。

妻 ： ちょっと秋子と電話でしゃべって(い)て。

夫 ： また長電話？

妻 ： 30分しゃべっただけよ。

夫 ： 毎日秋子さんと何をしゃべって(い)るの？ぼくは、おなかがすいて(い)るんだよ。

妻 ： ごめん、ごめん。すぐ作るから、ご飯の前にお風呂に入ってよ。

夫 ： ああ、いいよ。(He starts to undress in the bathroom.)

妻 ： あっ、ごめんなさい。お風呂をわかすの忘れた。

夫 ： え？本当に忘れっぽいね。

妻 ： ごめんなさい。私も忙しいから。

夫 ： 何が忙しいの？働いて(い)ないでしょう。

妻 ： でも、主婦はいろいろ忙しいのよ。

夫　：ああ、そう。それで、今日の晩ご飯は何を作るの？

妻　：何がいい？

夫　：まだ、考えて(い)ないの？

妻　：うん。お魚がいい？それとも、お肉がいい？

夫　：どっちが、あるの？

妻　：ええと。(The wife checks the inside of the refrigerator.) 魚だけ。

夫　：じゃあ、魚。

<Translation>

Husband : I'm home!

Wife : Hi! Ummm, the dinner is not ready yet. Sorry.

Husband : What? It's already 7 o'clock.

Wife : I was talking with Akiko on the phone a little.

Husband : Long telephone talk again?

Wife : I just talked for 30 minutes.

Husband : What are you talking about with Akiko every day? I am hungry.

Wife : Sorry, sorry. I will make it soon, so please take a bath before dinner.

Husband : Oh, okay. (He starts to undress in the bathroom.)

Wife : Oops, sorry. I forgot to heat the water in the bathtub.

Husband : What? You are really forgetful!

Wife : I'm sorry. I'm busy, too, so ...

Husband : What are you busy for? You are not working!

Wife : But housewives are busy for all sorts of things.

Husband : Oh, really. And what are you going to cook for dinner today?

Wife : What would be good?

Husband : You haven't thought about it yet?

Wife : Right. Is fish good? Or, is meat good?

Husband : Which one do you have?

Wife : Well. (The wife checks the inside of the refrigerator.) Just fish.

Husband : Then, fish.

Listening Comprehension

朝の日課

<u>3</u> 朝ごはんを食べる　　　<u>2</u> シャワーをあびる

<u>4</u> 新聞を読む　　　　　<u>1</u> はをみがく

CD recording:

ぼくは*毎朝*シャワーをあびます。シャワーをあびる前に、歯をみがきます。シャワーをあびた後に、朝ごはんを食べます。それから、新聞を読みます。

Reading Comprehension

おにぎりの作り方

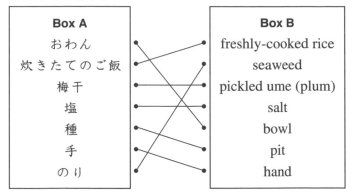

Box A	Box B
おわん	freshly-cooked rice
炊きたてのご飯	seaweed
梅干	pickled ume (plum)
塩	salt
種	bowl
手	pit
のり	hand

Chapter Nineteen

Kanji and Vocabulary

1. Reading and Writing Kanji Characters

C) 1. このかばんはとても<u>おも</u>いです。<u>おおき</u>いので、たくさんの<u>もの</u>を<u>いれ</u>られて<u>べんり</u>ですが、とても<u>もち</u>にくいです。

2. おいしい<u>たべもの</u>がたくさんあったので、ちょっと<u>たべ</u>すぎました。ケーキも3<u>こ</u> <u>たべ</u>ました。<u>くる</u>しくて、うごけません。

3. <u>きのう</u>は<u>たけした</u>さんと<u>えいが</u>を<u>み</u>にいきました。ぼくはチケットを<u>わすれ</u>たので、<u>たけした</u>さんは30<u>ぷん</u> <u>また</u>なくてはいけませんでした。

4. <u>いま</u>、<u>え</u>を<u>かい</u>ています。<u>どうぶつ</u>の<u>え</u>です。ライオンです。<u>しゃしん</u>を<u>み</u>てかいています。<u>1しゅうかんまえ</u>に<u>はじめ</u>ました。もうすぐ<u>お</u>わるところです。

5. まどは<u>あけて</u>ください。でも、ドアは<u>しめて</u>ください。

D) 1. 薬　　　お茶　　　苦しい

2. 行く　　　待つ

3. 持つ　　　待つ　　　時間

4. 間　　　開ける　　　閉める　　　聞く

5. 働く　　　男

E) 1. <u>動物</u>が好きです。　3. 宿題を<u>忘</u>れました。

2. <u>映画</u>を見ます。　　4. 勉強が<u>終</u>わりました。

2. Making Polite Requests

1. ちょっとかばんを<u>持って</u>下さい。

2. ちょっと<u>待って</u>下さい。

3. テレビを<u>けして</u>下さい。

4. <u>動か</u>ないで下さい。

5. カメラを<u>こわさ</u>ないで下さい。

3. Naming Common Objects in a Room

1. え　　　3. かべ　　　5. にんぎょう

2. かびん　　　4. てんじょう　　　6. ゆか

Grammar

1. 〜にくい and 〜やすい

Example answers:

1. このハンバーガーは大きくて、<u>食べ</u>にくいです。
2. このペンは<u>書き</u>やすいです。
3. この本は難しい漢字が少なくて、とても<u>読み</u>やすいです。
4. 先生はやさしくて、とても<u>話し</u>やすいです。
5. このくつは<u>はき</u>にくいです。

2. 〜すぎる

1. ビールを飲みすぎました。
2. ようふくを買いすぎました。
3. 父はきびしすぎます。
4. 兄はまじめすぎます。
5. このアパートはだいどころがせますぎます。

3. 〜しまう

1. happy   3. unhappy   5. neutral
2. unhappy   4. unhappy

4. 〜おく

Example answers:

1. お酒を買っておきます。
2. スーツケースに地図や、パスポートを入れておきます。
3. レストランをよやくしておきます。
4. スーツを買っておきます。
5. 勉強しておきます。

5. 〜ある

Example answers:

ドアがあけてあります。テレビがついています。ティーシャツがかべにかけてあります。くつしたがゆかにおいてあります。

Conversation and Usage

お別れ会

1. Ginger House   3. 10,000 yen
2. 10 people   4. necklace or wallet

<Translation>

Takahashi : Manager, why don't we have a farewell party for Ms. Kato next week?

Manager : I was just thinking about it, too. Where shall we have it?

Takahashi : How about Ginger House?

Manager : Oh, sounds good.

Takahashi : Then, I will make a reservation.

Manager : Oh, thank you. And it is better to buy some present.

Takahashi : You are right. Shall I collect 500 yen from each person?

Manager : Isn't it too little? I think it is okay to collect 1,000 yen from each.

Takahashi : Then, as there are ten people altogether, we will collect 10,000 yen, correct?

Manager : Right. What present would be good, I wonder.

Takahashi : I think a necklace or a wallet is good.

Manager : I agree.

Listening Comprehension

テレビでショッピング

1. two   2. black and red   3. 19,980 yen

CD recording:

このレザー・ハンドバッグは小さいですが、とてもじょうぶで便利です。前に小さいポケットが2つと、うしろに大きいポケットが1つあって、かぎや、ペンや、けいたいを入れるのにとても便利です。まん中には大きいものも入ります。とても持ちやすくて、りょこうにも便利です。どうぞ使ってみて下さい。色は くろと、あか。おねだんは、19,980円。今すぐ、お電話下さい。03-3333-1234です。

Reading Comprehension

私のたんじょう日

1. April 1st
2. a present that is not a surprise box
3. to place her grandmother's wig in her sister's handbag
4. Boo-boo cushion is a balloon-like cushion used to surprise someone. It is to be secretly placed under a seat and when the person to be tricked sits on it, it will make a loud blowing noise.
5. yes

<Translation>

My birthday is on April 1st. April 1st is April Fools Day. It is the day when we can play an innocent trick, so my birthday presents are 99% surprise boxes—figurines of snakes and frogs with springs jump out from inside a box wrapped with beautiful wrapping paper. As a result, I could create a collection of surprise boxes. Now, I usually expect my birthday present to be a surprise box, and therefore, I do not get surprised (by a surprise box) at all. I get very surprised when my present is not a surprise box. In my birthday cards from my friends, only lies are written.

As I get chagrined, I play tricks on my family, friends and colleagues. Last year, I left my grandmother's wig in my younger sister's handbag. When my sister put her hand in her bag, she felt the wig and screamed "Kyaa". And I left a boo boo cushion under my father's Japanese cushion. When he sat down, it sounded "boo" loudly.

My father was so shocked that he spilled his tea. I always prepare a camera secretly. I have been taking everyone's photo in the moment of a surprise and compiling a photo album.

My birthday is full of tricks every year, but it is a lot of fun.

Chapter Twenty

Kanji and Vocabulary

1. Reading and Writing Kanji Characters

C) 1. <u>そふ</u>と<u>そぼ</u>は<u>にゅうがく</u>のおいわいに<u>とけい</u>をくれました。

2. ぼくは ガールフレンド に<u>はな</u>をあげました。<u>ともだち</u>にはティーシャツをあげました。

3. <u>すいせんじょう</u>を<u>おく</u>りますから、<u>じゅうしょ</u>を<u>おしえて</u>ください。

4. <u>はは</u>は<u>えいが</u>を<u>み</u>てよく<u>なきます</u>。

D) 1. <u>祖父</u>と<u>祖母</u>　　　　　3. <u>友達</u>と勉強しました。

2. 電話番号と<u>住所</u>

2. Identifying Common Gifts

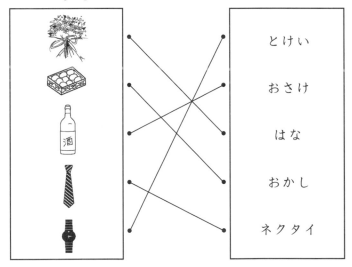

とけい

おさけ

はな

おかし

ネクタイ

3. Requesting a Letter of Recommendation

1. 日本に<u>りゅうがく</u>したいと思います。

2. <u>すいせんじょう</u>を書いて頂けないでしょうか。

3. <u>ようし</u>はこの封筒に入っています。

4. <u>じゅうしょ</u>は封筒に書いてあります。

5. <u>しめきり</u>は来月のはじめです。

Grammar

1. あげる and くれる

1. 私は田中さんに本を（<u>あげました</u>・くれました）。

2. 田中さんは私にペンを（あげました・<u>くれました</u>）。

3. 田中さんは母に花を（<u>あげました</u>・くれました）。

4. 田中さんはマイクさんにおかしを（<u>あげました</u>・くれました）。

5. 父は母にネックレスを（<u>あげました</u>・くれました）。

2. さしあげる, くださる and やる

1. 私は社長にお酒を（あげました・<u>さしあげました</u>）。

2. 私は父におかしを（<u>あげました</u>・さしあげました）。

3. 私はよう子ちゃんにTシャツを（<u>あげました</u>・さしあげました）。

4. 社長は私にかばんを（くれました・<u>くださいました</u>）。

5. 父は私に時計を（<u>くれました</u>・くださいました）。

6. 犬にステーキを（あげました・<u>やりました</u>・くれました）。

3. もらう and いただく

1. 社長にチョコレートを（もらいました・<u>いただきました</u>）。

2. 友達のおばさんから手紙を（もらいました・<u>いただきました</u>）。

3. 入学のお祝いに祖父から時計を（もらいました・いただきました）。

4. 姉はたんじょう日にボーイフレンドから花を（もらいました・いただきました）。

5. 母は父からネックレスを（もらいました・いただきました）。

4. 〜あげる, 〜くれる and 〜もらう

1. 私は妹に本を本を読んであげました。／私は妹に本を読んでやりました。

2. 先生は私に漢字を教えて下さいました。

3. 私は先生に漢字を教えていただきました。

4. 私は犬にセーターを作ってあげました。／私は犬にセーターを作ってやりました

5. 私は妹に買い物に行ってもらいました。

5. 〜ていただきたいんですが

1. お金をかしていただきたいんですが。

2. 父に会っていただきたいんですが。

3. メールアドレスを教えていただきたいんですが。

4. タバコをすわないでいただきたいんですが。

5. この仕事をてつだっていただきたいんですが。

Conversation and Usage

おみやげ

1. False　　2. False　　3. True　　4. False　　5. True

<Translation>

Miller　：Oh, Mr. Suzuki!

Suzuki　：Oh, Ms. Miller! It has been a long time! How are you?

Miller　：Yes. I'm fine. How about you, Mr. Suzuki?

Suzuki　：I'm fine thank you. I'm only 38 years old, but I became a grandfather this year.

Miller　：What? You got a grandchild?

Suzuki　：Yes. In March. A girl.

Miller　：Oh, congratulations!

Suzuki　：Thank you.

Miller : Then, your wife must be busy.

Suzuki : Yes. But she quit her job, so she is enjoying taking care of her grandchild.

Miller : Oh, really?

Suzuki : Are you busy, Ms. Miller?

Miller : Yes. I have lots of exhibitions in overseas this year, and what's more, I am teaching at a university.

Suzuki : Oh, really. That's wonderful.

Miller : Not at all. (I am) just busy. (Ms. Miller takes out something from her bag.) Well, this is just a little something, but please accept it.

Suzuki : Oh, you are so thoughtful (lit. polite). Thank you very much.

Miller : Not at all.

Suzuki : Oh, this is French wine, isn't it!

Miller : Yes, I went to France twice this year.

Suzuki : That's nice. Thank you for such a valuable gift.

Miller : Don't mention it.

Listening Comprehension

あげました・さしあげました

1. C   2. D   3. D   4. A   5. B

CD recording:

1. さしあげました。   4. くれました。

2. いただきました。   5. あげました。

3. 下さいました。

Reading Comprehension

お礼状

1. handbag   2. worker   3. Tokyo

<Translation>

Dear Kazuo,

It is cold every day, isn't it? How are you?

Thank you for sending a birthday present to me. I was surprised you remembered my birthday! It is a very cute handbag, so I'll used it for work (Lit. when I go to my company). When you have a chance to come to Tokyo again, please visit me.

I hope you stay well.

With appreciation,

Yoko

Chapter Twenty-one

Kanji and Vocabulary

1. Reading and Writing Kanji Characters

C) 1. せんたくと、りょうりと、そうじは<u>じ</u>ぶんで して<u>く</u>ださい。そのはこは<u>じ</u>ぶんで<u>へや</u>には こんで<u>く</u>ださい。

2. <u>さいきん</u>ジムで<u>うんどう</u>をし<u>はじ</u>めました。 ウエイトリフティングを30<u>ぶん</u>しています。 それから、<u>じてんしゃでかいしゃまでいって</u> います。<u>かいしゃのあと</u>はヨガのクラスに<u>い</u> きます。

3. <u>しょうがっこうのおんがく</u>のクラスでバイオ リンを<u>ひ</u>きました。いい<u>おとがで</u>なくて、と てもたいへんでした。

4. せんこうは<u>ぶんがく</u>でしたが、<u>すうがく</u>もす きだったので、<u>だいがく</u>でも<u>すうがく</u>のクラ スを2<u>つ</u>とりました。

5. <u>もりたまことともう</u>します。よろしく<u>おねが</u> いします。

6. <u>わたし</u>はいぬと、ねこは<u>す</u>きですが、<u>とり</u>は きらいです。<u>ともだち</u>のうちに<u>とり</u>がいるん ですが、あたまの<u>うえにの</u>るんです。とても いやです。

D) 1. <u>最近</u>よく勉強します。   3. 犬と、ねこと、<u>鳥</u>。

2. <u>数学</u>を<u>取</u>っています。   4. <u>自転車</u>に乗ります

2. Planning for Health

　父はいつも<u>けんこう</u>にいいことをしています。 朝はジムで30分<u>運動</u>します。エレベーターを使わ ないで、<u>かいだん</u>を使います。<u>たばこ</u>はすいませ ん。お酒も飲みません。肉や<u>たまご</u>はあまり食べ ません。やさいや、<u>なっとう</u>を食べます。

Grammar

1. ～ようにする and ～ようになる

1. 自分で宿題をするようになりました。

2. 電気をせつやくするようにしました。

3. クラスを休むようになりました。

4. 漢字が書けるようになりました。

5. たまごを食べないようにしました。

6. なまけないようになりました。／なまけなくなり ました。

2. ～ことにする and ～ことになる

1. 私がそうじをすることになりました。

2. ホンコンで働くことにしました。

3. 今日からここで働くことになりました。

4. オーストラリアにりゅうがくすることにしまし た。

5. 来月けっこんすることになりました。

6. ここでタバコをすってはいけないことになりま した。

3. ～と、～する and ～と、～した

1. When spring comes, it gets warm.

2. If you are a woman, you can get a discount on wine.

3. When I opened the door, there was a police officer standing there.

4. If you use this lotion, your skin becomes beautiful.

5. When I got home, the meal was already made.

Conversation and Usage

小学校の時の友達

1. Higashi High School   2. 10 years   3. Australia

<Translation>

Takako : Oh, Kenta?

Kenta : What?

Takako : Me! Takako! We were in the same class at Ishiyama Elementary School!

Kenta : Oh, Takako! I couldn't recognize you at all. Are you doing well?

Takako : Yes.

Kenta : Which high school do you go to now?

Takako : Higashi High School.

Kenta : Oh, really. You got in a good high school.

Takako : But I just practice figure skating all the time without studying.

Kenta : Wow. How many years have you been doing it?

Takako : Since I started when I was six, it will be 10 years this year.

Kenta : Really? Will you be at the Olympics?

Takako : I don't know. But I am making an effort every day so I can participate.

Kenta : You will be able to participate for sure. I want you to become famous. Try your best!

Takako : Thank you. How about you, Kenta?

Kenta : I decided to study abroad in Australia this year.

Takako : Wow, wonderful!

Kenta : My uncle is in Australia.

Takako : That's nice.

Listening Comprehension

自己紹介

1. Florida, United States

2. Asian Studies and mathematics

3. two

4. Kyoto

5. Japanese, literature, history

CD recording:

はじめまして。ショーン・コーエンと申します。アメリカのフロリダからです。今日からこの会社で働くことになりました。大学ではアジア学と数学を専攻しました。日本語のクラスは2つ取りました。それから、3年生の時に京都に一年留学しました。日本語や、文学や、歴史のクラスをとりまし

た。とても楽しかったです。アメリカに帰って、卒業しましたが、いつも日本で働きたいと思っていました。この会社で働けることになってとてもうれしいです。どうぞよろしくお願いいたします。

Reading Comprehension

手紙

1. Osaka

2. Tokyo

3. No.

4. Mr. Morita and Jenny

5. to take Japanese courses at Nakayama University

<Translation>

September 21

Dear Yuko,

The hot summer is over, and it is already fall. How are you doing, Yuko? How is your new job in Osaka?

I am home-staying at Mr. Morita's house in Tokyo now. Because Mr. Morita doesn't speak any English, I speak in Japanese every day. I became able to speak Japanese better than before. I am very happy about it. Mr. Morita is very kind and teaches me all sorts of things. We cook and eat dinner together every day. Last month, we climbed Mt. Fuji together. Jennie was with us, too. It was a lot of fun.

I decided to take Japanese language courses at Nakayama University starting next month. I am planning to study kanji a lot.

I hope you stay well, and wish you the very best.

(Sincerely,)

(From) David Wilson

Chapter Twenty-two

Kanji and Vocabulary

1. Reading and Writing Kanji Characters

C) 1. ようこさんはとても<u>しんせつ</u>で、やさしくて、<u>てんし</u>のような<u>ひと</u>です。たかこさんは<u>き</u>が<u>つ</u>よくて、ちょっとこわいです。としおさんは<u>き</u>が<u>よわ</u>くて、しずかですが、とてもいい<u>ひと</u>です。<u>むし</u>も<u>ころ</u>さないやさしい<u>ひと</u>です。

2. <u>こども</u>には<u>ちちおや</u>と<u>ははおや</u>はとても<u>たいせつ</u>です。

3. <u>わたし</u>の<u>こども</u>も<u>おとな</u>になって、<u>おや</u>になりました。

D) 1. <u>切手</u>を買います。   3. <u>強</u>い人と、<u>弱</u>い人。

2. <u>人間</u>と、動物。

2. Describing People

A)

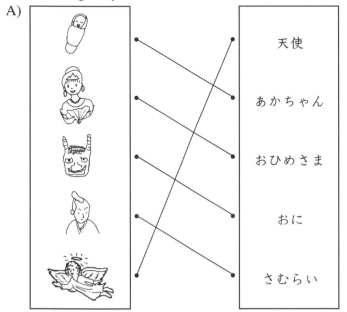

天使

あかちゃん

おひめさま

おに

さむらい

B) 1. 父はとても<u>こわい</u>です。よく子供をたたきます。

2. 母はとても<u>やさしい</u>です。天使のようです。

3. 姉はちょっと<u>気が強い</u>です。父の言うことを聞きません。

4. 兄は<u>せきにんかん</u>があります。約束は忘れません。

5. 弟は<u>ゆうき</u>があります。何もこわくありません。

6. 妹はちょっと<u>気が弱い</u>です。はっきり意見を言えません。

Grammar

1. ～そう(な)

1. あの人は新しいマネージャーですね。まあまあ<u>やさし</u>そうですね。

2. この車は<u>こわれ</u>そうです。へんな音がします。

3. 映画を見て、<u>泣き</u>そうになりましたが、泣きませんでした。

4. このきものはとてもきれいですが、<u>高</u>そうですね。

2. ～のよう(な)and ～みたい(な)

1. 山田さんはとてもやさしいです。<u>天使</u>のような人です。

2. 兄は遊んでばかりいて、せきにんかんがありません。大学生ですが、<u>子供</u>みたいです。

3. 私は母がいません。姉は私のせわをよくしてくれました。姉は私の<u>母親</u>のような人です。

4. あき子さんはいじわるで、こわいです。<u>おに</u>のような人です。

5. <u>犬</u>のような食べ方はいけませんよ。ちゃんとスプーンで食べて！

3. ～らしい

1. 私のボーイフレンドは（<u>男</u>・女）らしい人です。

2. 私のボーイフレンドは（男・<u>女</u>）のような人です。

3. 先生は（<u>かみさま</u>・先生）みたいな人です。

4. 父は（父親・<u>先生</u>）のような人です。

5. 母はとても（<u>母親</u>・父親）らしい人です。

4. ～たり

1. 昨日は音楽を聞いたり、映画を見たりしました。

2. 明日はりょうりをしたり、そうじをしたりします。

3. しゅうまつは新聞を読んだり、テニスをしたり、買い物をしたりします。(If しゅうまつ refers to a specific weekend in the past, the sentence should be in the past tense, as in しゅうまつは新聞を読んだり、テニスをしたり、買い物をしたりしました。)

4. 夏休みはアルバイトをしたり、りょこうをしたりします。(If 夏休み refers to a specific summer vacation in the past, like last summer vacation, the sentence should be in the past tense, as in 夏休みはアルバイトをしたり、りょこうをしたりしました。)

Conversation and Usage

ドレス

1. False   2. True   3. True

<Translation>

Atsuko   : How about this dress?

Tomiko   : What? It has too many ribbons. (I would) look like a princess (in it).

Atsuko   : Then, how about this?

Tomiko   : Oh, that's very elegant! But it looks expensive.

Atsuko   : No. It is not expensive. It's 9,800 yen.

Tomiko   : Really? It's cheap! And it is very feminine. I'll try it on. (Tomiko goes into the fitting room and comes out a few minutes later.)

Atsuko   : How is it? (Lit. How was it?)

Tomiko   : It is a bit too small. (Lit. It was a bit too small.) Is there a bigger one?

Atsuko   : (Atsuko looks for a bigger one.) There are many pink ones, but if you like black, that's the only one.

Tomiko   : Oh, really. I like this design, but pink is a bit ...

Atsuko   : Pink is also good.

Tomiko   : What? Pink? No way!

Atsuko   : Why?

Tomiko   : Pink is a bit too gaudy (for me).

Atsuko   : Not at all.

Tomiko   : But I have never worn pink before.

Atsuko   : You don't need to feel embarrassed.

Tomiko   : But ...

Atsuko   : It looks very good on you.

Tomiko   : Really?

Atsuko   : Yes.

Tomiko   : Okay. I will take (the) pink (one).

Listening Comprehension

機内アナウンス

1. East Airline	3. 2:55 p.m.
2. 2:45 p.m.	4. 25 degrees Celsius

CD recording:

ご搭乗の皆様、当機はあと10分ほどで東京国際空港に到着いたします。今一度、お座席のシートベルトをご確認ください。当地の時刻は8月24日月曜日午後2時45分、気温は摂氏25度です。本日はイースト・エアラインをご利用頂き、誠にありがとうございました。また、皆様と機上でお会いできること、心からお待ち申し上げます。それでは、皆様ごきげんよう。さようなら。*Attention please. Our plane will arrive at Tokyo International Airport in about ten minutes. Please check whether your seat belt is securely fastened. The time over there is 2:45 p.m. on Monday, August 24th. The temperature is 25 degrees Celsius. We appreciate your using our East Airline. We sincerely look forward to seeing you again on the plane. Have a nice day. Goodbye.*

Reading Comprehension

ももたろう

1. b	2. a	3. a	4. b	5. a

<Translation>

A long long time ago, there lived an old man and an old woman in some place. One day, the old man went to the mountain to gather firewood, and the old woman (his wife) went to the river to wash clothes. When the old woman was washing clothes in the river, a huge peach came floating down the river. She took the peach home. When the old man came home from the mountain, he saw the huge peach and was very surprised. They decided to try eating it. When the old woman brought out a knife and touch the peach with it (to try to cut it), the peach moved a little. The old couple was very surprised because the peach moved. Then, the peach split open and an energetic boy came out (of the peach). Since the old couple did not have a child, they were very happy with the encounter. Because the boy was born from a peach, they named him Momotaro. Momotaro ate well and grew up strong and big.

Around that time, there were very bad ogres in the village. They were stealing and kidnapping, and giving the villagers a hard time. The strong Momotaro decided to go to conquer them. The old couple was worried about him, yet they prepared the best clothes and dumplings called kibi-dango for him (for his long journey). Momotaro wore the best clothes, hung (the bag of) kibi-dango dumplings on his hip, and left his home for Ogre Island.

On the way, a dog approached Momotaro and said to him, "Momotaro-san, Momotaro-san, you have a bag of kibi-dango on your hip. Please give me a piece. (Then,) I'll follow you." Momotaro gave the dog a piece of kibi-dango, and the dog became his follower. After a little while, a monkey approached him. The monkey also became his follower by receiving a piece of kibi-dango. After a little while, a pheasant approached Momotaro, and it too became his follower by receiving one piece of kibi-dango.

Momotaro, the dog, the monkey, and the pheasant crossed over fields and mountains, took a boat and arrived at Ogre Island. First, the pheasant flew in to check what the ogres were doing. The pheasant came back and told Momotaro that the ogres seemed to be drinking sake. Then, the monkey got over the door of the gate and unlocked the gate (from inside). Momotaro and the dog went through the gate and sneaked inside. The ogres were very surprised. The dog, the monkey, and the pheasant instantly jumped onto the ogres, and did all sorts of things like scratching, biting and poking. Momotaro hit the ogres with all his might and the orgres were finally defeated. They gave back all the treasures they stole (from the villagers). Momotaro sent back the treasures to the villagers and returned home safely to the old couple.

Chapter Twenty-three

Kanji and Vocabulary

1. Reading and Writing Kanji Characters

C) 1. <u>とうきょう</u>を3<u>じ</u>に<u>で</u>たので、<u>おおさか</u>には6<u>じ</u>に<u>つ</u>きます。

   2. <u>いま</u>の<u>しごと</u>の<u>せんもん</u>はコンピューターです。<u>だいがく</u>では<u>すうがく</u>を<u>せんこう</u>しました。

   3. <u>ぶちょう</u>の<u>おく</u>さんはとてもいい<u>かた</u>です。

   4. うちの<u>かない</u>は<u>おおさか</u>で<u>うま</u>れました。

   5. <u>つま</u>と<u>おっと</u>はよく<u>はなし</u>をするべきです。

   6. テニス<u>ぶ</u>の<u>ぶちょう</u>は<u>き</u>が<u>つよ</u>いです。でも、いい<u>ひと</u>です。<u>ただ</u>しいことは<u>ただ</u>しい、<u>わる</u>いことは<u>わる</u>いといいます。

   7. <u>おっと</u>とは<u>かんが</u>えがいつも<u>ちが</u>います。でも、<u>いえ</u>のことを<u>き</u>める<u>とき</u>は、よく<u>はなしあ</u>いますから、だいじょうぶです。

   8. もう<u>すこ</u>し<u>べんきょう</u>の<u>しかた</u>を<u>かんが</u>えた<u>ほう</u>がいいですよ。

D) 1. 妻と夫　　　　　　　3. 正しいことと、悪いこと
　　2. 東京と大阪

2. Using the Terms for Spouses
1. 私の主人はゴルフばかりしていて、子供のめんどうをぜんぜんみません。
2. マリアさんのご主人は今どこにいらっしゃいますか？
3. うちの家内は母親なのに、りょうりも、そうじもしないんです。
4. マイクさんの奥さんは働いていらっしゃいますか。

3. Figuring Out Where to Eat on Yoko's Birthday
たけし　：ようこさんのたんじょう日はたしか5月31日だよね。
ようこ　：ええ。
たけし　：いっしょに食事をしませんか。
ようこ　：いいんですか。
たけし　：ええ。どこがいいか考えておいて下さい。
ようこ　：私が決めてもいいんですか。
たけし　：もちろん。
ようこ　：じゃあ、ピザハット。
たけし　：もっといいところにして下さいよ。
ようこ　：いいんですか。
たけし　：もちろん。
ようこ　：じゃあ、ラ・ベル・ヴィは？
たけし　：ああ、いいですよ。
ようこ　：本当に？ちゃんとさいふを持って来て下さいよ。

Grammar

1. ～なさいand ～ろ
Variation 1:
 1. 聞きなさい
 2. 来なさい（きなさい）
 3. しずかにしなさい
 4. 名前を書きなさい
 5. もんくを言うのをやめなさい
Variation 2:
 1. 聞け　　　　　　　4. 名前を書け
 2. 来い（こい）　　　5. もんくを言うのをやめろ
 3. しずかにしろ

2. ～はずだand ～べきだ
1. 子供は早くねる（はず・べき）です。
2. ひこうきは3時に着く（はず・べき）ですから、4時にはここに来るでしょう。
3. 大学生は勉強する（はず・べき）です。なまけてはいけませんよ。
4. 田中さんは今日来ない（はず・べき）ですから、うちに電話して下さい。
5. たばこはすう（はず・べき）じゃありません。

3. ～か(どうか)
1. 山田さんの専攻は何かしっていますか。
2. これはいくらかしっていますか。
3. 昨日のパーティーにだれが来たかしっていますか。
4. スミスさんは今何をしているかしっていますか。
5. 明日はしけんがあるかしっていますか。or 明日はしけんがあるかどうかしっていますか。

Conversation and Usage

1. ボーイフレンドとガールフレンド？
1. The university in Boston, which invited him, has a very strong program in mathematics.
2. He can receive a scholarship.
3. She thinks people should try their best and work hard when they are young.

<Translation>
Man　　　：As a matter of fact, a professor of mathematics in an American university invited me.
Woman　：To the graduate program?
Man　　　：Right. They will offer me a scholarship, too.
Woman　：Wow! That's wonderful! For mathematics, is America good?
Man　　　：It depends on the university, but that university is very good.
Woman　：Where in America?
Man　　　：Boston.
Woman　：Oh, really?
Man　　　：Right. But I'm wondering whether I should go or not.
Woman　：Go! You should try your best while you are young.
Man　　　：But wouldn't you feel lonesome?
Woman　：Not at all.
Man　　　：Is that true?
Woman　：Yes.
Man　　　：It cannot be the case! What does it mean that you wouldn't feel lonesome without me?
Woman　：Are you misunderstanding something?

2. 母とむすめ
1. Midori Tanaka　　4. 3:30 p.m.
2. Osaka　　　　　　5. take her mother (or Michiko's
3. a banker　　　　　　 grandmother) to the hospital

<Translation>
Child　　　：Mom, can you pass me that?
Mother　 ：Which one?
Child　　　：That one.
Mother　 ：Vegetable?
Child　　　：Nope.
Mother　 ：Meat?

Child : Yep.

Mother : Don't just eat meat, but eat vegetable, too.

Child : Yes, yes.

Mother : "Yes" should be (said) just once.

Child : Yes.

Mother : How was your school today?

Child : We got a transferred student from Osaka.

Mother : A girl?

Child : Yep. Midori Tanaka. (She said) that they move a lot because her dad works for a bank.

Mother : Oh, really? That's hard. Be friendly with her, okay?

Child : Yep. Is it okay to bring her to our home tomorrow?

Mother : Sure. But what time?

Child : We don't have club activity tomorrow, so at about 3:30 p.m.

Mother : I don't know whether I'll be there.

Child : Why?

Mother : I have to take your grandmother to the hospital tomorrow afternoon.

Child : Oh, really.

Listening Comprehension

メッセージ

1. Junko and George
2. 789-3344
3. to call her back
4. whether she can come to Ginger House tonight
5. 588-9477

CD recording:

1. もしもし、ゆきさん。ショーンです。今週の金曜日に僕のアパートでじゅんこさんと、ジョージさんと、いっしょに晩ご飯を食べます。ゆきさんもいかがですか。お電話下さい。789-3344です。では、また。

2. もしもし。ゆき。おかあさんよ。まだ帰ってないの？おそいわね。ちょっと電話ちょうだいね。

3. ゆき？私。みか。今晩、ジンジャーハウスに来れる？携帯に電話してね。588-9477。じゃあ、また。

Reading Comprehension

地球温暖化

1. • throwing away garbage anywhere
   • continuing war
   • creating exhaust gas

2. To try to save electricity, gasoline and other things, and not to throw away things in our daily life

3. She tries to do what she can do before telling other people what they should do.

<Translation>

1. **Kenichi Tanaka, 14 years old**

   We should consider protecting the earth more seriously. But most people don't do it. They have been doing things like throwing away garbage anywhere, continuing war and creating exhaust gas. If this continues, the earth will perish. I think it is better to think about protecting the earth.

2. **Keiko Yamaguchi, 13 years old**

   I think that global warming is something we can prevent. We should try to save electricity, gasoline and other things, and not to throw away things in our daily life. We should be able to prevent global warming by our effort.

3. **Emi Ishikawa, 13 years old**

   If global warming continues as it is, the earth may disappear. Before telling other people that they should do this and that, I myself want to start doing something. First, I will try not to throw away garbage (as much as I can).

Chapter Twenty-four

Kanji and Vocabulary

1. Reading and Writing Kanji Characters

C) 1. この<u>あいだ</u>、<u>にほんご</u> <u>能 力</u>（のうりょく）<u>しけん</u>の3<u>きゅう</u>を<u>うけよう</u>と<u>おもって</u>もう<u>しこみました</u>。3<u>しゅうかん</u>の<u>あいだ</u>、<u>まいにち</u> <u>としょかん</u>で<u>べんきょう</u>しました。<u>にほんご</u>の<u>せんせい</u>にも<u>たすけ</u>ていただきました。<u>きき</u>とりの<u>もんだい</u>はまあまあ<u>かんたん</u>でしたが、<u>かんじ</u>の<u>もんだい</u>はちょっと<u>むずかしかった</u>です。

2. <u>わたし</u>のそぼはなごやで<u>うまれました</u>。22<u>さい</u>のとき、<u>わかくて</u>かね<u>もち</u>の<u>男 性</u>（だんせい）と<u>結 婚</u>（けっこん）しました。

3. <u>きょうと</u>には<u>ふるい</u> <u>にほんてき</u>な<u>たてもの</u>がたくさんあります。

4. <u>ぎんざ</u>には<u>こうきゅう</u>なブティックや、レストランや、<u>みせ</u>がたくさんあります。

D) 1. <u>試験</u>を<u>受け</u>ました。　　3. <u>名古屋と京都</u>
   2. <u>図書館</u>や<u>映画館</u>

2. Using the verbs "To Take"

1. 薬を<u>のむ</u>
2. 日本語のコースを<u>取る</u>（と）
3. 試験を<u>受ける</u>
4. シャワーを<u>あびる</u>
5. 電車に<u>乗る</u>（の）

3. Sight-seeing

<u>かんこう</u>なら、京都がいいでしょう。<u>でんとう</u>的

なたてものがたくさんあります。JRパスを買うと、<u>しんかんせん</u>に安く乗れますよ。ニューヨークの<u>りょうこうがいしゃ</u>で聞いてみて下さい。それから、<u>りょかん</u>に泊まって下さいね。ふとんで寝られますよ。京都にはいろいろな<u>店</u>がたくさんありますから、おみやげをたくさん買って下さいね。

Grammar

1. ~よう

1. にげよう	4. 取ろう	7. 会おう
2. 飲もう	5. 運ぼう	8. 行こう
3. 歩こう	6. 待とう	9. しよう

2. ~ようと思う

1. スペインは行ったことがないので、来月<u>行こう</u>と思います。
2. 前の試験は悪かったので、今度の試験は<u>がんばろう</u>と考えています。
3. 今年は日本語能力試験の3級を受けたいので、来月<u>しんせいしよう</u>と思います。
4. あまり好きじゃありませんが、<u>食べよう</u>と思います。
5. 弟は日本にりゅう<u>学したい</u>と思っています。

3. ~ようとする

1. おきようとしましたが、おきられませんでした。
2. にげようとしましたが、にげられませんでした。
3. 言おうとしましたが、言えませんでした。
4. 飲もうとしましたが、飲めませんでした。
5. 乗ろうとしましたが、乗れませんでした。

4. ~ようにする

1. I am trying to eat fruit as much as I can.
2. When I was about to leave, Ms. Yamada came over.
3. I am thinking of studying Chinese next year.
4. I tried to eat it, but I couldn't.
5. Please try not to eat eggs.

5. ~たら

1. If you get a degree, it is easy to get a job.
2. If you don't like your job, it is better to quit it.
3. Once you use something, please put it away without fail.
4. If you press this button, a ticket will come out.
5. If I were rich, I would own a house.
6. When I went to the bookstore, I saw my senior in the tennis club.

6. ~なら

1. 日本語を勉強するなら、日本に住んだ方がいいでしょう。 *If you are going to study Japanese language, it is better to live in Japan.*
2. 漢字を2,000しっているなら、新聞が読めるでしょう。 *If you know 2,000 kanji, you can read newspaper (in Japanese), I guess.*
3. いいカメラを買いたいなら、あの店がいいですよ。 *If you want to buy a good camera, that store is good.*
4. お酒が好きなら、今度いっしょにいざかやに行きましょう。 *If you like sake, let's go to an Izakaya together.*
5. 新幹線を使うつもりなら、JRパスを買った方がいいですよ。 *If you are planning to use Shinkansen, It is better to buy a JR Pass.*

Conversation and Usage

北海道
1. because he wants to see snow
2. once
3. He has never tried hot spring.
4. ski
5. fish and crab

<Translation>

Wei Ming : I am thinking of going to Hokkaido this winter.

Akiko : Winter?

Wei Ming : Yep. I want to see snow.

Akiko : You have never seen snow?

Wei Ming : Right. Because I was born in Taiwan and grew up in Taiwan, I have never seen snow at all.

Akiko : Oh, I see. If you are going to Hokkaido, it is better to see the Snow Festival, too.

Wei Ming : Oh, right, right. The Snow Festival in Hokkaido is very famous, right?

Akiko : Yep.

Wei Ming : Have you ever seen the Snow Festival?

Akiko : Yep, once. About 5 years ago. It is very pretty.

Wei Ming : Oh, really.

Akiko : If you go to Hokkaido, it is better to enjoy hot spring, too.

Wei Ming : Oh, there are hot springs, too?

Akiko : Of course.

Wei Ming : Oh, really.

Akiko : In addition, you can ski, too.

Wei Ming : Oh, right. I have never tried hot springs or skiing, so I am looking forward to them very much!

Akiko : In addition, there are many delicious foods.

Wei Ming : Oh, really. For example?

Akiko : For example, crab, fish, etc.

Wei Ming : Oh, I love crab.

Listening Comprehension

デパートでの呼び出し
1. Yoshinori Motonaga

2. Camry, white color, license plate number: Kobe 83 ne 1108 (神戸83ね1108)

3. a girl who is about three years old, wearing a pink T-shirt and white skirt

CD recording:

1. お客様にお呼び出し申し上げます。名古屋市からお越しの元永喜紀さま。名古屋市からお越しの元永喜紀さま。お連れ様がお待ちです。いらっしゃいましたら、フロントデスクまでお越し願います。 *Attention please. This is a call for customers. Mr. Yoshinori Motonaga from Nagoya. Mr. Yoshinori Motonaga from Nagoya. Your company is waiting for you. Please come to the front desk.*

2. お車でお越しのお客様にお呼び出し申し上げます。お車ナンバー神戸83ね1108、白のカムリでお越しのお客様。至急、お車までお戻り下さいませ。 *Attention please. This is a call for customers who came by car. The customer who came by a white Camry whose plate number is Kobe 83 ne 1108. Please come back to your car as soon as possible.*

3. 店内のお客様に迷子のご案内をいたします。ピンクのTシャツをきて、白いスカートをはいた3歳ぐらいの女の子がお母さんを探しています。お心当たりがありましたら、1階のサービスカウンターまで至急お越し下さい。 *Attention please. This is to let the customers in the store know about a lost child. A girl with pink T-shirt and white skirt, about 3 years old, is looking for her mother. If you know anything about it, please come to the service counter on the first floor as soon as possible.*

Reading Comprehension

日記

1. Kenji   3. cooking class

2. her uncle from Kyushu   4. 2,000 yen

<Translation>

Friday, March 17, clear

I had lunch with Sachiko, Makoto and Kenji today. When I was about to pay for my lunch after eating, Kenji said that he would treat everyone. He seems to have gotten a bonus. I wish I can work in a nice company like Kenji's.

Saturday, March 18, rain

My uncle came to visit me from Kyushu today. He brought shochu (traditional Japanese distilled liquor) as a souvenir. I drank it with my uncle until late at night. It was a very rare kind of shochu and it was very good.

Sunday, March 19, cloudy

I went to the cooking class with Sachiko today. I could learn more than I thought and it was fun. If Sachiko is continuing with it, I will, too.

Monday, March 20, clear

I went to a pachinko parlor with Sachiko during lunch break today. I spent 2,000 yen. If it were not during lunch break, I would have spent 10,000 yen or so. After all, I will (decide to) quit pachinko.

Chapter Twenty-five

Kanji and Vocabulary

1. Reading and Writing Kanji Characters

C) 1. くうこうをまちがえて、ひこうきにのれませんでした。しかたがなかったので、うちにかえりました。

2. けっこんしたあとにふとってしまいました。こどもがうまれたあとはもっとふとりました。ちゅうごくのやせるくすりをもらいましたが、にがいのでぜんぜんのんでいません。

3. きょねんはかじやじこでたくさんのひとがしにました。

4. ちゅうかんしけんのへいきんてんはきまつしけんのへいきんてんよりたかかったです。

5. ジンジャーハウスはとうきょうでいちばんにんきがあるいざかやです。しゅうまつはともだちとよくジンジャーハウスにいきます。やすくて、おいしいです。

6. がいこくのきってが769まいあつまりました。

D) 1. 中間試験と期末試験

2. 家事や事故

3. 卒業して結婚します。

2. Describing Tastes

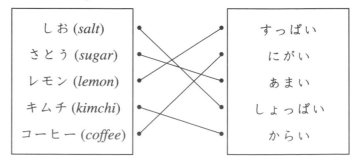

3. Identifying Disasters

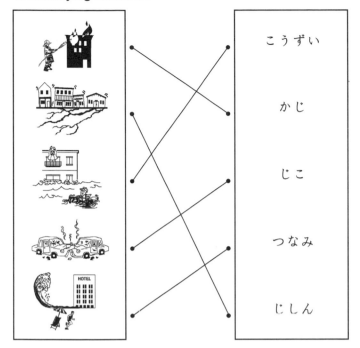

Grammar

1. ～でも

1. 私の兄は<u>何</u>でも食べます。からいものも、あまいものも食べます。姉は肉は食べませんが、魚なら、<u>何</u>でも食べます。
2. しょうがくきんがもらえるなら、<u>どの</u>大学にでも行きます。
3. 東京なら、ATMは<u>どこ</u>にでもありますよ。
4. <u>いくら</u>でもいいですよ。1万円でも、2万円でも、いいですよ。
5. わからないことがあったら、<u>いつ</u>でも私に聞いて下さい。

2. ～ても／～でも

1. どのじしょを<u>見</u>ても、この漢字はありませんでした。
2. <u>どこ</u>に行っても、安いホテルにとまります。
3. 父に<u>何</u>を言っても、わかってくれません。
4. いくら<u>勉強して</u>も、ぜんぜんわかりません。
5. ぜんぜん<u>勉強しなくて</u>も、わかります。

3. ～れば1

1. 待てば
2. 歩けば
3. 太れば
4. やせれば
5. 集まれば
6. くさっていれば
7. すれば
8. しなければ
9. 安ければ
10. あまければ
11. おいしくなければ

4. ～れば2

1. れいぞうこに入れなければ、くさります。
2. 早くよやくすれば、いいホテルがとれたはずです。

3. クレジットカードで買えば、安かったと思います。
4. パチンコをしなければ、よかったと思います。
5. 苦ければ、飲みません。

5. ～そうだ

1. メアリーさんはダンスが上手だそうです。
2. 林さんの車はトラックにぶつかったそうです。
3. 石田さんのねこは死んだそうです。
4. 森田さんはけがをしたそうです。
5. リーさんは中国人じゃないそうです。

6. ～ようだ and ～らしい

1. (a) 昨日サンフランシスコでじしんがあったようです。
   (b) 昨日サンフランシスコでじしんがあったらしいです。
2. (a) スミスさんはからいものは食べないようです。
   (b) スミスさんはからいものは食べないらしいです。
3. (a) 東京はぶっかが高いようです。
   (b) 東京はぶっかが高いらしいです。
4. (a) マイクさんはようこさんが好きなようです。
   (b) マイクさんはようこさんが好きらしいです。
5. (a) チェンさんのうちにきゅうきゅうしゃが来たようです。
   (b) チェンさんのうちにきゅうきゅうしゃが来たらしいです。

7. Particle で

1. 東京<u>で</u>ジョブ・フェアーがあります
2. 明日スミスさんと京都<u>に</u>行きます
3. 月曜日はカフェテリア<u>で</u>働きます
4. 大阪<u>で</u>大きい地震がありました
5. としょかん<u>に</u>コンピューターが30台あります

Conversation and Usage

てんぷら

1. No.
2. Spanish or Portugal missionaries, 16th century
3. Yes.
4. No.

<Translation>

Takeshi : Kate, do you like sushi?
Kate : Not so much. I don't care for raw fish. (Lit. I cannot easily become to like raw fish.)
Takeshi : Oh. Then, what do you like the best among Japanese foods?
Kate : Tempura.
Takeshi : Oh, really. Did you know this? Tempura was brought (to Japan) by Spanish and Portugal missionaries.
Kate : What? Really? About when?

Takeshi : About 16th century.

Kate : Isn't "tempura" Japanese (a Japanese word)?

Takeshi : It appears to be originally Spanish or Portugal.

Kate : Oh, really. I thought it was Japanese. By the way, is it true that Ieyasu Tokugawa ate tempura and died?

Takeshi : I don't know. Because there is another theory, stomach cancer.

Kate : Oh, I see. But tempura is delicious, so I guess Ieyasu had overeaten it and got a digestion problem.

Takeshi : Maybe. I also tend to overeat delicious things without thinking, and often get a digestion problem.

Kate : Oh, you are bad. (Lit. You cannot be helped.)

Takeshi : How about you, Kate?

Kate : I never get a digestion problem no matter how much I eat.

Takeshi : Wow. That's nice.

Listening Comprehension

ラジオのニュース

1. c   2. b   3. c   4. b   5. a

CD recording:

今日午前10時35分、東京都大田区桜通りで、タクシーがトラックにぶつかり、タクシーの運転手のたかだたろうさん42歳が頭を強くうって、大怪我をしました。トラックの運転手の森たかしさんによると、小学生が急に道に飛び出し、タクシーがそれをさけようと、急ブレーキをかけたところ、スリップしてトラックにぶつかったということです。*A taxi collided with a truck on Sakura Street, Ota Ward, Tokyo, at 10:35 a.m. today. The taxi driver, Mr. Taro Takada, 42 years old, hit his head hard and was severely injured. According to the truck driver, Mr. Takashi Mori, an elementary school student abruptly ran into the street and the taxi driver applied a sudden brake, trying to avoid him. As a result, the taxi slipped and crashed into the truck.*

Reading Comprehension

折鶴と禎子

1. two years old   4. twelve years old

2. no   5. 1958

3. folding paper cranes.

<Translation>

Have you ever made a folded paper crane? In Japan, people often make one thousand paper cranes when someone becomes ill. They pray for the recovery of the person, fold one thousand cranes, thread them, and give them (to the person).

The story about Sadako Sasaki in Hiroshima is very famous. On August 6, 1945, an atomic bomb was dropped in Hiroshima. At that time, Sadako was at her home, which was 1.7 kilometers from the ground zero. She was two years old. She did not have any (health) problem right after it. And she became an athletic and healthy elementary school student. But in 1955, when she was a 6th grader in elementary school, she got leukemia. It seems that the cause was the radiation, which she was exposed to at the time of atomic bomb when she was two. Sadako heard from her friend that her illness will be cured if she makes one thousand paper cranes, and she folded paper cranes earnestly while she was hospitalized. But she died in the same year, at the age of 12.

After that, there was some movement taken by Sadako's classmates (among other things), donation was gathered from everywhere in Japan and in the world, and "The Statue of the A-Bomb Children", which modeled Sadako and a folded paper crane, was built in Peace Memorial Park in Hiroshima in 1958. Since then, a folded paper crane became the symbol of the world peace.

Chapter Twenty-six

Kanji and Vocabulary

1. Reading and Writing Kanji Characters

C) 1. こんしゅうはあめやゆきがふって、いやなてんきでした。

2. とうきょうからしんかんせんにのって、なごやでおりました。それから、またしんかんせんにのって、きょうととおおさかにいきました。

3. ちいさいときにしゅうじをならったので、じをかくのがとくいです。てがみをかくときにじがきれいだと、とてもいいです。

4. にほんのこうこうせいはじゅけんべんきょうでたいへんです。わたしのあにはべんきょうがきらいで、いえでをしてしまいました。ですから、わたしのほうがさきにこうこうをそつぎょうして、だいがくににゅうがくしました。あにはいまもどこにいるのかわかりません。とてもかなしいです。

5. わたしのともだちはからてをならっています。まいにち2じかん れんしゅうします。からてのせんせいはとてもきびしいです。

6. ジェイソンというがくせいをしっていますか?いつもわるいことをしてこうちょうしつにい

かせられていた<u>がくせい</u>です。みんなはジェイソンの<u>わるぐち</u> (or <u>わるくち</u>) ばかり<u>いっ</u>ています。

7. この<u>あいだ</u>レストランで<u>お</u><u>きゃく</u>さんがけいたいでな<u>がでんわ</u>をしていました。

D) 1. <u>空手</u>の<u>練習</u>　　　3. <u>子供</u>が<u>家出</u>をした。

　　2. <u>受験</u>の<u>勉強</u>

2. What Can One Do to Others?

1. 弟が悪いことをしたので、父は弟を<u>しかり</u>ました。

2. 100点をとったので、母は私を<u>ほめて</u>くれました。うれしかったです。

3. 友達はいつも私を<u>からかって</u>、わらいます。とてもはらがたちます。

4. エープリル・フールの日はうそをついて、妹を<u>だまし</u>ます。おもしろいです。

5. 社長がひどいので、みんなは社長を<u>ひはん</u>しました。

Grammar

1. 〜られる1

1. ほめられる
2. たたかれる
3. からかわれる
4. しかられる
5. だまされる
6. しょうたいされる
7. ひはんされる

2. 〜られる2

1. 妹が母にほめられました。
2. 客がてんいんにだまされました。
3. 学生が先生にたたかれました。
4. ネックレスがどろぼうにぬすまれました。
5. 私のへやが兄に使われました。

3. 〜られる3

1. My younger brother graduated before me, (and I was a little embarrassed.)
2. Mr. Tanaka had a hard time because his girlfriend cried yesterday.
3. The person who was next to me in the train was talking on the cell phone for a long time. (It was annoying for me.)
4. Mr. Ishida's son ran away from his home, (which was a sad thing for Mr. Ishida.)
5. Mr. Hayashi's child died. (It was very sad for him, of course.)

4. 〜させる1

1. 読ませる
2. 勉強させる
3. 運動させる
4. 話させる
5. 習わせる
6. 待たせる
7. ふかせる
8. そうじさせる
9. 持って来させる

5. 〜させる2

1. 母は弟にさらを洗わせました。
2. 母は姉に車の運転を練習させました。
3. 母は妹にテーブルをふかせました。
4. 母は兄に習字を習わせました。

6. 〜させていただきたいんですが

1. 帰らせていただきたいんですが。
2. 食事をさせていただきたいんですが。
3. とまらせていただきたいんですが。
4. 会社の車を使わせていただきたいんですが。
5. レポートを読ませていただきたいんですが。

7. 〜させられる

1. Mr. Tanaka was made to drink by Mike.
2. My big brother was made to clean the yard by our father.
3. The elderly lady made me carry the heavy bag.
4. My girlfriend made me wait for her for three hours.

Conversation and Usage

書道

1. to draw horizontal lines, vertical lines and circles.
2. to sit and make ink
3. to clean

<Translation>

Kenta : Inhee, your handwriting is very good.

Inhee : Is it?

Kenta : Did you learn calligraphy?

Inhee : Yes. In Korea. But I hated it very much.

Kenta : Why?

Inhee : During the first year, I was made to draw just horizontal lines, vertical lines and circles.

Kenta : Really?

Inhee : Before the lesson, I was made to sit and make ink, and at the end (of the lesson), I was also made to clean.

Kenta : And how many years did you learn (take the lessons)?

Inhee : Because my mother didn't let me quit, I took the lessons for 10 years.

Kenta : Wow, that's amazing.

Inhee : Yes. I learned about patience more than calligraphy.

Listening Comprehension

お別れのことば

1. September in the previous year
2. Monday, next week
3. Mr. Nakayama
4. Kendo
5. Florida

CD recording:

来週の月曜日にアメリカに帰ることになりました。石山高校に来たのは去年の9月でした。この一年間皆さんに親切にして頂いて本当にありがとうございました。はじめの3ヶ月はぜんぜん日本語ができなくて、いろいろ困りましたが、山中先生や、友達のおかげで、今は日本語もまあまあ話せるようになりました。石山高校では大好きな剣道も習えて、とてもうれしかったです。皆さんとお別れするのは、とても悲しいです。アメリカに帰っても皆さんのことは忘れません。僕のうちはフロリダにありますから、皆さんも遊びに来て下さい。いっしょにディズニーワールドに行きましょう。どうぞお元気で。

Reading Comprehension

作文コンテスト

1. high school students
2. 1,000 or less
3. February 10, 2007 (Heisei 19)
4. four
5. 100,000 yen

<Translation>

Essay Contest

What does "international cultural exchange" mean to you? Do you like to make friends from foreign countries? Do you like to go to foreign countries? Why? Based on your experiences and your vision of the future, write an essay on international cultural exchange.

1. Submission period: 9/1/2006 - 2/10/2007
2. Qualification: High school students
3. Submission format:
   - The essay must be 1,000 characters or less.
   - One copy of the original essay and three photocopies are to be submitted to the following address by 2/10/2007.

   Essay Contest Organizing Committee
   Department of International Studies
   Nakayama University
   15 Ishikawa Town, Shinjuku Ward
   Tokyo 160-1234

   - Your full name, age, telephone number, e-mail address and mailing address must be submitted together.
4. Judges:
   Tetsuya Tanaka (Journalist)
   Yoko Yamada (Professor, Dept. of International Studies, Nakayama University)
   Makoto Kawaguchi (Director, Japan Club)
   Mariko Ishida (Director, Tokyo International Cultural Exchange Club)
5. Cash Prizes:
   The Best Essay Award (one essay) - 100,000 yen
   The Excellent Essay Award (three essays)–50,000 yen
6. Results:
   Winners will be contacted via e-mail by 3/31/2007.
   The award recognition ceremony will be held at the International Hall in Nakayama University on 4/25/2007.
7. Others:
   The essay must be original and unpublished.
   Nakayama University will hold the copyright of the award winning essays.